File Management
Techniques

File Management Techniques

Billy G. Claybrook

The MITRE Corporation
Bedford, Massachusetts

John Wiley & Sons

New York · Chichester · Brisbane · Toronto · Singapore

Library of Congress Cataloging in Publication Data:

Claybrook, Billy G. (Billy Gene), 1942–
  File management techniques.

  "Grew out of several courses . . . given at Virginia
Polytechnic Institute & State University from 1973–1977"
—Pref.
  Includes index.
  1. File organization (Computer science) 2. PL/I
(Computer program language) I. Title
QA76.9.F5C55 1983   001.64′2   82-24861
ISBN 0-471-04596-9

Printed in the United States of America

10 9 8 7 6 5 4 3 2

Preface

This is a book about file management. Specifically, it is about file organizations and the hardware and software involved in the creation and manipulation of files. It is intended to be of interest to computer science students and to professionals who are (or will be) applications programmers, systems programmers, or systems analysts. The book presents basic concepts, criteria for choosing between alternative file organizations, and other topics that are important for an understanding of file management. It discusses topics such as the evaluation of file organizations and new storage technologies.

Some of the material presented here is occasionally found in books on operating systems or database management systems; it is included here for completeness. On the other hand, I have tried to avoid topics that are of marginal importance for the study of file management. The book pertains to a specific topic that is an important part of any computer science curriculum; it is not a collection of topics that cover various areas of computer science.

This book grew out of several courses in file management given at Virginia Polytechnic Institute & State University from 1973–1977. Most undergraduate programs in computer science include a course in data structures that covers topics such as arrays, stacks, queues, trees, lists, and possibly internal sorting algorithms. Many computer science programs either have a separate course in file management or arrange for some of this material to be covered at the end of a data structures course or in an operating systems course.

Nearly all computer science programs have one or more course offerings in database management systems. It is natural for a course in file management to precede the study of database management systems (DBMSs) for several reasons. A solid understanding of file organizations and search mechanisms is necessary for physical database design because the problems encountered in database design involve defining access paths to sets of data that lead to satisfactory retrieval and update performance. The relationship between the file management system (FMS) of an operating sytem and a DBMS are important. A DBMS typically runs on top of an operating system and uses the FMS of the operating system to access files that compose a database. In DBMS courses there is so much material to cover concerning the three major data models and the commercial DBMSs that correspond to these models that little or no time is available for an in-depth look at external storage technology, external sorting, protection, or physical database design. One only need to examine some of the DBMS textbooks currently available to verify this. All of these topics, for example, external storage technology and external sorting, are usually covered in an ad hoc manner in data structure courses (again because of time limitations) or DBMS courses.

For students graduating from computer science programs, the topic of file management is probably the least understood topic in the area of systems software. I hope that this book addresses this problem by encouraging courses in file management to become part of more computer science curriculums.

The book was written with the following prerequisite courses in mind:

1. Introduction to programming.
2. Data structures.
3. A course that covers, in an introductory fashion, computer organization topics including I/O processors.

I have included some of the background material that a course in computer organization covers, in case such a course does not exist in a computer science program. The programming language used throughout the book is PL/I; however, the book is relatively independent of any programming language. A set of exercises at the end of each chapter serves as a review of the material in the chapter. In several chapters the exercises are oriented toward the computer systems available for student use. These should guide the instructor toward additional assignments appropriate for the course. In addition, at the end of each chapter is an annotated reference list which can be used to supplement the material covered in the chapter.

Billy G. Claybrook

Contents

File Management Techniques

1

Basic Concepts and Terminology

1.1 INTRODUCTION AND MOTIVATION

The material covered in this book is different from that covered in most other computer science books. It is not programming and it is not formalism. Rather, it is about real-world devices and logical forms of storage whose very existence is due primarily to cost and performance considerations.

The study of file organization and the management of files is important because almost all nontrivial programs manipulate data stored in external files. Failure to select the proper file organization for organizing data or failure to properly implement file management software can cause poor efficiency. Our experience with data structures tells us that the success or failure of a program often depends on the structures for organizing data in internal memory. The time to access a piece of data in internal memory may involve only a few microseconds, while the time to access data in external memory normally involves milliseconds or tens of milliseconds.

A solid understanding of file organizations and search mechanisms is necessary for physical database design. The problems encountered in database design involve defining access paths to sets of data that lead to satisfactory retrieval and update performance. Because databases are generally large objects that must be stored in external memory, it is important that the designer and user understand the complexities introduced by the use of external memory.

1.2 WHAT IS FILE MANAGEMENT?

All people who use a computer operate on data. The data may be read from cards, input from an interactive terminal, generated by a program, or stored on an external storage device. It is often desirable or necessary to store data from one execution of a program to the next. Large volumes of data are commonly stored in external memory as objects called files.

To effectively study the management of files, the following may be considered necessary background topics:

1. The physical characteristics and operation of storage devices.
2. The organization of data on the various types of available storage media.
3. Buffering techniques.
4. The functional characteristics of I/O processors (channels).

Topics 3 and 4 are discussed in this chapter and topics 1 and 2 are discussed in Chapter 2.

File management means different things to different people. Exactly what one understands the phrase "file management" to mean depends upon one's point of view. An applications programmer normally needs to be able to:

1. Sort files.
2. Search files.
3. Add records to files.
4. Delete records from files.
5. Alter values in existing records in files.
6. Copy files.

Thus, an applications programmer sees file management as dealing with the structuring of data so that these operations can be efficiently executed.

The systems programmer, on the other hand, has to worry about how such structured data is managed and must design software that:

1. Allocates and manages buffers.
2. Creates and maintains directories (catalogs) for locating files named by a user.
3. Accesses records.
4. Creates and updates tables in internal memory that indicate the status of files being used by a programmer.
5. Allocates, deallocates, and maintains storage space on secondary storage devices.

This book includes topics that should be of interest to both the applications and systems programmer.

1.3   TERMINOLOGY AND DEFINITIONS

The topics of data structures and file structures (file organizations) are closely related. However, the terminologies used in discussing these two topics differ considerably. For example, elements of files are referred to as *records,* while elements of lists are called *cells* or *nodes*. From an abstract point of view, a file and a list are essentially the same thing, and a cell and a record are the same thing. Historically, the view has been that a data structure resides entirely in internal memory (main memory) and is manipulated in internal memory, while a file is an object that resides on an external storage device and normally only part of it is brought into internal memory as it is being processed.

A file organization is usually considered the process of relating the stored-data requirements of a particular application to the physical characteristics of a particular type of external storage device. The selection of a data structure for an application usually does not take into consideration the physical characterisitics of external storage devices. When files are discussed, the terminology *file organization* and *physical organization* (or physical representation) are often used in place of data structure and storage structure.

The terminology used in this book for discussing files is similar to that used in the area of database management. This is not surprising since a database is essentially a collection of files. Real-world objects, for example, people and parts, about which information is stored are referred to as *entities*. Entities are represented in a computer system by data. Information about a particular entity is in the form of values, and the repository for the data is a file. Data about an entity are generally recorded in terms of attributes that describe the entity.

An *instance of an entity type* is a set of values for the attributes of the entity type. At the data description level, separate attributes are called data items. A data item represents an attribute and the attribute must be associated with the relevant entity type. A *data item* is the smallest named logical unit of data. A *record type* is a named collection of data items. An *instance of a record type* (an instance will be referred to simply as a record in the remainder of this book) is a set of values for the collection of data items in the record type definition. An instance of an entity type is represented by an instance of a record type whose data items represent the attributes of the entity type. A *file* is a list or collection of records representing a set of entities with certain aspects in common and organized for some specific purpose.

A file usually consists of one or more instances of a single record type; however, files can consist of instances of more than one record type. It is important to distinguish between a record type and an instance of a record type. The file PERSONNEL in Figure 1.1 has one record type with the name PERSONNEL_REC. There are no values associated with the data items SSN, NAME, DEPARTMENT, SALARY, AGE, START_DATE, and ADDRESS. When the data items have values associated with them, then an instance of a PERSONNEL_REC record exists. A record definition is like a template; it gives the names of the data items and their types. A simple description of a template is that it is a framework into which the values of data items can be inserted. Thus, the file named PERSONNEL is a collection of instances of the record type named PERSONNEL_REC, and each PERSONNEL_REC record is a collection of data items about a particular entity, an employee.

Data items are either simple items or group items. *Simple items* cannot be subdivided. A *group item* is a named collection of simple items within a record type definition. (NAME is a group item in Figure 1.1.) Certain data items (or attributes) in a record type may be designated as *keys*. A key may be used to identify an entity, to order the records in a file into ascending or descending order based on the value of the key in each record, or to specify records to be retrieved or updated. If each value of a key uniquely identifies a record in a file, then the key is called a *primary key*. An example of a primary key is SSN (social security number) defined as a data item in PERSONNEL_REC in Figure 1.1. Keys whose values do not identify a record uniquely are referred to as *secondary keys*. There may be many records in a file with the same secondary key value. Examples of secondary keys are DEPARTMENT and AGE in the PERSONNEL file defined in Figure 1.1.

As was mentioned earlier, keys may be used to specify records to be retrieved or updated. Retrieval requests made against a file are usually referred to as *queries*. There are various types of queries; a description of them is deferred until Chapter 3. Updating a file involves either adding (inserting) a record to a file, deleting a record from a file, or altering the values of data items in an existing record in a file.

The *logical structure* of a file is the view of a file as perceived by a programmer. A programmer may view a file as a collection of records ordered on some key or as a hierarchical structure consisting of master records with subordinate records. The *physical structure* of a file is concerned with the physical representation and organization of data on a storage medium. The physical representation is concerned with indexes, pointers, lists, and other means of storing and locating records. The logical order and the physical order of records in a file may be different.

Logically (that is, to the applications programmer), a file is considered a collection of logical records. A *logical record* is the unit of data transferred to the user program work area after the execution of a READ statement.

```
DECLARE PERSONNEL FILE INPUT;
DECLARE 1 PERSONNEL_REC,
          2 SSN FIXED DECIMAL(9),
          2 NAME
              3 FIRST CHARACTER(10),
              3 MI CHARACTER(1),
              3 LAST CHARACTER(12),
          2 DEPARTMENT CHARACTER(10),
          2 SALARY FIXED DECIMAL(7, 2),
          2 AGE FIXED DECIMAL(3),
          2 START_DATE CHARACTER(6),
          2 ADDRESS CHARACTER(20);

READ (PERSONNEL) INTO (PERSONNEL_REC);
        .
        .
        .
```

Figure 1.1. A PL/I file definition.

Physically (that is, to the systems programmer), a file is a collection of *physical records* or *blocks* that reside in external storage (external memory). A physical record is the smallest addressable unit of external storage. A physical record or block is a group of one or more logical records, and it is the basic unit of data that is read or written by a single I/O command executed at the I/O processor or channel level. A physical record can also be defined as the unit of interchange between internal memory and external storage. A physical record is said to be *blocked* if it consists of two or more logical records; otherwise, it is considered to be *unblocked*. The importance of blocking records is discussed in Chapter 2.

An *external storage device* consists of a drive unit (or storage unit) and a recording medium, referred to as an external storage medium. Drive units are hardware units, such as magnetic tape drives, disk drives, etc., that handle the storage and retrieval of data. Storage media are the material on which data are stored, for example, magnetic tape, disk packs, magnetic cores, etc. Some storage media, such as magnetic tape or disk packs, can be removed from a storage unit, or they may be a permanent part of the storage unit, as are most drums and all magnetic cores. The term *volume* refers to a unit of storage such as a reel of magnetic tape, a disk pack, a drum, etc.

1.4 BASIC CONCEPTS

In large modern computers, direct communication between internal memory and external memory is not feasible. The primary reasons for this are:

1. The difference in the data flow rate between internal memory (say, a few million characters per second) and that of an external storage device (a few hundred thousand characters per second).
2. The quantity of data handled by an external storage device (usually one character at a time) is different from internal memory (usually four or six characters).
3. There are occasions when several external devices want to communicate with internal memory at the same time.
4. Synchronization problems arise between an external storage device and internal memory, that is, the arrival of data usually does not correspond to when it can be stored in internal memory or when the device is free (not busy).

The four problems mentioned above are resolved by placing an interface between internal memory and an external storage device. For large computers, this interface is an *I/O processor* (or *channel*), and for smaller computers such as mini- and microcomputers, it may be a *bus*. A channel is effectively a small computer that has its own internal memory and an instruction set similar to an assembly language instruction set. A typical channel has only a few registers for internal memory and is capable of executing only a few simple instructions. A bus is a path for transferring data between internal memory and an external storage device. Only the channel is discussed in this chapter.

A channel is subordinate to the central processing unit in that each I/O task executed by the channel must be initiated by the central processing unit. The channel cannot initiate execution of any I/O tasks on its own. The central processing unit gives the channel an I/O task, and then the CPU is free to resume execution of another process while the channel is completing the I/O task. Each I/O task is defined by a channel program (I/O program). Since a simple channel has little internal memory, channel programs are stored in the internal memory of the main computer. The channel fetches the channel program instructions, one at a time, from internal memory and then executes them. A channel program for transferring N characters of data from a disk to internal memory may consist of one or more instructions to locate where the data reside on the disk, followed by a sequence of instructions that specify the locations in internal memory to which the data is to be transferred and when N characters of data have been transferred.

A *selector channel* can control, or be attached to, more than one external storage device. It may have several independent data transfer paths, but it can handle data transmission to or from only one device at a time, that is, it must complete execution of one channel program before beginning execution of another channel program. A *multiplexor channel* is a channel that can be used to transmit data to (from) several storage devices simultaneously, that is, the channel can simultaneously execute several channel programs. Actually, data are being transmitted to only one device at any given instant in time, but the multiplexor channel is time-shared among the devices, thus giving the appearance of the simultaneous transmission of data to more than one device. Multiplexor channels are usually attached to devices with low transmission rates, for example, card readers, line printers, and card punches.

The basic function of a channel on input is to collect data from an external storage device and format it into the appropriate unit of data for storing in a predetermined location in internal memory. On output, a channel obtains a word from internal memory and disassembles it into characters and transmits them in sequence to the proper external storage device. Figure 1.2 illustrates the flow of data from (to) internal memory to (from) an external storage device via a channel. The channel in Figure 1.2 has a single assembly register that can hold one word of data. No attempt is made in this book to cover all of the hardware characteristics of channels; only a brief description of their functional characteristics is provided.

Figure 1.2 introduces an element not yet discussed—the buffer. Each file that is being actively used by a programmer in a program, say a PL/I program, has at least one buffer associated with it. A buffer resides in internal memory, and it may be located within the space allocated to the user program by the operating system, or, more likely, it is located outside the user space as illustrated in Figure 1.2. The buffer size is large enough to hold the maximum-sized physical record stored in the file with which the buffer is associated. A central processing unit (CPU) memory cycle must be stolen by a channel to move a word from the assembly register of the channel to a buffer in internal

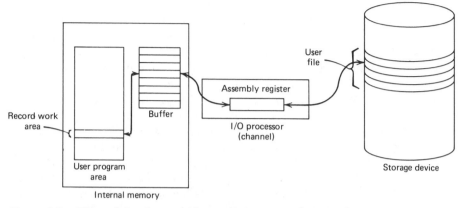

Figure 1.2.   Flow of data between internal memory and external storage.

memory. Complete physical records are generally transmitted between a file on an external storage device and internal memory. Storage devices transmit data at a constant rate until an I/O operation is complete. An important reason for having buffers is the apparent difference in an application program's read/write statements and the lower level read/write commands issued for an external storage device. The read/write statements in a program are associated with the movement of logical records between a buffer and a program's record work area, whereas, the read/write commands issued to an external storage device are concerned with the movement of physical records between external memory and a buffer. A *record work area* is the storage available for holding the most recent instance of a logical record from a file.

Since the user program read/write statements handle logical records, the physical record residing in a buffer must be deblocked (for a read) or blocked (for a write) to satisfy these requests. Deblocking is the reverse of blocking; that is, it is the division of a physical record into logical records.

When the first read statement for a file is executed in a user program, a block of records is moved from the external storage device, where the file is stored, to a buffer associated with the file. The first logical record in the buffer is transferred to the record work area in the user program's space. When the PL/I program segment in Figure 1.1 is compiled, the size of logical records defined by record type PERSONNEL_REC is determined, and at execution time this amount of storage (record work area) is available for holding the most recent instance of PERSONNEL_REC read from the file named PERSON-NEL. For each subsequent execution of the READ statement, the next logical record in the buffer is transferred to the record work area. Only after every logical record in the buffer has been moved to the record work area does the next execution of the READ statement cause another block of records to be transferred to the buffer from the external storage device. The new logical records in the buffer are moved, one at a time, to the work area as described above. This process is repeated for each block of records read. In a similar manner, WRITE statements issued in a user program cause the transfer of data from the record work area to the buffer. When the buffer becomes full, the block is written to the proper external storage device. Figure 1.3 illustrates the process of blocking and deblocking records.

In some programming systems such as COBOL, the record work area and the buffer area coincide. The buffer is within the user program space. The record work area can be considered to move through the buffer on successive reads. Regardless of whether the record work area is an individual area separate from the buffer or whether it coincides with the buffer, a pointer into the buffer area indicates the position of the next logical record to be read by a user program. After a logical record is read, the pointer is adjusted to point to the beginning of the next logical record in the buffer. This can be pictured as a template sliding across a physical record to define one logical record at a time.

The buffer(s) corresponding to a particular file are created (allocated) when the file is *opened,* and the buffer(s) corresponding to a file may be released (deallocated) when the file is *closed.* In some programming languages, such as COBOL and PL/I, a file is opened (closed) via an explicit OPEN (CLOSE) statement. In others, such as FORTRAN and the SYSIN and SYSPRINT files of PL/I, opening occurs implicitly when the first read or write for the file is executed; when a program terminates, all open files are closed. Opening a file is an indication by a programmer that the file is going to be used in some subsequent operations. Files can be opened for input only, output only, or for update. The use of the term update here means that as records are read, the record most recently read can also be rewritten on the same file. A file is closed when there are no more operations directed at it.

A file that is opened, say for input, may have only one buffer associated with it. This buffering technique (illustrated in Figure 1.3) is called single buffering. With the exception of the pooling of buffers technique described

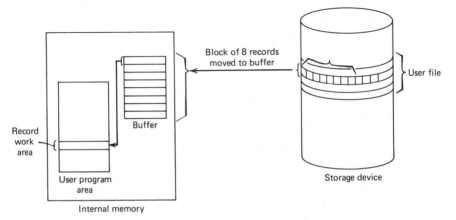

Figure 1.3.   Block of eight logical records moved to a buffer and moved one by one to the record work area.

below, the following remarks about buffering schemes assume that the file being processed is a sequential file with records accessed sequentially. A sequential file is a file in which the logical and physical order of the records on storage medium are the same. When the single buffering technique is used, the program may have to suspend computation until the buffer is filled. Another alternative is to allow the buffer to be emptied and filled simultaneously, that is, the user program can be reading logical records from it while it is being filled. This latter technique is illustrated in Figure 1.4. On input, the OUT pointer indicates the beginning of the next logical record in the buffer that is to be read by a user program, and the IN pointer indicates the last position in the buffer to be filled with data from an external storage device. Thus on input, a user program causes the OUT pointer to be advanced, and an access method routine causes the IN pointer to be advanced. An *access method* is a layer of software in an operating system that serves as the "go-between" for a user program and a file. The roles of the user program and the access method routine are reversed on output. A user program advances the IN pointer, and the access method routine advances the OUT pointer. The OUT pointer chases the IN pointer around the buffer in a cyclic fashion. When IN is incremented so that its value is equal to OUT, the buffer is full. When OUT is incremented so that its value is equal to IN, the buffer is empty.

A more common buffering scheme is called *double buffering*. With this scheme two buffers, BUF1 and BUF2, are allocated for a single file (see Figure 1.5). On the first read (if we assume the file is opened for input) against the file both buffers are filled, BUF1 and then BUF2. After all logical records in BUF1 are processed by a user program, the execution of a subsequent read statement uses BUF2, and at the same time a read command is issued by the operating system to refill BUF1, that is, the operating system anticipates the user needing the next block of records in the file. This form of buffering is called *anticipatory reading* or *anticipatory buffering*. Anticipatory reading is a meaningful opera-

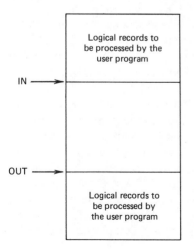

Logical records to
be processed by the
user program

IN ——→

OUT ——→

Logical records to
be processed by
the user program

Figure 1.4.   Single buffer with simultaneous empty and fill (assuming input).

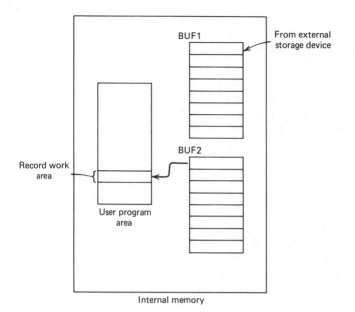

Figure 1.5. Double buffering.

tion only for files whose records are accessed sequentially. The technique of processing one buffer while the other is being filled and then switching the role of the buffers is called *buffer swapping*. Double buffering for a file opened for output works in a manner similar to input. While one buffer is being emptied to an external storage device, the other buffer can be filled by the user program. Double buffering facilitates computation-data transfer overlap.

Another buffering technique that is sometimes used is *multiple buffering*. Multiple buffering is similar to double buffering, but multiple buffering uses more than two buffers, say five buffers, all linked together in a circular manner. All buffers are filled on the first read against a file, and when a buffer is empty, a read command is issued by the operating system to refill the buffer. Output using multiple buffering works in a similar manner. Multiple buffering allows a higher degree of computer processing-data transfer overlap than may be achieved by double buffering.

The final buffering scheme uses a pool of buffers. *Pooling* allows two or more files or external storage devices to share a group (pool) of buffers from a common list. It becomes necessary to distinguish between input buffers and output buffers. Initially, all of the buffers in the pool are empty and are linked together. When a buffer is needed for output, it is removed from the empty buffer list, filled, and placed on an output buffer full list earmarked for a particular device on which the associated file is stored. When an output buffer is emptied, it is placed back on the empty buffer list. When a buffer is needed for input, it is removed from the empty buffer list, filled, and placed on an input buffer full list earmarked for a particular user program. When an input buffer has been processed, the empty buffer is returned to the empty buffer list.

A question of interest with respect to buffers is what is the appropriate number of buffers? As the number of buffers used increases, the execution time of a program will certainly not increase, but it will not continually decrease either; thus, there is a point of diminishing returns in which an increase in the number of buffers available does not reduce the execution time of a program. If the computation time between I/O requests is always greater than the time required to transfer a block from external memory, then double buffering is always satisfactory. If the computation time between I/O requests is always less than the block transfer time, then double buffering will keep the I/O device busy at all times. Multiple buffering is useful when the computation time between I/O requests varies from small values to large values.

1.5 SUMMARY

This chapter has introduced some of the terminology and basic concepts used throughout the remainder of the book. An attempt has been made to use standard terminology when possible. No attempt was made in the basic concepts section (Section 1.4) to discuss all of the techniques for buffering and data transfer. The discussion was confined to typical I/O methods that apply to many computers. A number of terms were defined in this chapter; among these are record, file organization, entity, data item, record type, file, key, logical record, physical record, blocking, I/O processor (or channel), buffer, open, close, and access method.

EXERCISES

1. Determine the types of buffering schemes used on one of your computer systems.
2. Determine the I/O architecture for the computer used in Exercise 1.
3. Describe some of the primary differences between the I/O schemes used in the PDP-11 Unibus structure and IBM I/O channels.

REFERENCES

1.1 Madnick, S.E. and Donovan, J.J. *Operating Systems,* McGraw-Hill Book Company, New York, 1974, 640 pages.

This is one of several good books on operating systems. It provides a relatively comprehensive coverage of operating systems, including buffering techniques, I/O programming, file systems, and external storage device management. It is oriented toward the IBM 360/370 operating systems.

1.2 Kuck, D.J. *The Structure of Computers and Computations,* Volume 1, John Wiley & Sons, New York, 1978, 611 pages.

A·comprehensive description of computer systems and how they are organized is given. Real I/O techniques are covered in detail. These include the DEC Unibus structure, IBM I/O channels, and the CDC Peripheral Processing Units.

1.3 Pfleeger, C.P. *Machine Organization,* John Wiley & Sons, New York, 1982, 227 pages.

A good introduction to computer organization is given in this book. The level of detail is appropriate for supplementing the material covered in this chapter.

External Storage Devices

2.1 INTRODUCTION

In the past 20 years on-line storage capacity has increased about three times as much as CPU power. However, memory represents perhaps the most limiting area in the development of more advanced computer systems.

Internal memory provides the storage requirements of central processing unit(s) for the execution of programs, including application programs and system programs such as assemblers, loaders, linkage editors, compilers, utility routines, and supervisory routines of the operating system. The storage capacity of internal memory is limited by the cost of internal memory units (0.1 to 0.7 cents per bit for semiconductor memory). The storage requirements for programs and the data on which they operate customarily exceed the capacity of internal memory of most computer systems. Thus, there is a requirement to provide other storage facilities on which to store programs and data.

Anyone creating files for storing programs and/or data should be capable of selecting (if the programmer is given or has the choice of selecting) the proper media on which to store the files and should also be aware of the appropriateness of a corresponding storage device for handling particular file organizations. For example, magnetic tapes allow only sequential access of data, while disks, drums, and magnetic core memory are random-access storage devices. With sequential access media, only the next record or the previous record can be located easily; this type of media excels when reading or writing the next record is the most common type of operation. With random-access media, a hardware address is used to position the access mechanism and each part of the recording medium can be addressed. Random-access devices excel in locating a particular data record having a known address.

As application and systems programmers select external storage devices for storing data files and program files, there are several areas of concern:

1. *Capacity.* The amount of data that can be stored on a storage medium.
2. *Portability.* Magnetic tapes and some disk packs are removable, permitting the off-line storage of files.
3. *Relative cost.* The cost of a device increases with the speed and convenience of accessing records.
4. *Record size.* The size of a set of contiguous data that can be addressed on a device.
5. *Accessing method.* The direct (random-) access of any record on a device may be possible, or the device may restrict the access of records to sequential access.
6. *Data transfer rate.* The rate, usually in bits, bytes, or characters per second, at which data can be transferred between internal memory and a device.
7. *Seek time.* Disk and drum devices with movable read/write heads often must precede each read/write operation by a seek that physically moves a read/write head over the track containing the desired record.
8. *Latency.* After a read or write command is accepted by a device, it normally takes an additional time increment, the latency time (or rotational delay time), before the beginning of the record to be accessed is under the read/write head and the data transfer can begin; this is either the start-up time for the magnetic tape to be accelerated to its rated speed from a dead stop or the rotational delay time of rotating disks or drums.

Another property of external storage devices that may be important for some applications is the ability of the device to be shared simultaneously by two or more users. A file that can be, or must be, accessed simultaneously by several users should be stored on a sharable device such as a magnetic disk. Sequential access storage devices are not appropriate for sharing.

Some of the properties mentioned above are not characteristic of all of the storage devices discussed in this chapter. For example, there is no seek time associated with fixed head disks and drums and large core stores.

Capacity, access time (the amount of time it takes to read data from a device), data transfer rate, and cost per bit are the basic performance characteristics of storage devices. When a storage technology is being measured, areal density (in bits per square inch) is the key figure to consider. The greater the areal density, the lower the cost per bit, and, correspondingly, the shorter the average access time for any given capacity.

The storage media and devices discussed in this chapter are magnetic tapes, fixed and removable disks and drums, magnetic bubble memories, charge-coupled devices, large core stores, and mass storage devices. The storage capacity and access time characteristics of each storage technology are presented. In addition, if appropriate, equations are given for calculating the storage space occupied by a file and the amount of time required to access a block of logical records. Space calculations are important for two reasons:

1. The programmer may have to explicitly specify the amount of storage space required for a file when it is created.
2. The programmer may want to know whether or not a file will fit on a single volume.

In some situations it is undesirable to span a file over more than one volume unless all of the volumes can be on-line together; otherwise, the volumes may have to be mounted and demounted several times during the processing of the file. Timing considerations for external storage devices are normally more important to a programmer than space considerations. Timing is important because a programmer may have access time constraints for the retrieval of data that must be considered when selecting the external storage on which to store a file. Another important reason for presenting and studying space and timing calculations is that it enhances the understanding of the operation of the devices.

2.2 MAGNETIC TAPES

The magnetic tape was the first external storage medium to be widely used and continues to be one of the most common storage media for storing data that can be processed in a sequential manner. Magnetic tapes are important external storage media for the following reasons:

1. They are inexpensive when compared with other storage media.
2. They are compact and portable, thereby facilitating off-line storage.
3. Because of their low cost, they are ideal for use in storing off-line backup and archival files.

The physical appearance of magnetic tape is similar to that of tapes used with tape recorders. A tape is made of a plastic material coated with a substance that is easily magnetized. Data are encoded on a tape, character by character. A number of tracks run the length of a tape, with one track required for each bit position in the coded representation of a character.

2.2.1 Parity

In addition to the tracks that record data, there is an additional track that records a *parity bit* used for error processing. Tapes can be either 7- or 9-track tapes. The 9-track is more commonly used than its predecessor, the 7-track tape. Figure 2.1 illustrates a portion of a 9-track tape. Data are recorded on a 9-track tape in either binary or EBCDIC mode, and each character is represented across the tape by a sequence of bits set to 0 or 1 in tracks 2 through 9. Data can be recorded in either even or odd parity mode. The bit in

Track

Figure 2.1.   Portion of a 9-track tape.

track 1 is the parity bit; it is written in track 1 by the tape drive unit as data are recorded on the tape. When a tape is written in odd parity mode, the parity bit is set to make the number of 1 bits in tracks 1 through 9 odd. The tape in Figure 2.1 is written in odd parity mode; the number of 1 bits on tracks 2 through 9 is even; therefore, a 1 bit is written in track 1 for the character. Even parity is similar, except that the bit in track 1 is selected to make the number of 1 bits in tracks 1 to 9 even.

A parity bit serves as a check on the accuracy of recorded data as it is read from a tape. When a tape is read, the tape drive unit checks that the number of 1 bits in tracks 1 though 9 agree with the parity of the tape. If this is not the case, then a parity error interrupt occurs. The interrupt routine that services the interrupt causes the record in which the parity error occurred to be reread several times by the tape drive unit until either the record is read without a parity error or the number of reread attempts has reached a system defined limit. The reason that the record is reread several times is that tapes are vulnerable to dust and other foreign substances and occasionally the mechanical tape drive unit can fail to function properly. Thus, in some cases a parity error may occur even though the data are recorded properly, and a subsequent reread will verify that it is recorded properly.

The parity described above is sometimes referred to as *simple parity* or *vertical parity*. Some tapes also have a *longitudinal parity* character generated as data are written on the tape. A longitudinal parity character, called a redundancy check character, is generated for each record in the following manner:

1. Each track is examined longitudinally, and the number of "1" bits in the track is counted.
2. If the number of "1" bits in a track is odd, then a one is written in the redundancy check character in the position corresponding to the track number.
3. If the number of "1" bits in a track is even, then a zero is written in the redundancy check character.
4. The redundancy check character is written at the end of the record.

When both vertical and longitudinal parity are used, it is less likely that an error will escape detection.

Data are recorded on a 7-track tape either in binary or BCD mode. A discussion on 7-track tapes parallels that of the 9-track tapes except that characters are recorded across the width of the tape in tracks 2 through 7. The parity bit is again recorded in track 1.

2.2.2 Interrecord Gaps

Data are written (read) on (from) a magnetic tape by a tape drive unit as the tape passes through the read/write head mechanism of the tape drive on which the tape is mounted. A tape drive unit is designed to read or write data only when a tape is moving at a specified speed. The data written on magnetic tapes are recorded in the format illustrated in Figure 2.2. Consecutive physical records are separated by an interrecord gap (IRG) that allows a tape to start and stop between individual read or write commands. No data are recorded in an IRG. At the completion of a read or write command, part of an interrecord gap passes through the read/write head. If the next operation for the same tape is initiated during this time, tape motion continues without interruption. However, if the next operation does not occur soon enough, the tape will stop, and it will require some time to accelerate the tape to full speed on the next command. The primary function of an interrecord gap is to provide space to allow a tape to stop after an I/O command, and to allow it to accelerate to the required speed necessary to read or write and avoid distortion. An interrecord gap is normally 0.75 inch in length for 7-track tapes and 0.6 inch for 9-track tapes. The effect of an interrecord gap is to decrease the amount of data that can be stored on a tape.

2.2.3 Tape Rewinding

A tape normally has a load point on it indicating the starting point on the tape where data can be recorded. When a tape is initially mounted, it is positioned at the load point ready for any ensuing I/O command. Magnetic tapes can be rewound back to their load point by a rewind command. Some magnetic tape drives have a high-speed rewind that applies only when the number of characters to rewind is greater than some number, say one or two million; for

Load point

| | Physical record 1 | IRG | Physical record 2 | IRG | Physical record 3 | IRG | Physical record 4 | |

Figure 2.2.   Magnetic tape format.

smaller numbers of characters, rewinding is done at the normal read/write speed.

2.2.4   Write Protection

Before a magnetic tape can be written on by a program, a computer operator must place a small plastic ring in a circular groove on the back side of the tape reel. This ring is called a write-protect (or write-enable) ring, and its absence prohibits a tape drive from writing data on the tape via a write statement issued in a program. A ring is a simple protection mechanism that may prevent a programmer from inadvertently writing on a tape that contains program code or data that should not be destroyed. It is a protection mechanism because a programmer must explicitly request an operator to place the ring in the tape reel.

2.2.5   Space and Timing Calculations for Magnetic Tape

The amount of data that can be stored on a magnetic tape depends on the size of the blocks and the density with which data can be recorded on the tape. Large blocks, resulting from a high blocking factor, result in more of a tape being used for storing data and less of the tape space being used for interrecord gaps. In addition, the average time to read/write a physical record is inversely proportional to the blocking factor since fewer interrecord gaps must be passed over. To efficiently utilize tape storage and to minimize read/write time, it appears that a blocking factor should be relatively large; however, one or more buffers large enough to hold a block must exist in internal memory. On the other hand, since internal memory is often at a premium, buffers cannot be arbitrarily large. Hence, block size is determined, to some extent, by the amount of internal memory available for buffers. A tradeoff exists between tape storage capacity and read/write time on the one hand, and the amount of internal memory available for buffers.

The density of a tape is expressed in bits per inch (bpi), bytes per inch (bpi), or characters per inch (cpi). Common recording densities for magnetic tapes are 556 cpi, 800 cpi, 1,600 cpi, and 6,250 cpi. Table 2.1 gives characteristics, including the density, of some commercial tape drive units.

2.2.5.1   Space Calculations

The space occupied by a block depends on:

1. Logical record length.
2. Blocking factor.
3. Density of the tape.

Table 2.1

Magnetic Tape Units

Manufacturer Model	CDC 626	Univac Uniservo 12	CDC 679-7	IBM 3420-4	Telex 6420-66
Speed	75 inches/ second	42.7 inches/ second	200 inches/ second	75 inches/ second	125 inches/ second
Density	800 characters/ inch	1600 characters/ inch	6250 bytes/ inch	6250 bytes/ inch	6250 bytes/ inch
Transfer rate	120K characters/ second	68K characters/ second	1.25M bytes/ second	470K bytes/ second	780K bytes/ second

Table 2.2 contains a list of the symbols, along with their descriptions, that are used in the equations given below for both space and timing. The total space (S_T) required for a file of N_L logical records is given by the equation

$$S_T = \frac{N_L}{BF} \left(IRG + \frac{BF \times LRL}{DEN} \right) \tag{2.1}$$

The quantity in parenthesis in (2.1) is the space occupied by a single block. The total space required for a sequential file with $N_L = 10,000$, $BF = 3$, $LRL = 160$ characters, $DEN = 800$ cpi, and $IRG = 0.75$ inch is

$$S_T = \frac{10000}{3} \left(0.75 \text{ inch} + \frac{3 \times 160 \text{ characters}}{800 \text{ cpi}} \right)$$

$$= 4500.9 \text{ inches} \cong 375 \text{ feet}$$

Table 2.2

Symbols Used in Space and Timing Equations for Magnetic Tape

Symbol	Description
N_L	Number of logical records in a file
BF	Blocking factor
IRG	Interrecord gap (in inches)
DEN	Density (cpi or bpi)
SPD	Speed (inches/second)
LRL	Logical record length (characters)
T_A	Start/stop time or time to fly across the IRG (ms)
S_T	Total space (inches)
T_T	Total time (seconds)

2.2.5.2   *Timing Calculations*

The time to read a block consists of:

1. The time to pass over an interrecord gap.
2. The time to read the block itself.

The total time to read a file of N_L records, if we assume there are no rewinds, is given by

$$T_T = \frac{N_L}{BF} \left(T_A + \frac{BF \times LRL}{SPD \times DEN} \right) \qquad (2.2)$$

The quantity in parenthesis in (2.2) is the amount of time required to pass over an interrecord gap plus the time to read a block. The product $SPD \times DEN$ is the data transfer rate. The data transfer rate for typical magnetic tape devices varies from about 30,000 to approximately 7,500,000 characters per second. For $SPD = 75$ inches/second, $T_A = 12.6$ ms (the value of T_A is the start/stop time rather than the fly time), $BF = 3$, $LRL = 160$ characters, $DEN = 800$ cpi, and $IRG = 0.75$ inch, the time to read a file of 10,000 logical records with a complete stop after each read is

$$T_T = \frac{10000}{3} \left(0.0126 \text{ second } + \frac{3 \times 160 \text{ characters}}{75 \text{ inches/second} \times 800 \text{ cpi}} \right)$$

$$= 68.68 \text{ seconds}$$

The space and access time requirements for a file on magnetic tape (and most other storage media) decrease as the blocking factor increases. This is illustrated in Figure 2.3.

2.2.6   Advantages and Disadvantages of Magnetic Tape

A limitation of magnetic tape is that records cannot be accessed randomly; that is, records must be processed in the order in which they reside on the tape. Accessing a record requires reading all of the records that precede it. Magnetic tapes have the advantage of being compact, portable, and suitable for off-line storage. In addition, they are a relatively inexpensive media. A 600-foot tape costs from $7 to 10 and a 2400-foot tape costs approximately $20 to 30. A low-performance magnetic tape unit (single drive with controller) with a data

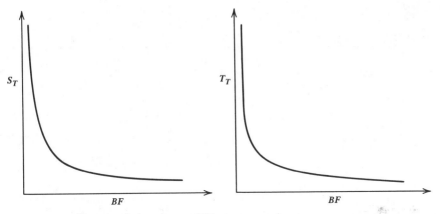

Figure 2.3.   Space and time versus BF.

transfer rate of 40,000 characters/second costs about $7500 to 10,000. A medium-performance unit (three drives with one controller) with a data transfer rate of 600,000 characters/second costs approximately $60,000 to 75,000. A high-performance unit (six drives with one controller) with a data transfer rate of 7,500,000 characters/second costs approximately $180,000 to 220,000.

2.3 MAGNETIC DISKS AND DRUMS

Disks and drums are direct access storage devices suitable for the on-line or off-line storage of data. Magnetic disks are more widely used than drums primarily because the cost/bit for disk storage is less than that for drum storage. When compared with magnetic tape, both the disk and the drum provide relatively low access times and high-speed data transfers. The manufacturers of disk and drum storage devices have been able to increase the areal density of the recording media for these devices by several magnitudes over the past several years; thus, they are still appropriate devices for storing large files. Table 2.3 shows how the areal density has increased over the past several years. The spectacular success and growth of magnetic disk and drum devices derives from certain inherent characteristics of this technology:

1. Low-cost storage media based on homogeneous magnetic surfaces.
2. Accessing that permits tens of millions of bits to share one read/write head.
3. The fundamental limits of the technology were far beyond the demands placed on the technology, thus allowing much room for growth and expansion in device capability and performance.

Table 2.3

Disk Storage Density

Year	Areal Density (bits/inch^2)
1955	2,200
1960	8,000
1965	220,000
1970	800,000
1975	2.24×10^6
.	.
.	.
.	.
1985	3.2×10^8

2.3.1 Magnetic Disks

Two types of disks are in common use: fixed disks (also called fixed head disks) and removable disks (also called movable head disks). Disk packs on fixed disk devices are not removed from a disk drive unit (except for maintenance purposes), whereas, removable disk packs can be easily removed from a disk drive unit and replaced, stored, or transported. Removable disks are the more common of the two types of disks because they facilitate off-line storage of files, and the cost/bit of storage is less.

2.3.1.1 Fixed Disks

The fixed disk in Figure 2.4 consists of six platters with a ferromagnetic material on each surface providing a storage media. The outermost surfaces of the top and bottom platters are sometimes not used for storing data since they can be easily damaged. Each surface is divided into concentric rings (see Figure 2.5) called tracks. The disk in Figure 2.4 has ten tracks per surface. Data are recorded on the tracks by read/write heads, one for each track, arranged on a read/write head comb assembly that is fixed in place and does not move. Each head floats just above or just below a surface (about 0.001 inch from the surface), while the disk is rotating at a high constant speed. Although tracks vary in length, all tracks for a given disk are capable of storing the same amount of data; the reason for this is that the recording density for inner tracks is greater than the recording density for outer tracks.

Since a fixed disk has one read/write head per track, no seek time is required to move a read/write head to the proper track on a surface; thus, the access time for a fixed head disk is comparable to that of fixed head drums because the seek time for both is zero. The major component of the access time for a fixed head disk is the latency time.

Fixed head disks are normally used in systems that are dedicated to one or a few applications and when files are required to be on-line with a low access

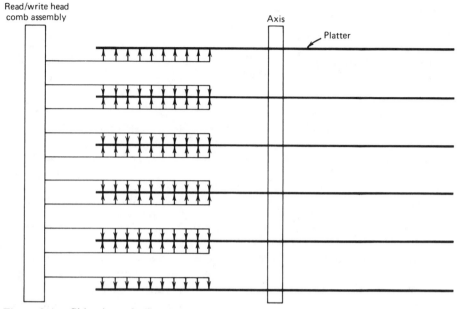

Figure 2.4.   Side view of a fixed head disk with 10 surfaces and 10 read/write heads per surface.

time requirement. Characteristics of some of the commercially available fixed disk units are given in Table 2.4.

2.3.1.2   Removable Disks

As was mentioned above, the movable head disk is the more common of the two types of disks because the disk packs are removable and the cost/bit of storage is less. There is only one read/write head per disk surface; the

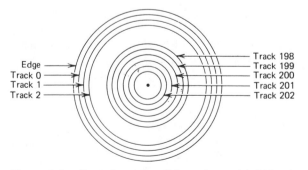

Figure 2.5.   Top view of a disk surface with 200 primary tracks and three alternate tracks (tracks 200, 201, 202).

Table 2.4

Characteristics of Fixed Disk Units

Manufacturer Model	Burroughs B9370-2	DEC R503	IBM 2305	Amcomp 8530/256
Surfaces/unit	2	1	12	4
Tracks/surface	100	64	32	128
Sector size	100 bytes	64 bytes	variable	—
Sectors/track	100	64	variable	—
Track capacity	10,000 bytes	4096 bytes	14,136 bytes	150K bits
Total capacity	2M bytes	262K bytes	5.4M bytes	76.8M bits
Average latency	17 ms	8.5 ms	2.5 ms	8.3 ms
Transfer rate	300K bytes/second	250K bytes/second	3M bytes/second	9M bits/second

read/write head comb assembly must be moved in and out in order to access all of the tracks on each surface. The read/write heads usually move together as a unit, and only one head can transfer data at a time. Figure 2.6 shows the side view of a movable head disk, and Figure 2.5 shows the top view of a movable head disk with 203 tracks.* In some movable head disk systems, the read/write heads are not rigidly fixed to the comb assembly (as they are in Figure 2.6), and they can be moved in and out among the surfaces independently off each other. If the disk in Figure 2.6 has 200 primary tracks per surface, then the movable comb assembly unit can move horizontally to 200 different positions. Each one of the 200 positions identifies a cylinder; a *cylinder* of data is the amount of data that is accessible with one positioning of the read/write head comb assembly unit. The time required to move the read/write heads from one cylinder to the next is referred to as the *seek time*.

Since the comb assembly mechanism moves, a large recording surface area can be covered with only a few read/write heads. A fixed head disk with the same recording surface area as a movable head disk has a higher cost/bit because of the cost of the many read/write heads required. Since the comb assembly unit on a movable head disk unit moves, it can be moved away from the surface areas of a disk pack, thus allowing the disk pack to be easily removed from the disk drive unit and replaced by another disk pack. The characteristics of some removable disk units are summarized in Table 2.5.

2.3.2 Magnetic Drum

A magnetic drum is a metal cylinder (10 to 36 inches in diameter) coated with a magnetic recording material. The surface of the drum is divided into circular

---

*The tracks numbered 0−199 are the primary tracks. Tracks 200−202 are alternate tracks that are used for replacing damaged and defective primary tracks.

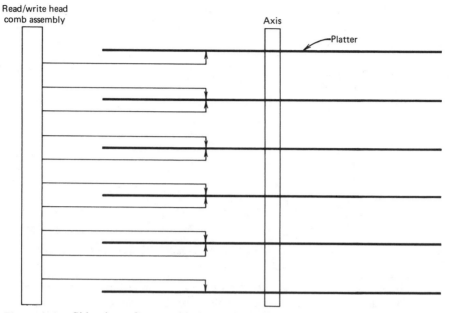

Figure 2.6.   Side view of a movable head disk with 10 surfaces.

tracks. Figure 2.7 illustrates a drum arrangement with each track having its own read/write head, and Figure 2.8 illustrates another, less common arrangement, with a fixed number of read/write heads that move along a read/write head assembly mechanism. A drum with fixed heads having 200 tracks has 200 read/write heads. In this case there is no seek time. A drum with movable read/write heads may have, for example, a group of five read/write heads, thus permitting five contiguous tracks to be accessed without moving the read/write head assembly.

Table 2.5

Characteristics of Removable Disk Units

Manufacturer Model	HP 2100	IBM 3330	IBM 3340	CDC 33801 AZ
Surfaces/unit	4	19	12	19
Tracks/surface	200	404	696	808
Sector size	256 bytes	variable	variable	—
Sectors/track	24	variable	variable	—
Track capacity	6144 bytes	13,030 bytes	8368 bytes	13,030 bytes
Total capacity	4.9M bytes	100M bytes	69.9M bytes	400M bytes
Average latency	12.5 ms	8.3 ms	12.5 ms	16.7 ms
Transfer rate	312K bytes/second	806K bytes/second	885K bytes/second	1.2M bytes/ second

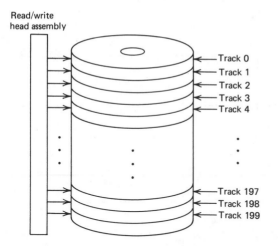

Read/write
head assembly

Figure 2.7. Vertical drum arrangement with one read/write head per track.

Drums are commonly used in situations in which a moderate amount of storage is required, and the access time must be relatively low. They are satisfactory storage media for system libraries consisting of systems programs such as loaders, compilers, etc. Table 2.6 gives the characteristics of some common drum units. Note that the Univac FASTRAND II drum in Table 2.6 is a movable head drum; this is the reason why it has a nonzero seek time.

2.3.3 Track Formats for Magnetic Disk and Drum

Each track on a disk or drum is subdivided into either fixed length sectors or variable length blocks. Sectors and blocks are synonymous with physical records, and they are the smallest addressable units on disk and drum devices.

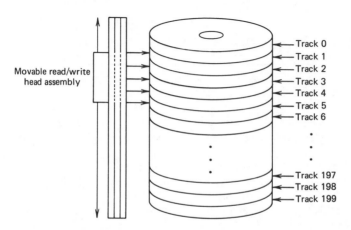

Movable read/write
head assembly

Figure 2.8. Vertical drum arrangement with five movable read/write heads.

Table 2.6

Characteristics of Magnetic Drum Units[a]

Manufacturer	IBM	UNIVAC	ICL
Model	2301	FASTRAND II	1964
Tracks	200	6144	512
Sector size	variable	168 characters	4 bytes
Sectors/track	variable	64	1024
Track capacity	20,483 bytes	10,752 characters	4048 bytes
Total capacity	4M bytes	132M characters	2M bytes
Average latency	8.6 ms	35 ms	20.5 ms
Transfer rate	1.2M bytes/second	153K characters/ second	100K bytes/second

[a]The seek time for all drums is zero except the FASTRAND II; the FASTRAND II has a seek time of 58 ms.

A complete sector or block is read into or written from a buffer upon the execution of an I/O command by an I/O processor.

2.3.3.1   Sector-Addressable Devices

Sectors are fixed length arcs of a track and there is an integral number of sectors per track. The number of characters of data that can be stored in a sector is fixed either in the hardware of a drive unit or is fixed when an operating system is generated. Subdividing tracks into fixed size sectors is appealing because:

1. It simplifies the allocation of storage space.
2. It simplifies address calculations.
3. It simplifies synchronizing CPU computation with record accessing from files, especially for sequential files.

Figure 2.9 illustrates a surface of a sector-addressable disk with eight sectors per track.

Some computing systems can be synchronized, for sequential file input, so that data records can be read in a manner that minimizes the latency time. The CPU processing speed and the data transfer rate of a device can be used to establish a sector size so that synchronization can be effected. Gaps or *hopscotching* are used in the synchronization process. Hopscotching makes more efficient use of space, but it is more difficult to organize than an organization that uses gaps to separate fixed length records. The following simple example illustrates hopscotching. Suppose there are ten physical records (R1, R2, . . ., R10) to be stored on a disk that has ten sectors per track. Suppose further that the serial access time per physical record is less than one millisecond and the job requesting the records takes two milliseconds to

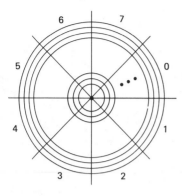

Figure 2.9. Surface of a sector-addressable disk.

process each record after reading it. The ten records can be stored on a track in the order:

Sector number	1	2	3	4	5	6	7	8	9	10
Record	R1	R8	R5	R2	R9	R6	R3	R10	R7	R4

By the time record R1 is read and processed, less than three milliseconds of time have expired. An I/O command to read record R2 can be issued by the operating system in time to read record R2 on the same rotation.

The CDC model 841 disk unit is an example of a device that has fixed length sectors and uses the concept of hopscotching for synchronization purposes. The 841 configuration described below has 14 sectors per track with each sector having a capacity of 322 characters. The operating system allocates space on the 841 disk in units of physical blocks (CDC terminology) of 56 sectors per physical block. This results in a physical block covering four tracks of the 841 disk, or it results in five physical blocks per cylinder (the 841 disk has 20 tracks per cylinder). Figure 2.10 illustrates the cylinder format for the 841 disk. The

Sectors

		0	1	2	3	4	5	6	7	8	9	10	11	12	13
	0	PB0 0	PB2 28	PB0 1	PB2 29	PB0 2	PB2 30	PB0 3	PB2 31	PB0 4	PB2 32	PB0 5	PB2 33	PB0 6	PB2 34
Tracks	1	PB0 7	PB2 35	PB0 8	PB2 36	PB0 9	PB2 37	PB0 10	PB2 38	PB0 11	PB2 39	PB0 12	PB2 40	PB0 13	PB2 41
	2	PB0 14	PB2 42	PB0 15	PB2 43	PB0 16	PB2 44	PB0 17	PB2 45	PB0 18	PB2 46	PB0 19	PB2 47	PB0 20	PB2 48
	3	PB0 21	PB2 49	PB0 22	PB2 50	PB0 23	PB2 51	PB0 24	PB2 52	PB0 25	PB2 53	PB0 26	PB2 54	PB0 27	PB2 55

Figure 2.10. Cylinder format for the CDC 841 desk unit.

Sectors

Tracks	0	1	2	3	4	5	6	7	8	9	10	11	12	13
4	PB0 28	PB3 0	PB0 29	PB3 1	PB0 30	PB3 2	PB0 31	PB3 3	PB0 32	PB3 4	PB0 33	PB3 5	PB0 34	PB3 6
5	PB0 35	PB3 7	PB0 36	PB3 8	PB0 37	PB3 9	PB0 38	PB3 10	PB0 39	PB3 11	PB0 40	PB3 12	PB0 41	PB3 13
6	PB0 42	PB3 14	PB0 43	PB3 15	PB0 44	PB3 16	PB0 45	PB3 17	PB0 46	PB3 18	PB0 47	PB3 19	PB0 48	PB3 20
7	PB0 49	PB3 21	PB0 50	PB3 22	PB0 51	PB3 23	PB0 52	PB3 24	PB0 53	PB3 25	PB0 54	PB3 26	PB0 55	PB3 27
8	PB1 0	PB3 28	PB1 1	PB3 29	PB1 2	PB3 30	PB1 3	PB3 31	PB1 4	PB3 32	PB1 5	PB3 33	PB1 6	PB3 34
9	PB1 7	PB3 35	PB1 8	PB3 36	PB1 9	PB3 37	PB1 10	PB3 38	PB1 11	PB3 39	PB1 12	PB3 40	PB1 13	PB3 41
10	PB1 14	PB3 42	PB1 15	PB3 43	PB1 16	PB3 44	PB1 17	PB3 45	PB1 18	PB3 46	PB1 19	PB3 47	PB1 20	PB3 48
11	PB1 21	PB3 49	PB1 22	PB3 50	PB1 23	PB3 51	PB1 24	PB3 52	PB1 25	PB3 53	PB1 26	PB3 54	PB1 27	PB3 55
12	PB1 28	PB4 0	PB1 29	PB4 1	PB1 30	PB4 2	PB1 31	PB4 3	PB1 32	PB4 4	PB1 33	PB4 5	PB1 34	PB4 6
13	PB1 35	PB4 7	PB1 36	PB4 8	PB1 37	PB4 9	PB1 38	PB4 10	PB1 39	PB4 11	PB1 40	PB4 12	PB1 41	PB4 13
14	PB1 42	PB4 14	PB1 43	PB4 15	PB1 44	PB4 16	PB1 45	PB4 17	PB1 46	PB4 18	PB1 47	PB4 19	PB1 48	PB4 20
15	PB1 49	PB4 21	PB1 50	PB4 22	PB1 51	PB4 23	PB1 52	PB4 24	PB1 53	PB4 25	PB1 54	PB4 26	PB1 55	PB4 27
16	PB2 0	PB4 28	PB2 1	PB4 29	PB2 2	PB4 30	PB2 3	PB4 31	PB2 4	PB4 32	PB2 5	PB4 33	PB2 6	PB4 34
17	PB2 7	PB4 35	PB2 8	PB4 36	PB2 9	PB4 37	PB2 10	PB4 38	PB2 11	PB4 39	PB2 12	PB4 40	PB2 13	PB4 41
18	PB2 14	PB4 42	PB2 15	PB4 43	PB2 16	PB4 44	PB2 17	PB4 45	PB2 18	PB4 46	PB2 19	PB4 47	PB2 20	PB4 48
19	PB2 21	PB4 49	PB2 22	PB4 50	PB2 23	PB4 51	PB2 24	PB4 52	PB2 25	PB4 53	PB2 26	PB4 54	PB2 27	PB4 55

Figure 2.10. *(continued)*

first physical block (PB0) starts at sector 0, track 0 and continues through sector 12, track 7. The second physical block (PB1) starts at sector 0, track 8 and goes through sector 12, track 15. When a physical block is written on alternate sectors beginning at sector 0, track 0, the even sectors are filled to the bottom of the cylinder and then a wrap-around takes place to begin filling odd sectors, top to bottom.

Gaps can be used in place of hopscotching for synchronizing. The gap length should be such that the time for passing over a gap is roughly equivalent to the time required by the CPU to process the current record and to start the data transfer for the next record. Otherwise, the medium must rotate all the way around for the next record to be accessed.

2.3.3.2 Block-Addressable Devices

Block-addressable devices differ from sector-addressable devices because a block can be a variable length record whose length is defined by a programmer. Thus, the number of blocks stored on a track can vary from track to track. Sector-addressable devices may be considered a special case of block-addressable devices in which there is an integral number of fixed size blocks per track. Since all sectors are the same size and there are an integral number of sectors per track, a specific sector can usually be located more quickly than a specific block. The primary motivation for using variable length blocks is that the size of programmer-defined physical records may not be the same length as a sector and space in a sector is wasted. On the other hand, a physical record may be defined by a programmer as larger than a sector, thus requiring more than one access to read or write a user-defined physical record. The use of variable-sized blocks, however, makes it very difficult to synchronize CPU computation with reading or writing records.

IBM disk and drum are block-addressable devices. A programmer defines the length of a logical record and block size via a job control language, a macro, or a data set label (see Chapter 6). Data are recorded on IBM direct access storage devices using one of two track formats: count-data or count-key-data formats. These two formats are illustrated in Figure 2.11. Each track contains sytem data as well as user data and has an index point that indicates its physical beginning.

The home address (HA) defines the track address (cylinder number and track number) and indicates the condition (operative or defective) of the track. The gaps in Figure 2.11 separate the individual areas on a track. The length of each gap varies with the device (because of the different rotating speeds of devices), the location of the gap, and the length of the preceding area. The address marker (A) indicates the beginning of a physical record or block.

A count area identifies a record's address (cylinder number, track number within cylinder, record number within track) and indicates the record's format (count-data or count-key-data) and length. If the records in a file are formatted with keys, then a one-byte field in the count area specifies the length of the key

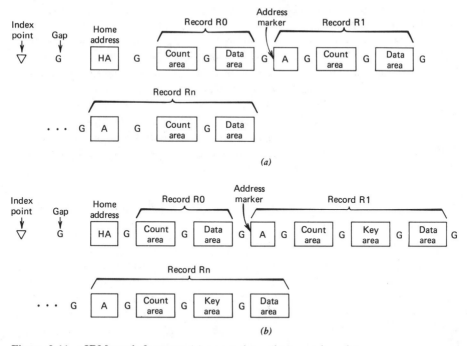

Figure 2.11. IBM track formats: (*a*) count-data; (*b*) count-key-data.

area. The key length for records formatted without keys (the count-data format) is 0. For records formatted with keys, the key area contains the key value of the last (rightmost) logical record in the associated data area. The data area is a block of one or more logical records. When a record is accessed, all the areas (count, key, data, etc.) are also accessed. The block size that a programmer specifies is the size of the data area only.

Each distinct area on a track has a two-byte field that is used for error detection. This field holds a cyclic check. The control unit for a device removes the parity bit from each byte of data as data are transferred from internal memory to a device, computes the cyclic check, and writes it at the end of each area. As data are transferred from a device to internal memory, the control unit recalculates the cyclic check for each area and compares it with the one retrieved from the area. Cyclic check bytes are not transmitted to internal memory, but parity bits are restored to the data bytes to maintain odd parity.

The first record on each track, R0, contains a count area and a data area. The count area is 11 bytes long, just as it is for all other records on a track. The key length in the R0 count area is always zero, and the data area is always 8 bytes long plus 2 bytes for the cyclic check. Record R0 does not hold user data; instead, it is used by an operating system for various purposes. For example, R0's count area (on nondrum devices) may be used to provide a cross-reference between a primary track that becomes defective and the alternate track that replaces it, or it can be used by an operating system to maintain a free space count for the track.

The total amount of gap space and system data per block on an IBM 3330 disk is 135 bytes if logical records are formatted without keys and 191 bytes if logical records are formatted with keys. The 135 bytes include the address marker, the count area, and two gaps. The additional 56 bytes for records formatted with keys is for the gap needed because of the existence of a key area. On an IBM 3350 disk, the gap space and system data require 267 bytes and 185 bytes for records formatted with and without keys, respectively. To utilize storage space on IBM disk and drum devices, record blocking, when appropriate, is recommended.

2.3.4   Space and Timing Considerations for Magnetic Disk and Drum

Space and timing calculations vary from device to device, file organization to file organization, and manufacturer to manufacturer. Therefore, the proper manufacturer manuals should be consulted for specific information on a particular disk or drum model. The equations given below for space and time calculations are intended to be general while at the same time typical of those supplied by manufacturers. In addition, the calculations are assumed to be for block-addressable devices with blocks containing gaps and system data areas in addition to the user data area. In order to keep the calculations simple, the equations are for sequential files allocated on contiguous tracks and cylinders. The equations also apply to sector-addressable devices since sector addressing can be considered to be a special case of block addressing. Table 2.7 contains a list of symbols, with their definitions, that are used in the space and timing calculations.

2.3.4.1   Space Calculations

Each disk and drum device medium has a track capacity that determines the number of blocks that it can hold. Maximum use of the space on a track can be achieved when there is one block per track. In general, the number of tracks required for storing a file is

$$N_T = \frac{N_B}{N_{B/T}}$$

where

$$N_B = \frac{N_L}{BF}$$

$$N_{B/T} = \left\lfloor \frac{T_{CAP}}{B_{SIZE}} \right\rfloor^*$$

$$B_{SIZE} = G_S + NDI + BF \times LRL$$

*⌊Brackets⌋ denote the mathematical floor function.

Table 2.7

Symbols Used in Space and Time Calculations for Disk and Drum

Symbol	Definition
N_L	Number of logical records in file
BF	Blocking factor
LRL	Logical record length (characters)
NDI	System data per block (characters)
G_S	Total gap space per block (characters)
B_{SIZE}	Block size (characters)
T_{CAP}	Track capacity
$N_{B/T}$	Number of blocks per track
N_B	Number of blocks per file
N_T	Number of tracks per file
N_C	Number of cylinders per file
$N_{T/C}$	Number of tracks per cylinder
T_B	Time to access a block
T_{SEEK}	Seek time
T_L	Latency time
T_{HS}	Head selection time
T_{DT}	Data transfer time
T_{TRK}	Time to access a track
T_{CYL}	Time to access a cylinder
T_{I-S}	Initial seek time to locate first cylinder of file
T_{CONT}	Seek time to move from cylinder i to cylinder $i+1$
T_T	Total time to access all blocks in a file

If the device is a disk and storage space for a file must be allocated in cylinders, then the total number of cylinders is

$$N_C = \frac{N_T}{N_{T/C}}$$

2.3.4.2 Timing Calculations

While space calculations are fairly straightforward, timing calculations are slightly more difficult. The time to access a block is

$$T_B = T_{SEEK} + T_L + T_{HS} + T_{DT}$$

For movable head disks, the seek time (T_{SEEK}) is usually the largest and most critical of the four components involved in T_B. The latency time (T_L) is the time for the correct block to rotate under a read/write head so that data transfer can begin. The latency time used in calculations is half the time required for one complete rotation of a disk platter or drum. The time to switch from read/write head to read/write head (T_{HS}) is considered negligible. The data transfer time (T_{DT}) is the time required to transfer data from the storage medium to internal memory after the correct block is located. (T_{HS}) is a function of the rotation speed of a device, the density at which data is recorded on the medium, and the block length.

Since disk and drum devices are random-access devices and are typically simultaneously shared by many processes, the timing calculations given below assume that more than one process is using the device on which the file resides. Thus, on the average, the access time of a block includes a seek time based on one-third the number of cylinders that the device has (note that for a fixed head disk and drum this seek time is zero). The total time required to access a file is

$$T_T = N_C \times T_{CYL}$$

where

$$T_{CYL} = N_{T/C} \times T_{TRK}$$
$$T_{TRK} = N_{B/T} \times T_B$$

The total time to access all the records in a sequential file stored on a dedicated device, that is, a device allocated to a single process, where the I/O operation is always read the next record, is

$$T_T = T_{I-S} + N_C \times T_{CYL} + (N_C - 1) \times T_{CONT}$$

The equations given above for computing both space and time are satisfactory for determining "ball park figures." Exact values for space requirements can be computed. But the exact amount of time for accessing a block on a shared, random-access storage device is virtually impossible to compute a priori since it depends on the activity of other users and this is unquantifiable.

2.4 CHARGE-COUPLED DEVICES AND MAGNETIC BUBBLE MEMORIES

Charge-coupled device (CCD) memories and magnetic bubble memories (MBMs) fill the access time gap between relatively fast core memories (3 to 5-microsecond access time) and cheap but relatively slow fixed disks and drums (8-millisecond access time). CCDs and MBMs can be placed into the category of accessing that includes the shift register type of devices with a serial-in/serial-out operation in which all shift registers are clocked simultaneously.

From their very inception, CCDs and MBMs have been heralded as storage devices to replace disk and drum. The cost per bit of both memories falls between the price categories of large core stores and fixed head disk and drum. These two new storage technologies may have many potential applications within the next few years. One potential use of these technologies is as a replacement of magnetic disk and drum storage as a cost-effective alternative in the capacity range overlapping large semiconductor and core memories at one end and small disks and drums at the other end.

The cost/bit price of CCDs and MBMs is nearly independent of storage capacity, whereas, the cost/bit of rotating magnetic memories is highly dependent on storage capacity, and it falls with increasing size. As a result, for applications that require low capacity external storage, not exceeding approximately 10^6 bits, the price per bit is high for rotating mass memory. The cost per bit is large, for small rotating mass memories, because of the fixed overhead costs of motor, power supplies, and electronic circuits. Thus, at low capacities, both CCDs and MBMs are very cost-effective—particularly since bit-price cost at low capacities of rotating memories is not likely to change substantially in the near future.

Although both CCDs and MBMs have the advantage of low cost per bit for small capacities, a low-cost removable medium is not available. Hence, low-cost off-line storage is likely to remain in the domain of rotating magnetic memories, specifically disk packs, for some time.

2.4.1 Charge-Coupled Devices

A serial shift register may be visualized as a set of flip-flops organized serially through which data are propagated, bit by bit, at a rate established by an external clock. In contrast to an ordinary digital shift register, however, a CCD is not a series of flip-flops; instead, data bits stored in the CCD are represented by variable quantities of electrical charge rather than on-off states of fixed magnitude.

Physically, a CCD is a linear array of closely spaced capacitors or gates. The presence of a clock pulse gates the charge of each capacitor cell into an amplifier; the amplifier, in turn, charges the next cell in sequence accordingly. The charging and discharging of this capacitance is the principal factor that limits the speed of CCDs. This capacitance is the storage site for charge in dynamic memories that must be refreshed every few hundred milliseconds (ms) as the charge leaks away from the capacitors. The frequency of refresh is a function of temperature, and at room temperature (25°C), the element storage time is about one second. At −30°C, the storage time is approximately 20 seconds. The frequency of a clock that shifts data through a CCD shift register can have a wide range, limited at one extreme by a circuit's maximum switching speed, and at the other extreme by the maximum allowable refresh time required to maintain the data bits.

There are at least three basic CCD memory organizations: the synchronous or serpentine organization, the serial-parallel-serial (SPS) organization, and the line addressable random-access memory (LARAM). The serpentine organization is the simplest of the three to describe (it also has the longest access time), and it is illustrated in Figure 2.12. In the serpentine organization, storage cells are laid out along a winding path with data refreshing stages at each corner. All bits traverse the same path through the loop at the same time-frequency with each bit passing through every storage element in one trip through the device.

The internal shift frequency and the I/O data rate are equivalent. The number of CCD storage elements between refresh stages depends on the transfer efficiency (the recoverable charge per bit shifted) and the lowest shift

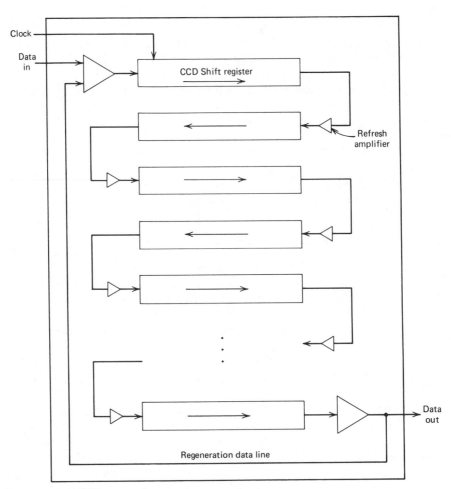

Figure 2.12.   CCD serpentine memory organization.

rate to be used in idle or standby mode. The highest shift rate and the number of bits between input and output stages determine the lowest access time, and for random addressing the average access time is half the maximum. Short access times can be obtained only at the expense of many I/O stages.

The performance of CCD memories is limited by access time, which is in the tens and hundreds of microseconds for small (16K bit) memories. Data can be accessed in a CCD by placing the address of the data in an address register, and when the data, specified by the contents of the address register, are shifted to an I/O stage, they are output bit by bit. In Figure 2.12 data are output via the Data-out line.

Most of the CCD memories range in size from 16K to 64K bits. To minimize latency (the access time to any given bit in the device), a 16K bit memory can be organized as 64 registers of 256 bits each. Any bit is accessible with a maximum of 255 shift operations. If the fastest shift cycle is 750 nanoseconds (ns) long, maximum latency time is less than 200 microseconds (μs).

As the cost of CCD memories decreases, a greater variety of CCDs will become available. Some manufacturers are developing stack CCD chips to build systems of 10^7 to 10^8 bits. A 64K bit chip is available with a cost per bit of about 0.1 cent, an access time of about 0.1 ms, and data transfer rates of 10^6 to 10^7 bits per second. To achieve a more attractive cost of 0.02 cent per bit, the full potential of CCD memories for high packing density must be demonstrated.

The primary question of whether CCD memories will find widespread use depends upon whether they will be cheap enough to compete with existing alternatives. Cost improvements for CCDs are 2 to 10 times better than semiconductor RAM (random-access memory). Currently, the cost of CCD memory is about one-fifth the cost of semiconductor RAM. With these projected cost improvements, CCD memories may be the future choice for medium- to large-scale internal memories; however, since CCD chips have serial access rather than random-access, cache memory might have to be used to accommodate their serial access characteristics.

2.4.2 Magnetic Bubble Memories

MBM may be viewed as the solid-state integrated analog of rotating electromechanical memories such as disks and drums. Data are stored in the form of magnetized regions. These regions are cylindrical domains in a thin layer of magnetic material with magnetization opposite to that of the surrounding area. Their presence or absence at specific locations correspond to binary digits stored at these locations. These bits are made accessible by moving the domains within the solid layer to an access device, as opposed to physically moving the storage media.

There are four basic functions required to operate a MBM: propagation, generation, detection, and annihilation/replication. Bubble propagation is required for access to information and bubble generation is the process of writing information into memory. The detection of bubbles is required to read the memory content. A bubble annihilator clears the memory data and is commonly combined with a replicator. The replication of bubbles allows a nondestructive read operation by duplicating information; one copy is read and discarded, while the original data remain in memory.

There are several ways to organize a MBM. The simplest organization is a single shift register. This is equivalent to a 1-track magnetic tape, and like magnetic tape, has the disadvantage of long access time. A better organization, illustrated in Figure 2.13, is the major/minor loop organization. Multiple shift registers like those in Figure 2.13 considerably reduce the access time from that of a serial organization, just as a fixed head disk has a lower access time than a tape. Disk tracks are, in effect, equivalent to minor loops.

To access data, bubbles (or the absence of bubbles) are transferred simultaneously from all minor loops to the major loop. Then they are shifted

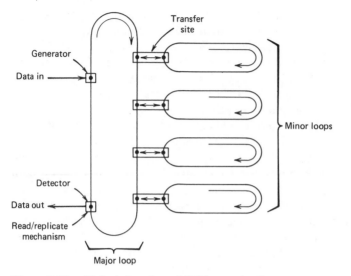

Figure 2.13. Major/minor loop MBM organization.

around the major loop, read, annihilated, or replicated, as required, and transferred back to the minor loops, regaining the same position previously occupied. Storing new information follows a reverse procedure.

Addressing requires two external counters, which are run at the rate of bubble shifting. One counter selects the position in a minor loop to be read; the other counter is started when a block is transferred to the major loop and indicates when bubble replication, annihilation, detection, and generation takes place.

Since bubble memories pack bits on small bubbles, the storage density of bubble memories is determined by the bubble size. A 92K bit MBM is available with a cost per bit of about 0.1 cent, an average access time of 2 to 4 ms, and a data transfer rate of 50K bits per second.

2.5 LARGE CORE STORAGE

Large core storage (LCS) is a directly addressable permanent addition to internal memory. It is implemented as magnetic core storage, is electronic, and has no moving or rotating parts. Three characteristics distinguish LCS from other storage devices:

1. LCS has no latency time.
2. LCS is addressable at the byte or word level.
3. Some LCSs are available to the CPU for instruction execution.

LCS usually has a larger access time than semiconductor internal memory (typically three or four times as long as semiconductor memory). When program instructions residing in LCS are executed or data stored in LCS are accessed, the performance of the CPU is degraded. For some applications it is important and efficient to transfer program instructions and data from LCS to internal memory before processing them.

There is usually a problem with addressing additional amounts of LCS because of the limitation of address length in the instruction word of a computer. Large address limits can usually be handled in one of two ways:

1. The LCS can be treated as a peripheral device like a disk; the LCS is divided into blocks and the address of a block is incorporated into a peripheral instruction with an appropriate device number.
2. Index registers can be used.

One manufacturer's LCS is packaged into units of one million 8-bit bytes of storage with each byte having a parity bit. Its cycle time is eight μs for each eight bytes (double word). Another manufacturer's extended core storage (ECS) is available in logically independent banks of 131K 60-bit words up to a maximum of two million words. Data transmission is directly between internal memory and ECS with no channel involved. The data transfer rate is 3.2 μs for the first word and eight words per μs thereafter. The CPU stops processing while transmission takes place.

The high speed of LCS makes it an obvious choice for the temporary storage of files, but the relatively high cost per bit makes it virtually impractical for the complete and permanent storage of large files. However, LCS can be used in several ways:

1. To store systems tables, such as job queue tables and file tables.
2. To store file indexes.
3. To store frequently used programs such as compilers, library routines, and parts of an operating system.
4. To store jobs in a swapped- (or rolled-) out state.
5. To use as an internal memory buffer.
6. To use for storing user programs or user data.

Using LCS as an internal memory buffer for other external storage devices in a three-level store hierarchy may be the most interesting and potentially useful application of LCS since there is usually a considerable penalty for buffering programs and data directly into internal memory from an external storage device.

2.6 MASS STORAGE DEVICES AND SYSTEMS

On-line database systems holding billions of characters of data are in existence. With such systems, it sometimes becomes expensive and impractical to store such large amounts of data on disk storage devices. Instead, it may be more realistic to store copies of often accessed programs and data on disk and to store all programs and data on a less expensive and slower mass storage unit. Mass storage systems, usually called mass stores or trillion-bit memories, provide on-line access to a trillion or more bits of data with no manual intervention involved. Access time to a randomly selected piece of data usually does not exceed 15 seconds.

Mass stores can normally be expected to occupy the lowest level in a storage hierarchy. Mass stores provide capacities of one to three orders of magnitude larger than drums and disks, and access times several orders of magnitude slower. Storage costs are about one order of magnitude less than those for disk and drum devices. The nature of these mass storage devices (or mass storage facilities) allows for an inexpensive cost per bit of on-line storage, provided the applications have the storage requirements to justify the devices. Their most obvious use is as a replacement of the conventional magnetic tape units for storing large sequential files or archival storage of random-access files.

One of the early mass storage devices, the IBM data cell, was introduced in the early 1960s. The principles of the data cell have been applied to the IBM 3851 Mass Storage Facility (MSF). The MSF provides a third level storage facility in the IBM 3850 Mass Storage System (MSS). The MSF holds archival information on tape cartridges, and they are the mass storage media. A tape cartridge is a spool (of magnetic tape) approximately four inches long and approximately two inches in diameter. Each cartridge holds about 770 inches of tape and has a capacity of about 50 million characters (half the capacity of an IBM 3330 disk pack). Access to a particular cartridge is gained after the cartridge is located from a library of cartridges and wrapped around a capstan so that it is properly positioned under a read/write head. Once a tape cartridge is mounted, data transfer is very fast, and it is comparable to disk data transfer rates. However, locating an item on a cartridge is comparable to locating an item on a magnetic tape. Data can be transferred cylinder by cylinder from the 3330 (the IBM 3330 disk is the second level of storage in the 3850 MSS) to a tape cartridge and vice versa. The 3851 MSF contains a maximum of 4,720 tape cartridges creating a total capacity of 236 billion characters.

Three other currently available mass storage systems that predate the IBM 3850 MSS are:

1. The Ampex Terabit Memory (TBM) System.
2. The Grumman Masstape System.
3. The Precision Instrument's Unicon System.

Maximum available system capacities for these systems range from 88×10^9 characters in the Precision Instruments Unicon to 110×10^9 characters in Grumman's Masstape to 362×10^9 characters for the TBM. The TBM random-access memory uses magnetic tape as the basic storage medium. Random-access is provided by using tape search speeds of 1,000 inches per second and by using packing densities of 700,000 bits/inch^2. The principle of the Unicon system is to create and detect information elements in two dimensions by means of signal modulated coherent laser radiation. The Unicon system has a packing density of 6.45×10^8 bits/inch^2.

Basic hardware prices (the prices given are 1973 prices) for these systems range from \$400,000 for a 14×10^9 character Masstape System (Masstape allows one to add on-line capacity in units of 14×10^9 characters) to \$4.6 million for the 362×10^9 character TBM. The Unicon System costs \$1.6 million for 88×10^9 characters.

The advantages of mass stores are several:

1. They provide relatively fast access to very large quantities of data.
2. They eliminate the human handling of data with the consequent elimination of human errors.
3. They provide the ability to share stored data among several host central processors.
4. They provide reliability improvements over conventional tape recording technology.
5. They reduce operating costs for a given level of service.

The disadvantages of mass stores include:

1. The inability to readily adapt to random processing or structured files.
2. The relatively small amount of experience with these devices in the user community.
3. The relatively large access time, about 10 to 15 seconds, to an arbitrary record.

A mass storage system is a complex system and the effective use of it and the host system(s) demand careful performance analysis. There are several factors of importance involving the implementation of mass storage systems within operating systems:

1. The total number of characters per second that can be transferred to and from the mass store (through-put capacity).
2. The storage capacity.
3. The cost of the mass store.
4. The mode of operation.
5. The directory alternatives.

2.7 STORAGE HIERARCHIES

A storage hierarchy can be thought of as an ordering of storage devices on the basis of speed and cost so that only the most important and most frequently accessed data are kept on the expensive and fast devices and the least important and less frequently accessed data are kept on the inexpensive and slow devices. The purpose of a storage hierarchy system is to increase the overall functional effectiveness of a computing system. In this context, functional effectiveness can take several forms. The one of primary interest is making large amounts of data available within a reasonably short period of time. The objective of a storage hierarchy is to maximize the frequency with which the faster devices are referenced so that access speeds approach those of the faster devices at a cost that approaches the slower devices. A storage hierarchy system may be characterized as follows:

1. Fast and slow devices are organized into blocks of data.
2. The first reference to a particular block requires that the entire block be transferred from the slow device and stored in the fast device. Subsequent requests to the block are made to the fast device.
3. The fast storage is capable of storing several blocks that are replaced on a dynamic basis by a block replacement algorithm.

Storage hierarchies operate in the following manner. When a program requests data, the request first goes to the highest level (level 1) of storage, internal memory, in the hierarchy. If the request is not satisfied at this level of storage, then the data request goes to level 2, etc. Table 2.8 illustrates a four-level storage hierarchy along with the capacity, cost, and access time of the storage at each level. In Table 2.8, the role of the large core store is to serve as a large buffer between internal memory and the slower disk device.

The IBM 3850 Mass Storage System (MSS) described in the previous section is an example of a three-level storage hierarchy system. The 3851 Mass Storage Facility (MSF) backs up the IBM 3330 disk units. The entire system appears to be a large array of virtual disk units. The objective of the 3850 MSS is to make the 3330 disk seem larger than it really is, or on the other hand, to make the large slow storage appear to have an access time comparable to that of the 3330 disk. The software of the IBM S/370 behaves as though it is using only 3330 disks as external storage devices. The 3330 disks at the second level of the hierarchy act as large buffers between the CPU and the third level storage, the 3851 MSF.

Table 2.8

Four-Level Storage Hierarchy

Level	Storage Technology	Capacity (bits)	Cost/bit ($\cent$)	Mean Access Time
1	Semiconductor memory	$10^6 - 10^7$	0.1	0.1 μs
2	Large core store	$10^7 - 10^8$	0.01	1 μs
3	Movable head disk	10^9	0.0001	20–75 ms
4	Mass store (tape cartridges)	10^{11}	0.000001	10 seconds

2.8   STORAGE TECHNOLOGY PERFORMANCE CHARACTERISTICS AND FUTURE PROSPECTS

Capacity, access time, data transfer rate, and cost per bit are the basic performance characteristics of storage devices. In measuring a storage technology, areal density (bits/inch^2) is the key figure to consider. The greater the bit storage density, the lower the cost per bit and correspondingly, the shorter the average access time for any given capacity. Typical size, access time, and cost per bit figures are given in Table 2.9 for some of today's storage technologies. The figures given in Table 2.9 are order of magnitude figures.

In spite of dramatic cost reductions projected for fast access memories, such as semiconductor, bubble memories, and charge-coupled devices, their costs are still significantly above the costs of storage with capacities in the range of 10^8 characters; thus, they cannot yet be considered competitive for situations requiring large capacities. The performance characteristics of rotating surface memories (disk and drum) have improved drastically over the past two decades, and even further improvements in large capacity rotating surface storage devices are certain to occur. For the foreseeable future, it is clear that disk and drum storage devices will be the dominant devices for applications requiring large capacity, on-line storage. MBMs and CCDs have been widely discussed as potential replacements for drum and fixed disk storage devices; however, to achieve widespread acceptance as replacements for drum and disk, the price per bit of the new storage technology must approach that of the devices they are to replace.

Table 2.9

Comparison of Storage Technologies

Type of Storage	Size (bits)	Access Time (seconds)	Cost/bit (¢)
Semiconductor memory	$10^6 - 10^7$	5×10^{-7}	$10^{-1} - 7 \times 10^{-1}$
Large core store	$10^7 - 10^8$	5×10^{-6}	10^{-2}
Bubble domain	$5 \times 10^5 - 2 \times 10^8$	$5 \times 10^{-4} - 10^{-3}$	$3 \times 10^{-2} - 5 \times 10^{-1}$
Charge-coupled device	$10^7 - 1.25 \times 10^8$	5×10^{-4}	5×10^{-2}
Drum and fixed disk	$5 \times 10^5 - 10^8$	10^{-2}	$10^{-3} - 5 \times 10^{-2}$
Movable head disk	$5 \times 10^7 - 10^{10}$	$0.5 \times 10^{-1} - 10^{-1}$	$10^{-4} - 2.5 \times 10^{-2}$
Magnetic tape	$10^8 - 10^{10}$	$1 - 10$	$10^{-5} - 10^{-4}$
Mass (tape cartridges)	$10^{11} - 10^{12}$	10	10^{-6}

Mass storage systems like the IBM 3850 Mass Storage System have not received wide spread use except in certain situations. One important reason for this may be the recent emphasis on distributing data rather than centralizing the storage of data.

EXERCISES

1. Given a magnetic tape drive with the manufacturer specifications: density = 1600 bytes/inch, IRG = 0.5 inch, and speed = 45 inches/second.

    (a) How many inches of tape are required to store 100,000 records, each 100 bytes with a blocking factor of 32?
    (b) How many records could be stored on a standard 2,400-foot tape if logical records of length 100 bytes and a blocking factor of 32 are assumed?
    (c) If a start/stop time of 10.6ms is assumed, how long will it take to read the 2,400-foot tape written in (b)?

2. Given a logical record length of 152 bytes, a magnetic tape density of 1,600 characters per inch, and an interblock (interrecord) gap of 0.5 inch, calculate the blocking factor necessary to have 95% of the tape (2400 foot) holding data.

3. If the manufacturer's specifications for the VAX RP06 disk drive are: surfaces = 19, tracks/surface = 815, sectors/track = 22, bytes/sector = 512, latency time = 8.3 ms, and seek time = 28 ms.

    (a) How many megabytes can be stored on an RP06 disk unit?
    (b) How many cylinders (either whole or partial) will be required to store 100,000 records, each of which is 100 bytes provided that no record is split across a sector boundary?

4. A given disk has 512 bytes in each sector, 55 surfaces on which to record information, 200 tracks per surface, and 20 sectors on each track. How many 120-byte logical records can be stored on 10 cylinders of this disk if we assume that no logical record is split across a sector boundary?

5. A certain disk drive has 200 tracks per surface and 5 surfaces. Each track has twenty 512-byte sectors. The disk rotates at 6,000 revolutions per minute.

    (a) What is the average latency time in milliseconds?
    (b) How many sectors are there on each cylinder?

6. A certain computer system has one disk controller attached to three disk drives. When three programs are executing, each of which is using a different disk drive, the I/O operations are too slow. Explain a possible cause for this effect.

7. Consider a disk storage device with a total capacity of 10,000 bytes per

track. It takes 10 milliseconds for one rotation. Suppose data are blocked into 1,000 byte blocks and interblock gaps are 100 bytes long. In addition, blocks cannot span tracks.

(a) Compute the maximum instantaneous data transfer rate in bytes/second.

(b) Compute the effective (average) data transfer rate in bytes/second for transferring an entire track.

8. Consider a disk track containing N unblocked records. A search operation starts at the beginning of a random block, looking for some other randomly located block. Derive an expression for rotational latency delay as an expected number of blocks that must be passed over to get to the desired block.

9. In this chapter, hopscotching was described for the CDC 841 disk unit. Describe how another manufacturer's disk system performs hopscotching.

10. Discuss the tradeoffs between fixed head disks and removable disks. What kinds of applications are more appropriate for each kind of disk?

11. Some people have suggested that frequently used data and programs should be placed on certain parts of a disk for fast access. Explain where these data and programs should be placed and give reasons for your answer.

12. One of the references at the end of this chapter describes three basic CCD memory organizations. The serpentine organization was described in this chapter. Give a written overview of the other two organizations with detailed illustrations.

13. It was suggested in this chapter that CCDs and MBMs will replace disk and drum storage in some applications. Locate descriptions of such applications in trade magazines and computer journals.

14. Read the references at the end of this chapter that describe MBMs and give a brief written overview of the technology behind this important storage device.

15. Describe some applications for which the use of mass storage systems are appropriate. Why, in your opinion, have mass storage systems failed to receive widespread use?

REFERENCES

2.1 Brechtlein, R. "Comparing Disc Technologies," *Datamation*, January 1978, pp. 139–150.

2.2 Hodges, D.A. "Microelectronic Memories," *Scientific American*, Vol. 237, September 1977, pp. 130–145.

2.3 Theis, D.J. "An Overview of Memory Technologies," *Datamation*, January 1978, pp. 113–131.

These three survey papers provide easy-to-read descriptions of the memory technologies covered in this chapter. Theis' paper gives several tables with manufacturer's specifications for random-access memories, charge-coupled devices, magnetic bubble memories, movable and fixed head disks, magnetic tape units, and mass storage systems. The Winchester disk and Josephenson device technologies are briefly discussed in Brechtlein and Hodges' papers, respectively.

2.4 Chi, C.S. "Advances in Computer Mass Storage Technology," *IEEE Computer,* May 1982, pp. 60–74.

This article describes magnetic recording technology and discusses some of the reasons why magnetic storage is still the dominant technology for external memories.

2.5 Amelio, G.F. "Charge-Coupled Devices for Memory Applications," *Proceedings of National Computer Conference,* 1975, Vol. 44, pp. 515–522.

2.6 Toombs, D. "CCD and Bubble Memories," *IEEE Spectrum,* Vol. 15, April 1978, pp. 22–30 and May 1978, pp. 36–39.

2.7 Ypma, J.E. "Bubble Domain Memory Systems," *Proceedings of National Computer Conference,* 1975, Vol. 44, pp. 523–528.

Good technical descriptions of CCDs and MBMs are given in these three papers.

2.8 Houston, G.B. "Trillion Bit Memories," *Datamation,* October 1973, pp. 52–58.

The discussion in this paper focuses on very large mass storage systems—in particular, the Ampex Terabit Memory System, the Grumman Masstape System, and Precision Instrument's Unicon System.

2.9 Johnson, C. "IBM 3850-Mass Storage System," *Proceedings of National Computer Conference,* 1975, Vol. 44, pp. 509–514.

The architecture of the 3850 Mass Storage System is examined to demonstrate its functional and performance capabilities.

2.10 IBM Student Text. "Introduction to IBM Direct-Access Storage Devices and Organization Methods," September 1976.

Provides a good description of direct-access storage devices for IBM computer systems.

2.11 Madnick, S.E. "Storage Hierarchy Systems," MIT Project MAC Report TR-105, Cambridge, Massachusetts, 1973.

2.12 Katzan, H., Jr. "Storage Hierarchy Systems," *Proceedings of SJCC,* 1971, Vol. 38, pp. 325–336.

These two papers discuss various storage hierarchy systems. Katzan's paper presents a 1971 state-of-the-art analysis of storage hierarchy systems.

2.13 Campbell, G., et al. "The Use of Extended Core Storage in a Multiprogramming Operating System," in *Software Engineering,* J. T. Tou (ed.), Vol. 1, Academic Press, New York, 1970.

2.14 Thornton, J.E. *Design of a Computer, the Control Data 6600,* Scott, Foresman and Company, Glenview, Illinois, 1970.

This paper and book discuss the use of Control Data Corporation's ECS as a bulk core storage between internal memory and secondary memory devices.

3

Common File Structures

3.1 INTRODUCTION

This chapter is the first of three that discusses file structures (organizations). The organizations discussed in this chapter are those that are commonly supported by the file (or data) management systems of many operating systems. These include the sequential, indexed sequential, and direct organizations. In addition to these common organizations, IBM's VSAM file organization is also described. Chapter 4 discusses search trees as a possible means for structuring files, and Chapter 5 discusses list-structured organizations that are feasible for satisfying multikey retrieval requests on secondary keys. The file organizations discussed in this chapter and in Chapter 4, with the exception of Bentley's k-d binary search tree, are satisfactory for satisfying only primary key retrieval requests. The file organizations discussed in these three chapters are supported by manufacturers through their operating systems, by software packages, or by database management systems such as SYSTEM 2000 and TOTAL that can be purchased or leased from manufacturers or independent software companies.

The primary objective of this chapter and the following two chapters is to present the characteristics of most of the file organizations currently available in order to allow an intelligent selection to be made for a particular application.

3.2 SELECTING A FILE ORGANIZATION

The primary objective of a file organization is to provide access paths to records during retrieval and update operations. Since requests against a file usually involve searching, access paths to records should make searching as efficient as possible. In applications that use the file organizations supported by the file system component of an operating system, the file selection problem is usually analyzed in the context of choosing one main access path to a collection of one or more records. The particular organization most suitable for any application depends upon such factors as:

1. The types of external storage devices available.
2. The types of queries allowed.
3. The number of keys.
4. The mode of retrieval.
5. The mode of update.
6. The need (or desire) to economize storage.

Computer systems with only sequential access devices restrict a programmer to using sequential files, whereas, if direct-access storage devices are available, then a programmer may have a number of file organizations from which to choose.

3.2.1 Types of Queries

There are three basic types of queries: the simple query, the range query, and the Boolean query. For a simple query, the value or negation of the value of a single key is specified. A range query involves specifying a range of values for a single key using the relational operators $<$, $\leqslant$, $>$, $\geqslant$. A Boolean query is a logical combination of simple and range queries using the logical operators $\wedge$ (AND) and $\vee$ (OR). An example of each type of query is:

1. Simple query: DEPARTMENT = 'AUTO'.
2. Range query: SALARY > 15000.
3. Boolean query: DEPARTMENT = 'AUTO' $\wedge$ SALARY > 15000 $\vee$ DEPARTMENT = 'SHOE'.

The file organizations discussed in this chapter and in Chapter 4, with the exception of Bentley's k-d binary search tree, are at best satisfactory for handling simple and range queries. The file organizations described in Chapter 5 are satisfactory for all three types of queries.

3.2.2 Mode of Retrieval and Update

The mode of retrieval may be either *real-time* or *batch*. For real-time retrieval, the response time for any query should be no more than a few seconds. For instance, in an airline reservation system, the availability of seats for a given flight must be determined in a few seconds. In batched mode retrieval, the response time is not usually critical. Retrieval requests are batched together, usually in a transaction* file, until either enough requests have been received or

*In general, a transaction may be either a retrieval request or an update.

a sufficiently long time period has elapsed. Then all retrieval requests in the transaction file are processed against the master file.

One of the programmer's first considerations when selecting a file organization is whether there is a real-time update requirement. If not, then the freedom of selecting a file organizaion is usually great. If real-time updates are required, file organization selection compromises must be effected that will enable the system to meet both retrieval and update requirements. Real-time update is necessary for an airline reservation system; however, there are some on-line systems that require real-time retrieval but do not require real-time update. Updates are batched, and updating is scheduled at a time when the on-line system is not operational. Bank systems are typical of systems requiring real-time retrieval but which permit updates, say for deposits, to be batched and made at the end of a day. Batched updating uses two files: a transaction file holding the updates and a master file representing the file status before the updates. The transaction file is processed against the current master file. The result is a new updated master file.

The simplest situation for batched processing occurs when records have only one key. The transactions are ordered on the same key as the master file. All records in the current master file are examined, retrieved if the transaction is a retrieval request, or modified if the transaction is an update. If a transaction file contains update transactions, then a new master file is normally created during the processing. A problem may arise if both retrieval requests and updates are indeed present in the same transaction file. The problem that must be resolved occurs when both a retrieval request and an update are present for the same record. Then a decision has to be made: Should the record be retrieved before or after the update? Batched processing is usually practical only when the number of transactions batched is reasonably large because it is inefficient to process an entire file for small batches. Batched processing is especially appropriate for sequential files.

3.2.3 Additional Factors for File Organization Selection

The availability of on-line external storage may not be a critical problem in many of today's large computer systems, but in some small systems the amount of on-line external storage space available may be limited. In situations where storage space is limited, the efficiency of retrieval and update may have to be sacrificed for economy of storage.

Some additional factors that should be considered when selecting a file organization suitable for an application include:

1. The frequency of use of a file.
2. The growth potential of a file.
3. The availability of file organizations supported by the programming system(s) available to a user.
4. The programming languages available for writing programs that require files.

The last two items, 3 and 4, may be the most important considerations for selecting a file organization for many applications. Most operating systems support sequential, indexed sequential, and direct organizations. While none of these may be the most satisfactory for a given application, one of them will probably be used since they are readily available. The programmer's preference for a language for developing an application program may determine the file organization(s) that can be used. Most Fortran IV implementations support both sequential and direct file organizations, and COBOL and PL/I support sequential, indexed sequential, and direct organizations.

Normally, it is desirable to evaluate and compare various file organizations during file organization selection. Some measures that can be used to evaluate a file organization include:

1. The storage required.
2. The time required to read an arbitrary record.
3. The time required to read the next record.
4. The time required to add a record.
5. The time required to alter data item values in a record.
6. The time required to read all records in a file.
7. The time required to reorganize a file.

A method for selecting a file organization for an application is:

1. Determine the file processing requirements of the application problem.
2. Select the file organization that appears to best satisfy the requirements determined in 1.
3. Is the file organization, determined in 2, supported by available programming system(s), either by an operating system or by a package available on the system?
4. If the answer to 3 is yes, then use the organization selected in 2.
5. If the answer to 3 is no, then select one of the three alternatives given below. The choice of the alternative should be governed by two considerations: the importance of the requirements in 1 for an application and the time period permitted for developing the application program.
   (a) Purchase a system that supports the desired file organization.
   (b) Develop an in-house system to support the desired file organization.
   (c) Select the most satisfactory of the file organizations supported by an available programming system and use it.

3.3 SEQUENTIAL FILE ORGANIZATION

The sequential file organization is the best known and most frequently used organization. The logical and physical order of the records stored in a sequential file are the same. Sequential files on disk are stored on tracks within contiguous cylinders, and on drums they are stored on adjacent tracks. Since records in sequential files are stored in continuous succession, accessing the nth record in a file (starting at the beginning of the file) requires that the previous n-1 records also be read.

Historically, sequential files have been associated with magnetic tapes because of the sequential nature of the recording medium. But sequential files are commonly stored on random-access devices such as disk and drum when high-speed successive record access is a requirement of processing. A word of caution is warranted for the immediately preceding remark because for multiprogramming systems in which a disk device is being shared by several users, reading the next record from a sequential file may involve considerable seek time to position the read/write heads over the cylinder containing the "next" record. Of course, how much the read/write head movement actually affects the processing of an associated application or system program depends to some extent on the buffering scheme used, and whether or not anticipatory reads are done on the sequential file by the operating system's access routines.

The principal use of sequential files is the serial or sequential processing of records. If a read/write mechanism is positioned to retrieve a particular record, then it can rapidly access the next record in the file. The advantage of being able to rapidly access the next record in a file becomes a disadvantage when the file is to be searched for a record other than the "next" record. On the average, half of a sequential file must be read to retrieve a particular record. Sequential files are useful for sorting and searching large volumes of data that for economic reasons are stored on magnetic tape.

Sequential files may be keyed or nonkeyed. Each logical record in a keyed file has a data item called a key that can be used to order the records. The records in nonkeyed sequential files are in serial order, with each new record usually placed at the end of a file.

3.3.1 Opening and Closing Sequential Files

Files can be "opened" for input, output, or update. When a file is opened for input, only read operations are accepted for the file, that is, records can only be read from the file. Similarly, when a file is opened for output, only write operations are accepted for the file. When a file is opened for update, the record most recently read can be rewritten.

A sequential file stored on magnetic tape can be opened only for input or output. A sequential file stored on disk or drum can be used for input, for output, or for update. This means that a programmer can open a file for output and write records to the file and then later, in the same program, open the file for input and read records from it. Before this can be done, however, in either COBOL or PL/I, the file must be "closed" and then reopened. The close function causes a sequential file to be rewound. An explicit rewind operation is provided in Fortran IV for rewinding sequential files since there is no close function. Logically, a rewind operation positions a file so that a "read next record'' operation causes the first record in the file to be read. Rewinding a sequential file residing on a magnetic tape is a physical operation that causes the tape to be rewound back to the load point of the file. The open and close functions mentioned above cause several things to happen when they are executed in a program. Both functions are discussed in detail in Chapter 6.

3.3.2 Sequential File Updating

Adding records to or removing records from a sequential file is straightforward but often time-consuming. For nonkeyed files, new records can be added (inserted) at the end of the file, but for keyed files with records maintained in key value sequence (sorted order), the insertion process requires that room be made for a new record in its proper sorted position. The only way to insert a record and maintain both the sort order and the physical sequence of the file is to copy the original file down to a point of insertion, insert the new record, and then copy the remainder of the file. Since inserting one record at a time in a sorted sequential file is costly, records to be inserted are usually batched (in sorted order) and one pass made over the original file, thus creating an updated file with new records inserted in the proper positions. A second alternative for inserting records is to insert the new records serially at the end of the file and then sort them into proper sequence at a later time.

Removing (deleting) records from a sequential file, whether it is a keyed or nonkeyed file, requires that records be pushed together to compact space occupied by the deleted records. This space is normally compacted by making a copy of the file with the deleted records absent.

Altering (updating) values of a data item in a record can be difficult. If an updated record is longer or shorter than the original record, then adjacent records have to be moved either to make room for a longer record or to compact space for a shorter record. It is expensive to update one record at a time. In most cases, updates are batched, sorted into the same order as the file, and then a single pass is made over the file, updating data items in specific records as they are encountered. Batching updates make it possible to process sequential files at a low cost per update.

In summary, the sequential file organization provides for the rapid access of the next record in a file, but presents some difficulties when retrieving records out of sequence and updating records.

3.3.3 Sequential Files in PL/I

The example to demonstrate the use of sequential files in PL/I involves updating a personnel file (MASTER). The allowable updates are add, delete, and modify. Each record in MASTER is an instance of PERSONNEL_REC (see Figure 3.1). Updates to MASTER are collected in a transaction file (TRANSACTION). In Figure 3.1, the procedure PERSONNEL_UPDATE uses the MASTER and TRANSACTION files to produce a new personnel file,

```
PERSONNEL_UPDATE:  PROCEDURE OPTIONS(MAIN);
  /*THIS PROCEDURE USES A TRANSACTION FILE CONTAINING UPDATES TO A PERSONNEL
  MASTER FILE TO UPDATE THE MASTER FILE, THUS CREATING A NEW MASTER FILE.
  ALL FILES ARE SORTED ON THE SOCIAL SECURITY NUMBER (SSN).  EACH RECORD
  IN THE TRANSACTION FILE HAS A CODE (1 = ADD, 2 = DELETE, AND 3 = MODIFY)
  THAT INDICATES THE TYPE OF UPDATE THAT IS TO BE APPLIED TO THE MASTER
  FILE.  THE OLD MASTER AND TRANSACTION FILES ARE RETAINED AS BACKUPS TO
  THE NEW MASTER FILE.*/

  DECLARE 1 PERSONNEL_REC,
            2 SSN FIXED DECIMAL(9),
            2 NAME,
              3 FIRST CHARACTER(10),
              3 MI CHARACTER(1),
              3 LAST CHARACTER(12),
            2 DEPARTMENT CHARACTER(10),
            2 SALARY FIXED DECIMAL(7, 2),
            2 AGE FIXED DECIMAL(3),
            2 START_DATE CHARACTER(6),
            2 ADDRESS CHARACTER(20);

  DECLARE 1 TRANSACTION_REC,
            2 CODE FIXED DECIMAL(1),
            2 TRANS_DATA,
              3 SSN FIXED DECIMAL(9),
              3 NAME,
                4 FIRST CHARACTER(10),
                4 MI CHARACTER(1),
                4 LAST CHARACTER (12),
              3 DEPARTMENT CHARACTER(10),
              3 SALARY FIXED DECIMAL(7, 2),
              3 AGE FIXED DECIMAL(3),
              3 START_DATE CHARACTER(6),
              3 ADDRESS CHARACTER(20);

  DECLARE MASTER FILE RECORD ENV(CONSECUTIVE F(70, 1400)),
          TRANSACTION FILE RECORD ENV(CONSECUTIVE F(71, 710)),
          NEW_MASTER FILE RECORD ENV(CONSECUTIVE F(70, 1400)),
          (MASTEREOF, TRANSEOF) BIT(1) INITIAL('0'B);
```

Figure 3.1. Updating sequential files in PL/I.

NEW_MASTER. All three files are sorted on the social security number (SSN).

The algorithm used in procedure PERSONNEL_UPDATE to update MASTER is straightforward. Records are copied from MASTER to NEW_MASTER until the SSN of the current MASTER record matches the SSN of the current TRANSACTION record (for delete and modify updates), or until the current TRANSACTION record is itself copied to NEW_MASTER (for an add update). Each record in TRANSACTION has a code indicating the type of update (1 = add, 2 = delete, 3 = modify). After a TRANSACTION record has been processed, another TRANSACTION record is read and the update process described above is repeated.

If the end of TRANSACTION is reached before the end of MASTER is reached, the remaining MASTER records are copied to NEW_MASTER. On the other hand, if the end of MASTER is reached first, the remaining records in TRANSACTION (they should only be add updates) are copied to NEW_MASTER.

The procedure PERSONNEL_UPDATE performs error checking to detect

```
ON ENDFILE(MASTER) DO;
                     MASTEREOF = '1'B;
                     CALL FINISH_TRANSACTION;
                     STOP;
                 END;

ON ENDFILE(TRANSACTION) DO;
                     TRANSEOF = '1'B;
                     CALL FINISH_MASTER;
                     STOP;
                 END;

OPEN FILE(MASTER) INPUT;
OPEN FILE(TRANSACTION) INPUT;
OPEN FILE(NEW_MASTER) OUTPUT;

/*BEGIN READING MASTER AND TRANSACTION FILES*/
READ FILE(MASTER) INTO (PERSONNEL_REC);
READ FILE(TRANSACTION) INTO (TRANSACTION_REC);

/*PERFORM THE FOLLOWING STATEMENTS UNTIL AN END OF FILE CONDITION IS
  RAISED ON EITHER THE MASTER FILE OR THE TRANSACTION FILE*/
DO WHILE(¬MASTEREOF & ¬TRANSEOF);
  DO WHILE(PERSONNEL_REC.SSN < TRANS_DATA.SSN);
    WRITE FILE(NEW_MASTER) FROM (PERSONNEL_REC);
    READ FILE(MASTER) INTO (PERSONNEL_REC);
  END;
  SELECT (CODE);
    WHEN(1)
      CALL ADD;
    WHEN(2)
      CALL DELETE;
    WHEN(3)
      CALL MODIFY;
    OTHERWISE
      PUT SKIP EDIT('INVALID TRANSACTION CODE FOR RECORD
                    WITH SSN = ', TRANS_DATA.SSN) (A, F(9));
  END;
  READ FILE(TRANSACTION) INTO (TRANSACTION_REC);
END;
```

Figure 3.1. (Continued)

and record errors incurred while MASTER is being updated. Typical errors include trying to delete or modify MASTER records that do not exist. Each update operation in Figure 3.1 is implemented as an internal procedure.

In PL/I, sequential files are declared with the CONSECUTIVE environment (ENV) attribute. An environment attribute identifies the file organization: CONSECUTIVE for sequential files, INDEXED for indexed sequential files, and REGIONAL(n), where n = 1, 2, 3, for direct files. In addition, an environment attribute can define block size (and thus the blocking factor). For example, MASTER has a blocking factor of 20.

Since MASTER and TRANSACTION are read-only, they are opened for INPUT. NEW_MASTER is write-only; thus, it is opened for OUTPUT. All three files are closed after processing.

An ENDFILE condition defined by an ON statement is raised when the end of the named file is reached. Either of the DO groups in Figure 3.1 is executed if the ENDFILE condition is raised. Upon normal completion of ON statements, control passes to the statement immediately following the statement that caused the condition to be raised.

```
ADD: PROCEDURE;
      IF PERSONNEL_REC.SSN = TRANS_DATA.SSN
         THEN PUT SKIP EDIT('ATTEMPT TO ADD RECORD WITH DUPLICATE KEY
                            = ', TRANS_DATA.SSN) (A, F(9));
         ELSE WRITE FILE(NEW_MASTER) FROM (TRANS_DATA);
      END ADD;

DELETE: PROCEDURE;
          IF PERSONNEL_REC.SSN ≠ TRANS_DATA.SSN
            THEN DO;
                 PUT SKIP EDIT('ATTEMPT TO DELETE A PERSONNEL RECORD
                               WITH SSN = ', TRANS_DATA.SSN,
                               ' THAT DOES NOT EXIST IN THE MASTER')
                               (A, F(9), A);
                 WRITE FILE (NEW_MASTER) FROM (PERSONNEL_REC);
              END;
          READ FILE(MASTER) INTO (PERSONNEL_REC);
        END DELETE;

MODIFY: PROCEDURE;
          IF PERSONNEL_REC.SSN ≠ TRANS_DATA.SSN
            THEN DO;
                 PUT SKIP EDIT('ATTEMPT TO MODIFY A PERSONNEL RECORD
                               WITH SSN = ', TRANS_DATA.SSN, ' THAT
                               DOES NOT EXIST IN THE MASTER') (A, F(9), A);
                 WRITE FILE(NEW_MASTER) FROM (PERSONNEL_REC);
              END;
            ELSE WRITE FILE(NEW_MASTER) FROM (TRANS_DATA);
          READ FILE(MASTER) INTO (PERSONNEL_REC);
        END MODIFY;
```

Figure 3.1.   (Continued)

A PL/I manual should be consulted if some of the other statements in procedure PERSONNEL_UPDATE are unfamiliar.

3.4   INDEXED SEQUENTIAL FILE ORGANIZATION

The development of direct-access storage devices made it feasible to transform a sequential file into a file that could be accessed both sequentially and randomly via a primary key. The indexed sequential file organization is such a file organization. Two variations of the indexed sequential file organization are presented: the first developed by IBM and the second by CDC.

3.4.1   The IBM Indexed Sequential File Organization

An indexed sequential organization is a sequential organization with two additional features. One feature is an index to provide random-access to keyed records, and the other feature is an overflow area that provides a means for handling record additions to a file without copying the file. IBM indexed sequential files have both of these features. They are commonly referred to as ISAM (indexed sequential access method) files, and such terminology is used in this chapter for the purpose of brevity. An ISAM file consists of three component areas: an index area, a prime area containing data records and related track indexes, and an overflow area.

```
FINISH_TRANSACTION: PROCEDURE;
                    /*THE END OF MASTER HAS BEEN REACHED.  IF
                    TRANSACTION HAS ALSO BEEN COMPLETELY PROCESSED THEN
                    STOP, OTHERWISE COPY THE VALID RECORDS FROM
                    TRANSACTION TO NEW_MASTER.*/

                    IF TRANSEOF
                       THEN DO;
                            CLOSE FILE(MASTER), FILE(NEW_MASTER),
                                  FILE(TRANSACTION);
                            RETURN;
                            END;
                    DO WHILE(¬TRANSEOF);
                       IF CODE = 1 & PERSONNEL_REC.SSN < TRANS_DATA.SSN
                          THEN DO;
                               WRITE FILE(NEW_MASTER) FROM (TRANS_DATA);
                               PERSONNEL_REC.SSN = TRANS_DATA.SSN;
                               END;
                          ELSE;
                             PUT SKIP EDIT('ATTEMPTED TO ADD A RECORD FROM
                                          TRANSACTION TO NEW_MASTER WITH CODE =
                                          CODE, 'AND SSN = ', TRANS_DATA.SSN)
                                          (A, F(1), F(9), A);
                          READ FILE (TRANSACTION) INTO (TRANSACTION_REC);
                       END;
                    END FINISH_TRANSACTION;

FINISH_MASTER: PROCEDURE;
               /*THE END OF TRANSACTION HAS BEEN REACHED.  IF THE END
               OF MASTER HAS NOT BEEN REACHED THEN COPY THE REMAINING
               RECORDS TO NEW_MASTER*/

               IF MASTEREOF
                  THEN DO;
                       CLOSE FILE(MASTER), FILE(NEW_MASTER),
                             FILE(TRANSACTION);
                       RETURN;
                       END;
               /*COPY REST OF MASTER TO NEW_MASTER*/
               DO WHILE (¬MASTEREOF);
                  WRITE FILE(NEW_MASTER) FROM (PERSONNEL_REC);
                  READ FILE(MASTER) INTO (PERSONNEL_REC);
               END;
               END FINISH_MASTER;
END PERSONNEL_UPDATE;
```

Figure 3.1.   (Continued)

Access to an ISAM file can be made in either sequential mode or direct mode. When the access mode is sequential, records are retrieved in basically the same manner as they are for a keyed sequential file. Sequential accessing can begin at any record in the file. To start sequentially accessing an ISAM file at a specific record in the file, a programmer must specify the key value of the record. When the access mode is direct, the primary key value of the desired record is supplied by a programmer, and an index translates the key value into a block address. The block is accessed and brought into internal memory where it is scanned for the logical record containing the specified primary key value. An index is created automatically by an operating system as records are written into the prime area. Records are written into a prime area in the lexical order determined by the value of the primary key in each record. An index is created on the same primary key that is used to order the records in the prime area.

3.4.1.1 ISAM Indexes

A number of index levels can exist in the index area of an ISAM file. The ISAM file illustrated in Figure 3.2 has three levels of indexes counting the track index. The track index is the lowest level of the index, is always present, and is written on the first track(s) of the cylinder that it indexes. A track index contains two entries for each prime track of a cylinder: a normal entry and an overflow entry. A normal entry contains two elements: (1) the address of a prime track with which the entry is associated, and (2) the key value of the last record on the track. When an ISAM file is created, the highest key value that can appear on a prime area track is fixed, and it is maintained in the key value part of the related overflow entry. For example, in the file in Figure 3.2 no record with a key value exceeding 36 can appear on track 01 of cylinder 01. This track is the prime track (or home track) for all records with key values less than or equal to 36. The key value of an overflow entry can change only if the file is reorganized. The track address part of an overflow entry is initially set to contain the value 255, and it is changed when the addition of a record to the home track causes the last record on the track to be placed in an overflow area. The last entry of each track index is a dummy entry indicating the end of the index.

Just as a track index describes the storage of records on the prime tracks of a cylinder, a cylinder index indicates how records are distributed over the cylinders that make up an ISAM file. There is one cylinder index entry per track index, that is, if the data records in a file are stored on 20 cylinders, there will be 20 entries in the cylinder index. Each cylinder index entry contains the key value of the last record in the related cylinder and the corresponding cylinder address.

A final level of indexing that can exist, but does not have to exist, in this hierarchical indexing structure is the master index. Each entry in a master index contains the address of a track in a cylinder index and the key value of the highest keyed cylinder index entry on that track. The master index is used when the number of entries in a cylinder index is large, thus causing a time-consuming serial search through the cylinder index for the correct cylinder containing a desired record. The master index forms the root node of the indexes used in ISAM files. The indexes for ISAM files partition the prime area into small groups of records (tracks of records) so that an individual record can be accessed without accessing all the records that precede it.

The record with key value 421 in the ISAM file in Figure 3.2 is located in the following manner. The master index is searched (a master index may be retained in internal memory during file processing) to locate the proper cylinder index with which the record is associated—in this case, the second track of the cylinder index. Track two of the cylinder index is brought into internal memory and searched to find the cylinder on which the record is located, that is, cylinder 5. The track index for cylinder 5 is accessed and brought into internal memory and searched to determine the address of the track on which the record resides, that is, track 2. Finally, a search of track 2 in cylinder 5 is required to locate the record with key value 421.

Master index

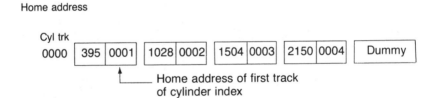

Cylinder index

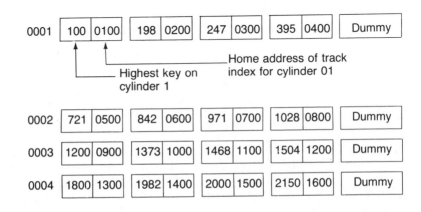

Cylinder 1

Figure 3.2. ISAM file organization.

Cylinder 5

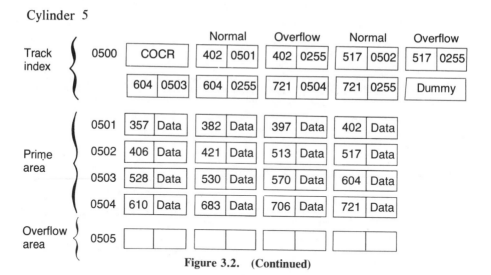

Figure 3.2.   (Continued)

3.4.1.2 ISAM Overflow Areas

The problems associated with adding records to sequential files are partially avoided in ISAM files by the provision of an overflow area. Two organizations of overflow areas are possible: a cylinder overflow area (illustrated in Figure 3.3a) and an independent overflow area (illustrated in Figure 3.3b). An advantage of the cylinder overflow area is that additional seeks are not required to locate overflow records. A disadvantage is that space may be wasted if additions are not evenly distributed throughout a file. An advantage of an independent overflow area is that less total space need be reserved for overflows, and a disadvantage is that accessing overflow records requires additional seeks. A suggested approach is to have cylinder overflow areas large enough to contain the average number of overflows, and an independent overflow area to be used as cylinder overflow areas are filled.

3.4.1.3 Updating an ISAM File

Updating an ISAM file may affect both the prime area and the indexes. For example, the addition of a record to an ISAM file may cause one or more of the key values in the index entries to be altered. ISAM files can be updated either in sequential or direct mode. Sequential mode should be used when updates can be batched. In this case one pass is made over the file. When updates must be made on an individual basis, they should be done in direct mode.

When a record is added to an ISAM file, the prime track on which it should be placed is determined by the access method—ISAM in this case. The addition is placed on the prime track itself if the key value of the added record is less than the key value kept in the normal entry of the related track index entry. If the added record must be placed on the prime track, then a record already on the track may have to be removed and placed in an overflow area. All overflow

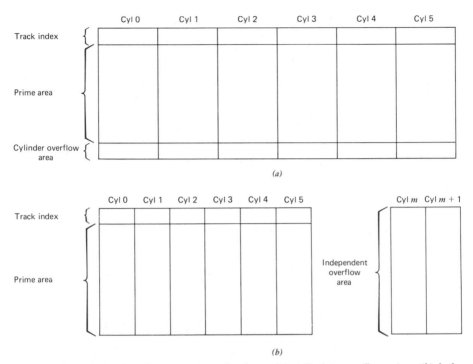

Figure 3.3. ISAM overflow area organizations: (*a*) cylinder overflow area; (*b*) independent overflow area.

records for a prime track are linked together in the overflow area, and a pointer to this list of overflow records is maintained in the address field of the overflow entry. The list of overflow records, if any, for each track is maintained in sorted order on the primary key. Thus, all records associated with a prime track, whether they are on the prime track or in the overflow area, are in logical sorted order. If the key value of an added record is greater than the key value in the normal entry of the related track index entry, then the added record goes directly to the overflow area. Records are never moved from an overflow area to a prime track, unless a file is reorganized.

To clarify some of the remarks made in the preceding paragraph, suppose that a record with a primary key value of 40 is added to the ISAM file in Figure 3.2. The prime track for this record is track 02 of cylinder 01, that is, the home address of the track is 0102. This record must be placed between the two records with key values 39 and 42. This means that the record with key value 45 must be removed from the prime track and placed in the overflow area for cylinder 01. The normal track index entry for track 02 is modified to reflect the current highest key value on track 02, namely 42. The address item in the overflow index entry for track 02 is modified to contain the address of the overflow record (the record with key value 45). The address in the overflow entry is the address of the record with key value 45 since it is the only overflow record for prime track 02 in the overflow area. Figure 3.4 illustrates cylinder 01

Cylinder 1

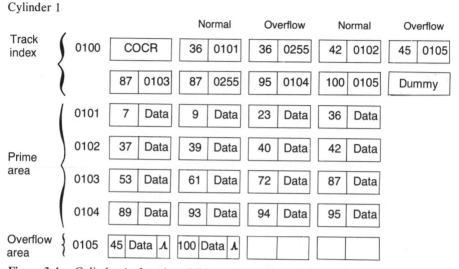

Figure 3.4. Cylinder 1 after the addition of records with key values 40 and 93.

after records with key values 40 and 93 are added to the ISAM file in Figure 3.2.

Deleted records are not physically removed from an ISAM file; instead, deleted records are marked by placing '11111111'B (B indicates a binary constant) in the first byte of a fixed length record or in the fifth byte of a variable length record. If a marked record is forced off its prime track during a subsequent update, it is not rewritten in the overflow area unless it has the highest key value on that cylinder. If a record that has the same key value as a previously deleted record is later added, then the space occupied by the deleted record may be recovered. When an ISAM file is processed in sequential mode, marked records are not retrieved. During direct processing, marked records are retrieved and the programmer must check them for the delete code.

A record in an ISAM file can be modified in either sequential or direct processing modes. Section 3.4.1.4 illustrates how this can be done using PL/I.

An ISAM file may have to be reorganized occasionally for two reasons:

1. The overflow area(s) becomes filled.
2. Additions increase the time required to directly locate records.

Reorganization can be accomplished by sequentially copying the records of a file, leaving out all records that are marked deleted, into another storage area and then recreating the file by sequentially copying the records back into the original file area. The reorganization of an ISAM file with records in the overflow area usually causes new indexes to be created.

3.4.1.4   Processing ISAM Files in PL/I

The example used to illustrate ISAM file processing in PL/I is the personnel update example used in Section 3.3.3. Whereas in Section 3.3.3, a new master file was created, here the master ISAM file is updated in place. This form of updating has the disadvantage that a backup file does not remain; however, MASTER can be copied prior to being updated.

The MASTER file in Figure 3.5 is declared to be indexed via the environment attribute INDEXED. The transaction file (TRANSACTION) is again a sequential file. MASTER is opened for UPDATE with DIRECT access and TRANSACTION is opened for INPUT. A file opened for UPDATE can be either read or written. When the DIRECT attribute is specified for an ISAM file, the file's indexes are traversed to locate records.

The KEY condition in the ON KEY statement in Figure 3.5 can be raised during operations on keyed records in any of the following cases:

1. A keyed record cannot be found.
2. An attempt is made to add a duplicate key value.
3. A key value is out of sequence (for an ISAM file).
4. A key value has not been specified correctly.

MASTER does not have blocked records in this example. The reason for this is that the DELETE statement should not be used in PL/I to process ISAM files with blocked records. A subset of PL/I input/output statements that can be

```
PERSONNEL_UPDATE: PROCEDURE OPTIONS(MAIN);
    /*THIS PROCEDURE UPDATES A PERSONNEL MASTER FILE (MASTER)
     ORGANIZED AS AN INDEXED SEQUENTIAL FILE.  THE UPDATES ARE IN A
     FILE (TRANSACTION).  BOTH FILES ARE ORDERED ON THE SOCIAL SECURITY
     NUMBER (SSN).  THE RECORDS IN TRANSACTION CONTAIN A CODE (1 = ADD,
     2 = DELETE, AND 3 = MODIFY) THAT INDICATES THE TYPE OF UPDATE.*/

    DECLARE 1 PERSONNEL_REC,
                2 DELETE_FLAG BIT(8) INITIAL(8'0'B),
                2 SSN FIXED DECIMAL(9),
                2 NAME,
                  3 FIRST CHARACTER(10),
                  3 MI CHARACTER(1),
                  3 LAST CHARACTER(12),
                2 DEPARTMENT CHARACTER(10),
                2 SALARY FIXED DECIMAL(7, 2),
                2 AGE FIXED DECIMAL(3),
                2 START_DATE CHARACTER(6),
                2 ADDRESS CHARACTER(20);

    DECLARE 1 TRANSACTION_REC,
                2 CODE FIXED DECIMAL(1),
                2 SSN FIXED DECIMAL(9),
                2 NAME,
                  3 FIRST CHARACTER(10),
                  3 MI CHARACTER(1),
                  3 LAST CHARACTER (12),
                2 DEPARTMENT CHARACTER(10),
                2 SALARY FIXED DECIMAL(7, 2),
                2 AGE FIXED DECIMAL(3),
                2 START_DATE CHARACTER(6),
                2 ADDRESS CHARACTER(20);

    DECLARE MASTER FILE RECORD KEYED ENV(INDEXED F(71)),
            TRANSACTION FILE RECORD ENV(CONSECUTIVE F(71, 1420)),
            TRANSEOF BIT(1) INITIAL('0'B);
```

Figure 3.5. Updating ISAM files in PL/I.

```
ON ENDFILE(TRANSACTION) DO;
                         TRANSEOF = '1'B;
                         CLOSE FILE(TRANSACTION), FILE(MASTER);
                         STOP;
                      END;
ON KEY(MASTER) PUT SKIP LIST('ATTEMPTED TO DELETE A RECORD OR MODIFY A
                         RECORD THAT DOES NOT EXIST OR ADD A
                         A RECORD WITH DUPLICATE KEY. IT HAS SSN = ',
                         TRANSACTION_REC.SSN) (A, F(9));

OPEN FILE(MASTER) DIRECT UPDATE;
OPEN FILE(TRANSACTION) INPUT;

/*UPDATE MASTER FILE*/
DO WHILE(¬TRANSEOF);
  READ FILE(TRANSACTION) INTO (TRANSACTION_REC);
  SELECT (CODE);
    WHEN(1)
        DO;
           PERSONNEL_REC = TRANSACTION_REC, BY NAME;
           DELETE_FLAG = 8'0'B;
           WRITE FILE(MASTER) FROM(PERSONNEL_REC) KEYFROM(TRANSACTION_REC.SSN);
        END;
    WHEN(2)
        DELETE FILE(MASTER) KEY(TRANSACTION_REC.SSN);
    WHEN(3)
        DO;
           READ FILE(MASTER) INTO(PERSONNEL_REC) KEY(TRANSACTION_REC.SSN);
           PERSONNEL_REC = TRANSACTION_REC, BY NAME;
           REWRITE FILE(MASTER) FROM(PERSONNEL_REC) KEY(TRANSACTION_REC.SSN);
        END;
    OTHERWISE
        PUT SKIP EDIT('INVALID TRANSACTION CODE FOR RECORD WITH SSN = ',
                         TRANSACTION_REC.SSN) (A, F(9));
  END;
 END;
END PERSONNEL_UPDATE;
```

Figure 3.5.   (Continued)

used to perform operations on ISAM files is given in Table 3.1. Since ISAM files are keyed, the input/output statements have clauses, for example, KEY, KEYFROM, etc., that indicate either the name of a variable containing the key value or the name of the variable into which a key value is to be placed (for a READ).

Each record in MASTER has an 8-bit DELETE_FLAG item. Initially, DELETE_FLAG is set to all zeros. When a record is deleted using the DELETE statement, this flag is set to all ones.

To modify the contents of a record in an ISAM file opened for UPDATE with DIRECT access, the record must first be read and then rewritten with the appropriately modified record. This is illustrated in Figure 3.5.

The procedure in Figure 3.5 is significantly shorter and less complex than the corresponding procedure in Figure 3.1. While these two procedures perform the same functions, their differences are several. First, in Figure 3.1 MASTER is a sequential file instead of an indexed sequential file. Second, MASTER in Figure 3.1 automatically serves as a backup for NEW_MASTER,

Table 3.1

Summary of PL/I Accessing Modes and I/O Statements for ISAM Files[a]

Type of Processing	Access Mode	Purpose	I/O Statements
INPUT	SEQUENTIAL	Process all records in sequence.	READ FILE (PERSONNEL) INTO (PERSONNEL_REC) or READ FILE (PERSONNEL) INTO (PERSONNEL_REC) KEYTO(SSN)
INPUT	DIRECT	Process selected records.	READ FILE (PERSONNEL) INTO (PERSONNEL_REC) KEY(SSN)
OUTPUT	SEQUENTIAL	Create a new ISAM file.	WRITE FILE (PERSONNEL) FROM (PERSONNEL_REC) or WRITE FILE (PERSONNEL) FROM (PERSONNEL_REC) KEYFROM(SSN)
UPDATE	SEQUENTIAL	Modify all records.	REWRITE FILE (PERSONNEL) or REWRITE FILE (PERSONNEL) FROM (PERSONNEL_REC)
UPDATE	DIRECT	Modify selected records.	REWRITE FILE (PERSONNEL) FROM (PERSONNEL_REC) KEY(SSN)
UPDATE	DIRECT	Add new records.	WRITE FILE (PERSONNEL) FROM (PERSONNEL_REC) KEYFROM(SSN)
UPDATE	DIRECT	Delete a specific record.	DELETE FILE (PERSONNEL) KEY(SSN)

[a]Similar tables containing I/O statements for sequential and direct files can be found in the PL/I language manual included in the references at the end of this chapter.

whereas, there is no backup for the ISAM file in Figure 3.5 unless one is created prior to update. Third, the update algorithm used in Figure 3.1 causes every record in MASTER to be accessed to locate the records that must be deleted or modified or to determine the position where new records are added. In contrast, the records in ISAM MASTER for which no updates are specified are not accessed. Fourth, since the sequential MASTER is not keyed, an ON KEY statement cannot be used to detect errors. The programmer must include all error detection statements.

There are a number of tradeoffs that can be discussed with respect to the two procedures in Figures 3.1 and 3.5. Enumerating these tradeoffs is left as an exercise to the student (the material in Section 3.2 should be of use in this exercise).

While the above example has dealt with updating ISAM files, a few words should be said about creating ISAM files. ISAM files are normally (but not required to be) created sequentially. For example, to create the MASTER file defined in Figure 3.5 sequentially, it would be opened for output with the sequential processing mode as in

OPEN FILE(MASTER) SEQUENTIAL OUTPUT

MASTER would be loaded with PERSONNEL_REC records in sorted order on the primary key, SSN.

3.4.2 SCOPE Indexed Sequential Files

A SCOPE Indexed Sequential (SIS) file is organized as a collection of data blocks and index blocks. Both types of blocks are handled as "SCOPE Logical Records," and they are the unit of data transferred by a single I/O command. A programmer does not have control over the physical placement of blocks on an external storage device, but a programmer does have control over the size of both types of blocks. A programmer can allow SIS to determine an index block size by giving it the expected number of data records (logical records) and the number of levels desired in the index. The larger an index block, the fewer the number of index levels created; and, therefore, the fewer the number of accesses required to obtain a desired data record. An SIS file may have up to 63 levels of indexes.

3.4.2.1 SIS Data Blocks

Data blocks contain data records in the leftmost (topmost) part. Key values, with pointers to the corresponding data records within the data block, are contained in the rightmost (bottom) part of a block. Any padding (free space) in a data block exists between the data records and the key values. A programmer may specify, at file load time, the percentage of each data block (and index block) that is to be padding. Figure 3.6 illustrates the organization of data blocks. Data records cannot span data blocks, that is, a data record cannot be

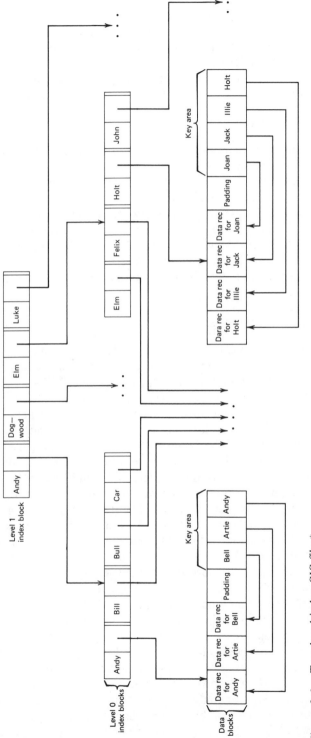

Figure 3.6. Two-level index SIS file.*

*The key values in the key area of each data record are arranged in descending order so that a single padded area can be used to allocate space for both data records and key values in the key area.

67

split. The number of data records and their key values that can be contained within data blocks is variable and depends on the size of each data record. Data blocks may contain fixed length or variable length records as defined by a user. The data block size (and index block size) remains constant per file, and each data record contains a header word defining its size in characters.

3.4.2.2 SIS Index Blocks

An index block contains pairs of key values and addresses and padding space for the addition of such pairs. A key value/address pair consists of the lowest key value of a particular data block or lower level index block and the address of the data or index block in which this key value resides. The lowest level index blocks, that is, level 0 index blocks, contain pointers to data blocks, whereas level 1 index blocks, contain pointers to the level 0 index blocks. Figure 3.6 illustrates a two-level index file. If an SIS file contains more index levels, each level's index blocks contain pointers to the next lower level index blocks. The highest level index block for any given file is called the primary index.

3.4.2.3 Updating SIS Files

Data records are maintained in sequence within a data block. All update functions imply a change to data blocks and only in the case of data block splits or deletion of the first record in a data block are index blocks modified.

When updating requires a record to be inserted in the middle or at the end of a filled data block, SIS reapportions the records between two data blocks, the original data block and a new data block, in order to accommodate the new record and key value. Half of the data records remain in the original data block, with the header word of the block changed to reflect the altered contents. The remaining records are written to a newly created data block or rewritten in a data block left vacant by a previous series of data record deletions. The new low key value entry for the new data record is placed in a level 0 index block, and the index block header revised. Figure 3.7 illustrates data block splitting.

An index block may also overflow if the number of key value entries exceed the index block capacity. When overflow occurs, another index block at the same level is created, with SIS spreading the entries between the original block and the new block and making an entry in the parent index block. Retrieval times are not affected by an index block split unless the primary index is full. Splitting overflowed blocks eliminates the problem of continually having to move overflow records from a full block into a separate overflow area, as is done with prime area overflows in ISAM files. However, the splitting process requires more memory than a record-at-a-time overflow process.

The deletion of a data record causes the record and its key value to be removed from a file. SIS eliminates the key value entry in the data block and deletes the record from the data block. The space occupied by deleted records is automatically garbage collected. That is, the holes left by deleted records are

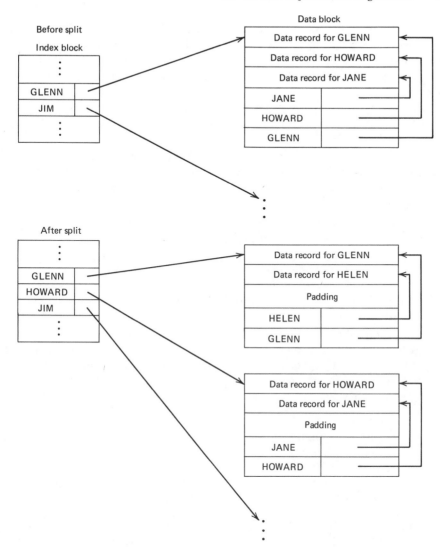

Figure 3.7. Splitting data records after the insertion of a data record with key value HELEN.

replaced by active records with higher key values in the block. Thus, both the active record area and the padding area are always contiguous areas in a block. If the record deleted is the only one in a block (data or index block), then the block is linked to a chain of empty blocks for use when new blocks are required by overflows. If a deleted key value is the low key value in a block, it causes a·modification to be made to the parent index block.

When a data record is modified and the number of characters in the record after modification is the same as in the original record, the modified record is rewritten in its original position in the data block and no record movement occurs. When a new record is smaller or larger than the original record, all of the succeeding records in the data block are adjusted to accommodate the newly modified record. If a data block does not have the space to hold a record whose length increases as a result of modification, then a data block split occurs.

One or more address parts of key value/address pairs in the key area of a data block are altered to indicate the new positions of data records that are moved as the result of updates.

SIS files are created by using successive insert operations. Data records must be in ascending key value sequence as they are placed in a file. Level 0 index blocks are created first as the data blocks are being built.

3.5   DIRECT FILE ORGANIZATION

In direct files there is a definite relationship between the primary key value of a record and its address on a direct-access storage device. Records are stored and retrieved through the use of this relationship. Direct files allow individual records to be accessed very quickly, but the sequential processing of a direct file is a difficult task. Section 3.6 analyzes both indexed sequential and directly organized files with respect to sequential and direct processing so any comments concerning their relative efficiency for accessing records are deferred until then. Three methods for accessing records in direct files on direct-access storage devices are discussed in this section:

1.   Direct addressing.
2.   Dictionary lookup.
3.   Indirect addressing.

3.5.1   Direct Addressing

Direct addressing, in its simplest form, consists of a programmer supplying the hardware address (either relative or absolute) of a desired record and then allowing an operating system to access the record. The hardware address of a record on a disk is a triple (cylinder number, track number, record number). This is in contrast to indirect addressing in which a programmer performs a transformation on a key value prior to its use by an operating system. With direct addressing, a programmer does not transform a key value in any way prior to its use in locating a record.

In some instances, key values cannot be formatted easily such that they directly represent hardware addresses of records. A more common approach to direct addressing is to treat a key value as a relative record number that can be translated into a hardware address by the system. Treating a key value as a relative record number has its drawbacks but a relative record number does uniquely identify the address of a record. For example, suppose that a directly organized file has records with primary key values in the range 0 to 9999 (these key values could be part numbers). Since a key value is treated as a relative record number, space must be reserved for 10,000 records, one corresponding to every possible key value between and including 0 and 9999.

An operating system determines the direct address of a record from its relative record number (that is, the key value) in the following manner. A key value is divided by the number of records per track producing a quotient that gives a relative track number and a remainder giving the relative record number on that track. The relative track number is divided by the number of tracks per cylinder (for a disk) to determine a relative cylinder number (the quotient) and a relative track within cylinder (the remainder). The result is a triple (cylinder #, track #, record #) that is a relative hardware address. An absolute hardware address is determined by "adding" a relative hardware address to an absolute hardware address that is the starting address of a file on a storage device. For this form of direct addressing, primary key values must be numeric, in ascending order, and the records must be fixed length.

The disadvantage of the above technique for direct accessing is that large amounts of storage space may be wasted since a record slot must exist for every possible key value. In practice, the number of actual key values may be only a small percentage of the possible key values. To see the magnitude of this problem, consider the possibility of a directly organized personnel file for a company with 20,000 employees that is keyed on the social security number. The number of possible key values is about one billion and the number of actual key values is a small percentage of this.

When the number of possible key values is relatively close to the number of actual key values, this form of direct accessing is very effective. But more often than not, the number of actual key values is much less than the number of record slots that must be maintained. When this happens, dictionary lookup or indirect addressing should be used to access a direct file.

3.5.2 Dictionary Lookup

With the dictionary lookup form of direct addressing, each record in a direct file is assigned a unique address. On occasion, address assignment may be made prior to file creation. This may occur when a file consists of a collection of system library procedures whose locations on external storage are fixed. However, this is not the normal way that dictionary lookup is used. Normally, address assignment for each record is performed by an operating system when a record is added to a file. Then, it is a programmer's responsibility to place the key value of an added record and its address in the dictionary, forming a key value/address pair. To retrieve a record, the key value of a desired record is used to search the dictionary (the dictionary can be thought of as an associative table) for an entry with that key value. If a match occurs, the related direct address is used to access the desired record. A direct address in a dictionary may be a relative hardware address or an absolute hardware address. A relative address is normally used because movement of a file on an external storage device could cause all of the absolute addresses in a dictionary to be updated.

A dictionary must be large enough to hold all the addresses of records in a file. Thus, a dictionary may become quite large, and it may be stored as a file itself. When a record is deleted, the related entry in the dictionary is also removed.

The organization of a dictionary and a dictionary search strategy have considerable influence on the effectiveness of this approach to direct file organization. If a dictionary is not maintained in sorted order on the key values, then a sequential scan or hashing are the only practical ways of locating a particular entry. If a dictionary is maintained in sorted order, a binary search is possible, but adding entries to a sorted dictionary is time-consuming, especially if entries must be moved to make room for a new entry.

In order to use a dictionary effectively, the entire dictionary should be kept in internal memory. But for large files, a dictionary may be too large and this may be impractical. An alternative is to segment a dictionary and keep only the most frequently and recently referenced segments in internal memory. If large core storage (LCS) is used as a buffer between internal memory and a disk, then several of the referenced segments could be stored there while a file is active.

When a dictionary is small and a file is nonvolatile, that is, it is subject to few changes, a dictionary may be a printed list of key values and related addresses. The addresses of records are looked up manually by a programmer and provided as input to programs. One instance in which a direct file may have a manually maintained dictionary occurs when a file contains system library procedures.

A dictionary lookup technique for converting key values into direct addresses is effective only for small files. Like the method of direct addressing, dictionary lookup has the advantage of producing a unique direct address for each record in a file. An indexed sequential file organization is a variation of this method in which a dictionary is organized as a hierarchical structure with two or more levels of indexes.

3.5.3   Indirect Addressing

Indirect addressing requires that a programmer apply a transformation function to a key value to convert the key value into a direct address to be used by the operating system to locate the desired record. This is in contrast to direct addressing and dictionary lookup in which a programmer does not perform any transformation on a key value prior to its use by an operating system.

The available storage space for a direct file using indirect addressing is divided into sections called home buckets. A bucket can hold one or more logical records, and a file designer can select a bucket capacity.

3.5.3.1   Key-to-Address Transforms

Every logical record is mapped into one of the home buckets by a *key-to-address transform* (also commonly referred to as a key transformation function or hashing function). The direct addressing and dictionary lookup methods always yield unique direct addresses, but indirect addressing using a key-to-address transform does not necessarily produce unique direct addresses. Transforms may map more than one key value to the same home bucket address. An attempt to place a record in a full bucket causes an overflow. A record that cannot be placed in its home bucket is referred to as an overflow record (this phenomenon is termed a *collision* in the context of hashed symbol tables). A procedure for handling overflow records is discussed later in this section. A complete key-to-address transform algorithm for indirect addressing consists of two main parts:

1. A mapping (function) for transforming key values into direct addresses.
2. A technique for handling overflows.

The factors that have a substantial effect on the efficiency of a direct file using indirect addressing are:

1. The bucket size and loading factor.
2. The key value set.
3. The key-to-address transform.
4. The method of handling overflow records.

If a file designer chooses a small bucket size, a relatively high proportion of overflows may occur that will necessitate additional bucket reads and quite possibly, additional seeks. A larger bucket capacity will incur fewer overflows, but a larger bucket will have to be read into internal memory and searched for the required record when a retrieval request is issued. Unless the bucket size is relatively large, records need not be maintained in sorted order within a bucket. In practice, bucket capacity is tailored to the hardware characteristics of the storage device on which a file resides; for example, bucket capacity may be a sector, one half of a track, or even an entire track.

The *loading factor* of a file is defined as the ratio of the number of records currently in a file to the number of record slots available in the file. Another definition of a loading factor is that it is the percentage of record slots in a file that are occupied. As the loading factor increases, the probability of an added record becoming an overflow record increases; for example, if the loading factor is 0.90 (that is, the file is 90 percent full), a record added to the file will very likely become an overflow record.

Several key-to-address transform techniques, for example, division-remainder, digit analysis, mid-square, folding, etc., are available for transforming a key value into a direct address. A performance evaluation for transform techniques for large files has produced the following results:

1. The best way to select a key-to-address transform is to take the key value set for the file in question and simulate the behavior of several possible transforms, recording the percentage of overflows for given bucket sizes.

2. The ideal transform is a transform that distributes the key value set uniformly across the home bucket address space.
3. The number of accesses per record and the percentage of overflow records increase with high loading factor and decrease with large bucket size.
4. The simple division-remainder technique gives the best overall performance of the transforms considered.

Key-to-address transforms for direct files are similar to the hashing functions used to search tables stored in internal memory. The main difference is due to the characteristics of external storage, which differs from directly addressable internal memory. The time to access a table entry in internal memory is measured in terms of microseconds, while the time to access a record in external memory is usually on the order of tens of milliseconds. Thus, the merit of a key-to-address transform is measured by how few accesses are required, on the average, to locate a desired record. For internal hashing, the amount of computation time required to compute an address is sometimes critical, but for direct files stored in external memory, the computation time is negligible when compared to the access time for records.

3.5.3.2 Handling Overflows

Overflow records can be handled by a technique called overflow chaining. When the overflow bucket capacity is one, overflow chaining is simple. A record mapped by a transform to a full home bucket is stored in an overflow bucket in an independent overflow area. The overflow bucket's address is recorded in the home bucket. Another record mapped to the same full home bucket is stored in another overflow bucket. This overflow bucket is chained to the tail of the overflow list for the home bucket. The home bucket in the case just described can have a capacity of one or more records while an overflow bucket capacity is just one.

Attempts should be made to select an appropriate overflow bucket capacity so that the mean overflow bucket chain length can be kept small. The longer a chain, the greater the possibility that multiple seeks will be required to find a record. The risk of multiple seeks can be reduced if overflow buckets have a capacity greater than one. When overflow buckets have a capacity exceeding one, the first home bucket to overflow is assigned a bucket in an overflow area. The next home bucket to overflow is assigned the same overflow bucket unless it is full. When an overflow bucket is filled, it is itself assigned an overflow bucket. Each home bucket contains a pointer to the overflow bucket that is the head of its overflow record list. This technique for handling overflow records utilizes the space allowed for overflow records in an efficient manner, but multiple seeks may still be required to find a record.

Another technique that utilizes overflow storage space less efficiently but reduces the possibility of multiple seeks involves choosing an overflow bucket size greater than one and linking together only the overflow buckets for a particular home bucket. This is similar to the technique described above for overflow buckets holding only one record. If the bucket size is properly chosen, then relatively efficient use can be made of overflow storage space, and the risk of multiple seeks to locate overflow records is reduced.

3.5.3.3 An Example

The following example illustrates the method of indirect addressing for determining the direct address of records in direct files. The key-to-address transform used is the simple division-remainder transform. This transform is expressed as the function

$$F(KV) = Rem(KV/N)$$

Rem is the remainder function; *KV* is a record key value; and *N* is the largest prime number not exceeding the number of home buckets for a file (this transform works best when *N* is prime or *N* has few small divisors). Not only does this transform give good overall performance for large files, but it can be evaluated with low computing costs. The bucket capacity for this example is assumed to be one.

The file used in this example has 10,000 records in it with a key value range of 0000000 to 9999999. Space for 12,000 records is allocated for the file to reduce the probability that overflows will occur. The record addresses are numbered from 00000 to 11999. The divisor used is the largest prime not exceeding 11999, that is, the divisor is 11987. The home bucket address of the record with key value 0235671 is calculated below.

The division of the key value 0235671 by the divisor 11987 gives a quotient of 19 plus a remainder of 7918. The remainder, 7918, is the home bucket address of the record with the key value 0235671. The operating system computes a hardware address from the home bucket address. If there are 10 records per track and 20 tracks per cylinder, then the relative hardware address of the record with key value 0235671 is the triple (cylinder 39, track 11, record 8). If the first record of the related direct file is at absolute hardware address (40,0,0), then the record with key value 0235671 has absolute hardware address (79,11,8).

An advantage in using indirect addressing over direct addressing for calculating the direct address of a record is that it compresses a possibly large key value range such as 0 to 9999999 to a smaller range, for example, 0 to 11999. This situation occurs quite frequently in applications where records are identified by part numbers or social security numbers.

3.5.4 Updating Direct Files

Records may be added to a direct file without affecting any other records in the file. When dictionary lookup is used, an entry must be made in a dictionary for an added record. Adding a record to a direct file using indirect addressing results in the record being placed in its home bucket unless the home bucket is full. Then it is placed in an overflow bucket.

Deleted records may be marked and physically removed when a file is reorganized, or deletions may be marked and the space recovered when a new record is added to the file at a position occupied by a marked record. Deleting a record from a direct file using the dictionary lookup technique requires that the entry related to the deleted record also be removed from the dictionary. Deleted records that are marked but not physically removed adversely affect performance when a chain of overflow records is searched for a particular record.

Altering the value(s) of one or more data items in a record may cause the record to increase or decrease in size, necessitating record relocation. When this occurs, an altering operation is essentially a delete of the old record followed by an insert of the newly altered record.

3.5.5   General Comments on Direct Files

The usual statement made about direct files is that any record can be retrieved by a single access, and other records in a file do not have to be accessed as in sequential files. This statement is true only if the direct addressing and table lookup techniques are used. In general, the statement is not always true for indirect addressing since more than one record will have to be accessed if the desired record is an overflow record.

For direct files, the ability to access all records in a file very quickly in key value sequence is relinquished in favor of the quicker direct access. Also, a change in the distribution of key values, especially in a volatile file, may adversely affect the results of indirect addressing and the speed with which records in a file can be accessed. For this reason, direct files may require frequent reorganization. A programmer should periodically calculate the average number of reads per record to ensure that an existing organization continues to provide the desired degree of efficiency.

Difficulties associated with direct files include:

1. Handling overflow records when indirect addressing is used.
2. Manipulating large dictionaries when dictionary lookup is used.
3. Poor space utilization when direct addressing is used, and when more space is allocated than needed to prevent an excessive number of overflow records when indirect addressing is used.
4. Selection of a key-to-address transform (for indirect addressing) because the performance of a direct file is closely related to it.

3.5.6   Processing Direct Files in PL/I

The personnel file update example used in Sections 3.3.3 and 3.4.1.4 is used to illustrate direct files in PL/I. There are only a few differences between the direct file program in Figure 3.8 and the ISAM file program in Figure 3.5. The directly organized MASTER file has the REGIONAL(1) environment attribute. REGIONAL(1) files treat a key value as a relative record number. A PL/I language manual should be consulted for an in-depth discussion of the direct file organizations provided in PL/I.

Directly organized files have unblocked records. The other major difference between ISAM and direct files in PL/I occurs during the modification of existing records. With direct files, records to be modified do not have to be read prior to being rewritten.

3.6 A COMPARISON OF THE INDEXED SEQUENTIAL AND DIRECT FILE ORGANIZATIONS

The modeling of file organizations for evaluating their performance has received a great deal of attention because of the increasing complexity involved in designing files for the storage and retrieval of data. This complexity is due to the increasing demands made on systems and their increasing size. It is important to have some idea of what file organizations are appropriate for a

```
PERSONNEL_UPDATE: PROCEDURE OPTIONS(MAIN);
    /*THIS PROCEDURE UPDATES A PERSONNEL MASTER FILE (MASTER)
    ORGANIZED AS A DIRECT FILE.  THE UPDATES ARE IN A FILE (TRANSACTION).
    THE TRANSACTION FILE IS ORDERED ON THE SOCIAL SECURITY
    NUMBER (SSN).  THE RECORDS IN TRANSACTION CONTAIN A CODE ( 1 = ADD,
    2 = DELETE, AND 3 = MODIFY) THAT INDICATES THE TYPE OF UPDATE.*/

    DECLARE 1 PERSONNEL_REC,
              2 DELETE_FLAG BIT(8) INITIAL(8'0'B),
              2 SSN FIXED DECIMAL(9),
              2 NAME,
                3 FIRST CHARACTER(10),
                3 MI CHARACTER(1),
                3 LAST CHARACTER(12),
              2 DEPARTMENT CHARACTER(10),
              2 SALARY FIXED DECIMAL(7, 2),
              2 AGE FIXED DECIMAL(3),
              2 START_DATE CHARACTER(6),
              2 ADDRESS CHARACTER(20);

    DECLARE 1 TRANSACTION_REC,
              2 CODE FIXED DECIMAL(1),
              2 SSN FIXED DECIMAL(9),
              2 NAME,
                3 FIRST CHARACTER(10),
                3 MI CHARACTER(1),
                3 LAST CHARACTER (12),
              2 DEPARTMENT CHARACTER(10),
              2 SALARY FIXED DECIMAL(7, 2),
              2 AGE FIXED DECIMAL(3),
              2 START_DATE CHARACTER(6),
              2 ADDRESS CHARACTER(20);

    DECLARE MASTER FILE RECORD KEYED ENV(REGIONAL(1) F(71)),
            TRANSACTION FILE RECORD ENV(CONSECUTIVE F(71, 1420)),
            TRANSEOF BIT(1) INITIAL('0'B);
```

Figure 3.8.   Updating direct files in PL/I.

```
ON ENDFILE(TRANSACTION) DO;
                         TRANSEOF = '1'B;
                         CLOSE FILE(TRANSACTION), FILE(MASTER);
                         STOP;
                      END;
ON KEY(MASTER) PUT SKIP LIST('ATTEMPTED TO DELETE A RECORD OR MODIFY A
                          RECORD THAT DOES NOT EXIST OR ADD A
                          RECORD WITH DUPLICATE KEY.  IT HAS SSN = ',
                          TRANSACTION_REC.SSN) (A, F(9));

OPEN FILE(MASTER) DIRECT UPDATE;
OPEN FILE(TRANSACTION) INPUT;

/*UPDATE MASTER FILE*/
DO WHILE(¬TRANSEOF);
  READ FILE(TRANSACTION) INTO (TRANSACTION_REC);
  SELECT (CODE);
    WHEN(1)
      DO;
        PERSONNEL_REC = TRANSACTION_REC, BY NAME;
        DELETE_FLAG = 8'0'B;
        WRITE FILE(MASTER) FROM(PERSONNEL_REC) KEYFROM(TRANSACTION_REC.SSN);
      END;
    WHEN(2)
      DELETE FILE(MASTER) KEY(TRANSACTION_REC.SSN);
    WHEN(3)
      DO;
        PERSONNEL_REC = TRANSACTION_REC, BY NAME;
        DELETE_FLAG = 8'0'B;
        REWRITE FILE(MASTER) FROM(PERSONNEL_REC) KEY(TRANSACTION_REC.SSN);
      END;
    OTHERWISE
      PUT SKIP EDIT('INVALID TRANSACTION CODE FOR RECORD WITH SSN = ',
                          TRANSACTION_REC.SSN) (A, F(9));
  END;
END PERSONNEL_UPDATE;
```

Figure 3.8. (Continued)

given application. In many instances, an application requires that a file be organized so that both efficient sequential and direct processing can be performed. Two file organizations that are candidates for satisfying these processing requirements are the indexed sequential and direct organizations.

Simulation models of these two file organizations for both batch and direct (or random) processing have been developed. The models have been used to analyze the performance of the organizations. When a file organization is selected, both the storage space and the processing time must be considered. The storage space required for both organizations is approximately the same. The indexed sequential organization requires space for indexes, a prime area, and an overflow area, while the direct organization requires space for home buckets and an overflow area (indirect addressing is assumed). The overflow requirements are slightly larger, in most cases, for direct files. A decision concerning which of the two file organizations should be selected is mainly dependent on the processing times of each.

When both batch and direct processing are required, the general tendency is to select the indexed sequential organization, since for batch processing the indexed sequential organization is many times faster than the direct organization. The indexed sequential organization is faster for batch processing than the direct organization because transactions can be sorted into the same sequence as the file itself, and the average update time per record is low when compared with updating a direct file with a batch of transactions. In addition, for direct processing, the indexed sequential organization is only a few times slower than the direct organization.

A direct file can, however, be as efficient as an indexed sequential file, with respect to batch processing, provided the transactions are placed into the same physical sequence as the master file and then processed. This can be done by: (1) generating the relative address of each record associated with a transaction (through the application of a key-to-address transform on the key value), (2) attaching the address to the transaction, (3) sorting transactions on the addresses, and (4) processing the transactions sequentially. This technique is called "batch random."

Simulation results using models of the indexed sequential and direct file organizations suggest that an indexed sequential file organization is better than a direct organization when both batch and random processing are required. On the other hand, when the batch random technique is used for processing records in a direct file, the simulation results indicate that batch random is faster than indexed sequential for modifying a record in batch mode and also faster for reading a record when transactions are batched.

The decision to process a given file in batch or random mode is dependent upon the percent of the file that is to be processed. The batch times (for both read and modify) per record increase as the percent of the file processed decreases. The random processing times are not affected.

3.7   VSAM FILES

In 1972 IBM released a new access method, VSAM (Virtual Storage Access Method), for its series of S/370 virtual memory machines. VSAM files are designed to replace IBM sequential, indexed sequential, and direct files. VSAM is a set of programs that:

1.   Provides a format for storing data independently of a storage device.
2.   Provides routines for sequential or direct access and for access by key, by relative address, or by relative record number.

Records in VSAM files are addressable without respect to the physical attributes of external storage. Instead, each record is addressed with respect to its displacement from the beginning of a file.

VSAM files can be key-sequenced, entry-sequenced, or relative record files. The basic difference among the three types of files involves the order in which records are loaded. A key-sequenced file is basically the same as an IBM ISAM file, an entry-sequenced file is basically a sequential file, and a relative record file is a version of the direct file organization.

VSAM stores the records of each type of file in a fixed-length contiguous area of external storage called a *control interval*. In addition to containing data records, a control interval contains control information describing the records. A control interval is the unit of data that is transferred by VSAM between virtual and external storage; its size may vary from one file to the next but for a given file its size is fixed either by VSAM or a programmer. VSAM chooses the size of a control interval based on:

1. The type of external storage device used to store a file.
2. The record size.
3. The amount of virtual storage space provided by a programmer for VSAM's buffers.

The maximum control interval size is 32,768 bytes. A control interval is relatively independent of the type of storage device. A control interval that fits on a track for one device might span two or more tracks on another device. A group of control intervals make up a *control area*. A control interval can be thought of as a track and a control area as a cylinder. VSAM fixes the number of control intervals for each control area in a file.

A storage area on external storage for VSAM's use is called a *data space*. A VSAM file is stored in one or more data spaces on one or more volumes of external storage devices of the same type. When additional space is needed, VSAM can automatically extend a file by the amount of space indicated by the data space area size (the automatic extension of a file in the manner just described may not be implemented on every system supporting VSAM files; instead, only a single data space may be allocated for a file with no automatic extension). A VSAM file can be extended to a maximum size of 2^{32} bytes (approximately 4.29×10^9 bytes).

Records of a key-sequenced or entry-sequenced file may be either fixed-length or variable length, whereas the records of a relative record file are always fixed-length. VSAM treats them all the same and places control information at the end of each control interval to describe the records contained in it. The combination of a record and its control information, though not physically adjacent, is called a *stored record*. Adjacent records of the same length share the same control information, thus for VSAM files with fixed-length records only one set of control information is needed per control interval. Figure 3.9 illustrates how records and their control information are stored in a control interval.

A record in a VSAM file is addressed by its displacement in bytes, called its

Control information

R1	R2	R3	R4	• • •	Rn	Free space		• • •	

Figure 3.9.   A control interval.*

*At load file time, the programmer can specify the percentage of each control interval to be initially allocated as free space.

relative byte address (RBA), from the beginning of a file, and not by a physical hardware address on an external storage device. For relative byte addressing, VSAM considers all control intervals in a file to be contiguous as though the file were stored in virtual storage beginning at address 0.

3.7.1   Key-Sequenced Files

Records are loaded into a key-sequenced file in key sequence. A key-sequenced file is always defined with an index that relates key values to the relative location of records in a file. An index is similar to an index for indexed sequential files, and it is used to locate a record for retrieval or to locate the correct position for the insertion of a new record. An index can have one or more levels. The size of index records is set by a programmer at file load time. Index records in the lowest index level are called the *sequence set,* and they give the location of control intervals. Records in all higher levels are collectively called an *index set;* they give the location of index records. Figure 3.10 demonstrates the relationship of a file and its index.

Each entry in an index-set record consists of the highest key value that an index record in the next lower level contains and a pointer to the beginning of that index record. Each entry in a sequence-set record consists of the highest key value in a control interval and a pointer to the beginning of that control interval. For direct access by key, VSAM follows vertical pointers from the highest index level down to the sequence set to find a vertical pointer to a control interval containing the desired record. For the sequential access of a key-sequenced file, VSAM refers only to the sequence set, using horizontal pointers to get from one sequence set record to the next in an attempt to locate the pointer to the control interval containing the desired record. Figure 3.11 gives a macro-view of a sequence-set index record. The number of entries in a

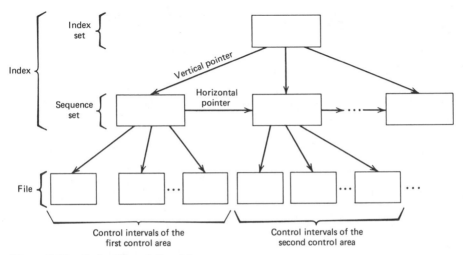

Figure 3.10.   Index-file relationship.

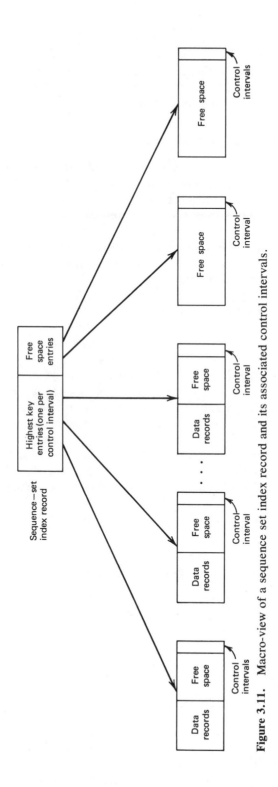

Figure 3.11. Macro-view of a sequence set index record and its associated control intervals.

sequence-set index record is the same as the number of control intervals in a control area.

3.7.2   Entry-Sequenced Files

Records are loaded into an entry-sequenced file serially without respect to the contents of the records. The sequence of records in a file is determined by the order in which they are placed in the file. New records are stored at the end of a file. No index is associated with this type of VSAM file. When a record is loaded during file creation, or subsequently added, VSAM indicates its RBA to a programmer. If a programmer desires to access records directly, then the RBAs must be stored in a programmer-created and maintained dictionary or cross-reference table. Entry-sequenced files are useful only for applications that require no particular ordering of records; they are useful for recording data about events in the order that they occur, for example, computer logs.

3.7.3   Relative Record Files

Records are loaded into a relative file in relative record number sequence. A relative record file has no index. It has a string of fixed-length record slots, each of which has a relative record number from 1 to n (n is the maximum number of records that can be stored in a file). Each record is stored and retrieved via the relative record number of a slot. When a record is inserted, a programmer can assign a relative record number or allow VSAM to assign the record to the next available numbered slot in sequence.

Records in a relative record file are grouped together in control intervals just as they are for the other two types of VSAM files. The number of records per control interval is identical; VSAM determines this from the logical record length and the control interval length. Relative record files can be processed by key with the relative record number treated like a key value.

Figure 3.12 illustrates the first control interval in a file with eight record slots per control interval. The record slots in succeeding control intervals in the file are numbered 9–16, 17–24, etc.

3.7.4   Updating and Maintaining VSAM Files

While a key-sequenced VSAM file is similar to an ISAM file in several ways (actually it is more closely related to the SIS file organization), updating and space maintenance on the two are dissimilar. An update such as the deletion of

Relative record 1	Relative record 2	Relative record 3	• • •	Relative record 8	Control information
Slot 1	Slot 2	Slot 3		Slot 8	

Figure 3.12.   First control interval within a relative record file.

a record or the modification of an existing record that results in the record being shortened causes succeeding records in the control interval to be moved to the left and their RBAs changed so that the vacated space can be combined with the free space in the control interval. An update, such as the insertion of a new record or the modification of an existing record that lengthens the record, causes any succeeding records in the control interval to be moved to the right into the free space. In addition, it causes their RBAs to be changed. Movement of records in a control interval to claim space or reclaim space occurs only with key-sequenced files.

When a record to be inserted into a key-sequenced file will not fit in a control interval, VSAM moves some of the records in the control interval to an empty control interval in the same control area and inserts the new record in its proper key value sequence. If these control intervals are not physically adjacent, the physical sequence of records is no longer the same as the key value sequence. When there is not a free control interval in the control area, record insertion causes VSAM to establish a new control area, either by using space already allocated or by extending the file.

Deleting a record in a relative record file does not cause the unused space to be automatically reclaimed, that is, the RBAs of relative records do not change during updates. The reason for this is that a programmer expects a particular record to be in a particular slot and any automatic movement of records in a relative record file by VSAM could disrupt a programmer's work. Records can be inserted in empty record slots, and the modification of an existing record does not result in shortening or lengthening the record since all records in relative record files are fixed-length.

The update and maintenance characteristics of VSAM files are summarized in Table 3.2. Key-sequenced VSAM files and ISAM files achieve essentially the same results, although in many cases better performance can be achieved from key-sequenced VSAM files. There are two important differences between these two file organizations that generally lead to better performance from VSAM files:

1. VSAM does not distinguish between primary and overflow areas as does ISAM.
2. Deleted records in ISAM files are marked and the space reclaimed at file reorganization time, whereas, VSAM automatically reclaims space and combines it with any existing space in the affected control interval, thus generally requiring fewer file organizations.

EXERCISES

1. An indexed sequential file is organized on a primary key, PKEY. Describe a simple method for answering range queries involving this primary key such as:

   "find all records with PKEY > 100"

Table 3.2

Summary of Characteristics of VSAM Files

Key Sequenced	Entry Sequenced	Relative Record
(1) Records in collating sequence by key values.	Records are in the order in which they are entered.	Records are in relative record number order.
(2) Access is by key value through an index or RBA.	Access is by RBA.	Access is by a relative record number that is treated like a key value.
(3) A record's RBA can be changed by an update.	A record's RBA cannot change.	A record's relative record number cannot change.
(4) Free space is used for inserting records and changing their length in place.	Space at the end of the file is used for adding records.	Empty slots in the file are used for adding records.
(5) Space given up by a deleted or shortened record is automatically reclaimed within a control interval.	Space occupied by a deleted record is not reclaimed, but its space can be reused for a record of the same length.	Space occupied by a deleted record can be reused.

2. For a certain disk drive, the maximum seek time is 20 milliseconds and the maximum time to search a track is 50 milliseconds. What is the maximum time to locate a given record in an ISAM file stored on this disk where the file has three levels of indexing (master, cylinder, and track). Give your answers in milliseconds.

3. Shown below is the track index, prime tracks, and overflow area (track 5) for cylinder number 1 of an ISAM file. Show what changes would be caused by inserting a record with key value 52 into this file.

Track Index

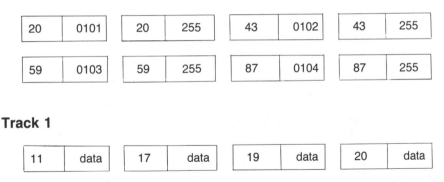

| 20 | 0101 | | 20 | 255 | | 43 | 0102 | | 43 | 255 |

| 59 | 0103 | | 59 | 255 | | 87 | 0104 | | 87 | 255 |

Track 1

| 11 | data | | 17 | data | | 19 | data | | 20 | data |

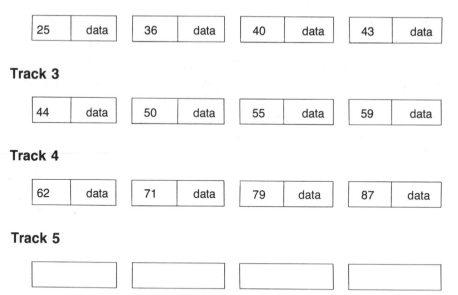

Track 2

Track 3

Track 4

Track 5

4. Given a direct file with N home buckets, each containing K records, what is the worst case number of accesses to locate a record that is known to be in the file?
5. Enumerate some tradeoffs that exist between the two update procedures in Figures 3.1 and 3.5.
6. Rewrite the programs in Figures 3.1, 3.5, and 3.8 in a language other than PL/I; for example, rewrite them in COBOL.
7. A common file management application involves merging two sorted files to form a third sorted file. Create two sequential files with records having the format of PERSONNEL_REC in Figure 1.1 sorted on the SSN and then merge them to create a third file.

REFERENCES

3.1 Behymer, J.A., et al. "Analysis of Indexed Sequential and Direct Access File Organizations," *Proceedings of 1974 ACM SIGMOD Workshop*, pp. 389–417.

The indexed sequential and direct file organizations are analyzed. The authors' results are summarized in this chapter.

3.2 Cardenas, A. F. "Evaluation and Selection of File Organizations—A Model and System," *Commun. ACM*, Vol. 16, September 1973, pp. 540–548.

The factors that affect file organization are discussed. A methodology and a model to estimate the storage costs and mean access time of file organizations is given.

3.3   IBM Reference Manual, *Data Management Services Guide,* Form GC26-3746.

3.4   IBM Student Text, *Introduction to IBM Direct-Access Storage Devices and Organization Methods,* September 1976.

These two IBM manuals describe the file organizations supported by current IBM operating systems; in particular, the sequential, indexed sequential, direct, and VSAM organizations.

3.5   IBM System/360 *Operating System PL/I(F) Language Reference Manual,* Order No. GC28-8201-4, December 1972.

This language reference manual defines the PL/I language used in this chapter to illustrate the processing of sequential, indexed sequential, and direct files.

3.6   Lum, V. Y. "General Performance Analysis of Key-to-Address Transformation Methods Using an Abstract File Concept," *Commun. ACM,* Vol. 16, October 1973, pp. 603−612.

3.7   Morris, R. "Scatter-Storage Techniques," *Commun. ACM,* Vol. 11, January 1968, pp. 38−44.

These two papers discuss algorithms that can be used to convert key values into direct addresses for the indirect addressing approach discussed in Section 3.5.3.

4

Tree-Structured File Organizations

With the exception of the k-dimensional binary search tree, the tree-structured file organizations discussed in this chapter are suitable only for primary key retrieval. The tree structures described are binary search trees and multiway (m-way) search trees. A binary tree is one of the best known and most frequently used data structures for organizing data that are stored entirely in internal memory while being processed. Table 4.1 compares a binary search tree with some of the other well-known ways to organize data.

Binary search trees have seldom been used for organizing large files in two-level storage. On the other hand, the multiway tree, which is essentially a generalization of the binary tree, has received widespread use for organizing indexes for large files in external memory.

The indexes associated with the ISAM and SIS file organizations described in Chapter 3 are examples of organizations having tree-like indexes. In fact, not only are the indexes organized as multiway trees but the overall organization in each case is a multiway tree with data records as terminal nodes. Trees are useful for organizing indexes because of their good search and update characteristics. By comparison with other organizations such as the sequential organization, additional memory is required for links between nodes. But from a cost-effective viewpoint, this is generally more than compensated for by the savings in searching.

The principal reason for the frequent use of the multiway search tree and the infrequent use of the binary search tree in two-level storage involves the number of accesses to external memory to locate a record with a specific key value. Multiway trees with a large number of records per node, say 100 records, can be used to store a large number of records in a tree of small height, whereas a binary search tree storing the same number of records but storing one record

Table 4.1

Comparison of Binary Search Trees with Other Methods of Organizing Data

	Operation		
File Organization	Random Access of a Single Record	Sequential Processing of Entire File	Insertion/Deletion of a Single Record (Search Time Excluded)
Sequentially allocated linear list	$O(\log_2 n)$	$O(n)$	$O(n)$
Linked linear list	$O(n)$	$O(n)$	Constant
Scatter storage	Constant	$O(n \log_2 n)$	Constant
Binary search tree	$O(\log_2 n)$	$O(n)$	Constant

per node requires several more levels. Thus, several more accesses to external memory are required to locate a record with a given key value. However, if storage for the nodes is allocated properly, some, but not all, types of binary search trees offer a feasible alternative to multiway search trees. A method of allocating storage for nodes should try to minimize the number of accesses to external memory to retrieve a desired record.

Tree structures that can be modified dynamically and accessed efficiently from external memory are of primary interest in this chapter. Some of the tree structures discussed in this chapter are of limited practicality for organizing large files, but they are included here for two basic reasons:

1. Completeness of discussion.
2. To encourage the investigation of strategies for storing trees on external storage devices.

4.1 THE O NOTATION

Before tree-structured files are addressed in the remainder of this chapter, a bit of notation must be discussed. This notation, the *O* (read big "oh") is used to express the time and space complexities of algorithms. The complexity of an algorithm is very much related to the structure(s) used to organize the data processed by the algorithm. In fact, the algorithm and the structure(s) are inseparable when the time and space requirements are computed. The complexity problem is described in the following few paragraphs.

Given a problem, a programmer seeks an efficient algorithm for its solution. Two important questions arise: (1) how can algorithms that solve the same problem be compared?, and (2) how can the "goodness" of an algorithm be judged? Both are commonly answered by associating with a problem a value, called the *size of the problem,* that is usually a measure of the quantity of input

Table 4.2

Values for Various Complexity Functions

$\log_2 n$	n	$n \log_2 n$	n^2	n^3	2^n
0	1	0	1	1	2
1	2	2	4	8	4
2	4	8	16	64	16
3	8	24	64	512	256
4	16	64	256	4096	65,536
5	32	160	1024	32,768	4,294,967,296

data (but not necessarily limited to this). For example, size may also be the quantity of output data or the sum of the quantities of input and output data. The time and space needed by an algorithm, expressed as a function of the size of a problem, are called the *time* and *space complexities,* respectively, of the algorithm.

When an algorithm solves a problem of size n in time cn^2 for some constant $c,$ then the time complexity of that algorithm is $O(n^2)$. More precisely, a function $f(n)$, which represents the computing time of some algorithm, is said to be $O(g(n))$ if there exists a constant c such that $f(n) \leq c \times g(n)$ for all sufficiently large values of n. The O notation means "proportional to" or "on the order of." In other words, if the computing time of some algorithm is expressed as $O(n^2)$, then this is equivalent to saying "the computing time of the algorithm is on the order of n^2."

The two most important measures of an algorithm are its time and space complexities. Of primary interest are the worst-case complexity and the expected (or average) complexity. Both the worst-case and average complexities should be known for proper algorithm selection.

Time and space complexities frequently seen in some chapters of this book are $O(1)$, $O(\log_2 n)$, $O(n)$, $O(n\log_2 n)$, $O(n^2)$, $O(n^3)$, and $O(2^n)$. $O(1)$ is written to mean a complexity that is a constant. $O(n)$ is called linear, $O(n^2)$ is called quadratic, $O(n^3)$ is called cubic, and $O(2^n)$ is called exponential. If the time complexity of an algorithm is $O(\log_2 n)$, then it is faster, for sufficiently large n, than if the time complexity is $O(n)$. Similarly, $O(n\log_2 n)$ is better than $O(n^2)$, etc. The O notation hides a constant factor that can be of considerable importance, especially for small values of n.

Table 4.2 shows how the time complexities grow with $c=1$. Note that the times $O(n)$ and $O(n\log_2 n)$ grow rather slowly. For large sets of data, algorithms with a time complexity greater than $O(n\log_2 n)$ are usually impractical.

4.2   THE PATH LENGTH OF TREES

The efficiency of search trees is usually measured in terms of the average search path length and/or the complexity associated with inserting and deleting nodes. There are two basic types of search trees: those built with unrestricted growth patterns and those built with restricted growth patterns. The restricted growth trees almost always have better search characteristics than unrestricted growth trees because the average search path length is less, but the complexity associated with inserting and deleting nodes is normally much greater.

The number of branches that have to be traversed in order to proceed from the root of a tree to a node x is called the *path length of node x*. The root has path length 1, its direct descendants have path length 2, etc. A node at level i has path length i. The *path length of a tree* is defined as the sum of the path lengths of all its nodes. The path length of a tree is also called the *internal path length*. The internal path length of a tree can be expressed as

$$P_I = \sum_i (n_i \times i), \tag{4.1}$$

where n_i is the number of nodes at level i. The average path length is given by

$$\overline{P}_I = \frac{1}{n} P_I \tag{4.2}$$

where $n = \sum_i n_i$ is the number of nodes in the tree. The internal path length of the tree in Figure 4.1 is

$$P_I = 1\times1 + 2\times2 + 2\times3 + 1\times4 + 3\times5 = 30$$

and the average internal path length is

$$\overline{P}_I = 30/9 = 3.33$$

There are two different conventions that may be used to measure path length; they amount to defining the level of the root as being 0 or 1. Some

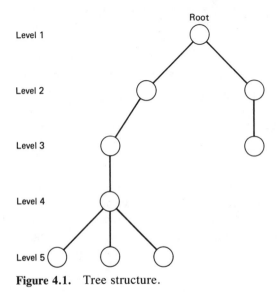

Figure 4.1. Tree structure.

formulas, for example, the average search path length for search trees, may differ in a trivial way depending on whether the level of the root is assumed to be 0 or 1. In this book the level of the root is 1.

The above summation (4.1) gives the internal path length of a tree. In order to define the *external path length,* the tree in Figure 4.1 is extended by a special node, called an extended node (or blank node), wherever a null subtree is present in the original tree. An assumption that must be made in creating the extended tree is that each node has the same branching factor. The branching factor is the number of branches that can emanate from a node in a tree. Figure 4.2 illustrates the extended tree corresponding to the tree in Figure 4.1. The *external path length of a tree* is now defined as the sum of the path lengths over all extended nodes, or

$$P_E = \sum_i (m_i \times i) \qquad (4.3)$$

where m_i is the number of extended nodes at level i. The average external path length is

$$\bar{P}_E = \frac{1}{m} P_E \qquad (4.4)$$

where $m = \sum m_i$ is the number of extended nodes. For the extended tree in Figure 4.2, the external path length and the average external path length are given by

$$P_E = 0 \times 1 + 1 \times 2 + 4 \times 3 + 2 \times 4 + 9 \times 6 = 76$$

$$\bar{P}_E = 76/16 = 4.75$$

Extended nodes have no data values associated with them. New data values are inserted into an existing search tree as the value of the first extended node encountered while traversing the path from the root. A path terminates when an extended node is encountered.

For binary trees some interesting results have been developed relating a binary tree and its corresponding extended tree. Two of the most important are:

1. $m = n + 1$, that is, the number of extended nodes is one greater than the number of nodes in the original binary tree.
2. $P_E = P_I + (2n+1)$ if the level of the root is 1 (or $P_E = P_I + 2n$ if the level of the root is 0).

The terminology, average path length, average number of comparisons, or average search time, is used in various references to express the search characteristics of trees. For example, the search characteristics of a random binary search tree may be expressed as "the average path length is $1.4\log_2 n$," "the mean number of comparisons is $1.4\log_2 n$," or "the average search time is $1.4\log_2 n$." In terms of O notation, the average path length for a random binary search tree is $O(\log_2 n)$.

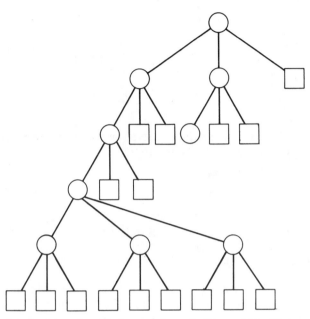

Figure 4.2. Extended tree (of tree in Figure 4.1) with branching factor 3 (square nodes indicate extended nodes).

4.3 BINARY SEARCH TREES

A *binary tree* is a finite set of nodes that is either empty or consists of a root node with two distinct binary trees called the left and right subtrees of the root. A binary search tree is a binary tree organized so that for each node x all key values in the nodes in the left subtree of node x are less than the key value of node x and those in the right subtree of node x are greater than the key value of node x.

4.3.1 Random and Perfectly Balanced Binary Search Trees

An unrestricted growth binary search tree constructed with key values arriving in random order is called a *random binary search tree*. An algorithm, TREE_INSERT, for searching for a specified argument and/or inserting a record (node) with a new key value into a random binary search tree is given below (for convenience the assumption ROOT $\neq \Lambda$ is made). KEYVALUE, LLINK, RLINK, and DATA are functions that give the values of key value, left link, right link, and data, respectively, in a record. The function ALLO-CATE allocates storage for a new record. KV is the argument key value; Λ is a null pointer; and P, Q, and ROOT are pointers to records.

Algorithm TREE_INSERT

1. [Initialize] $P \leftarrow$ ROOT.
2. [Compare] If KV = KEYVALUE(P), the search terminates;
       if KV < KEYVALUE(P), go to Step 3;
       if KV > KEYVALUE(P), go to Step 4.
3. [Move left] If LLINK(P) $\neq \Lambda$ set $P \leftarrow$ LLINK(P) and go to Step 2;
       otherwise, go to Step 5.
4. [Move right] If RLINK(P) $\neq \Lambda$, set $P \leftarrow$ RLINK(P) and go to Step 2.
5. [Insert key value KV into tree] ALLOCATE(Q),
      KEYVALUE(Q)$\leftarrow KV$,
      LLINK(Q)$\leftarrow \Lambda$,
      RLINK(Q)$\leftarrow \Lambda$,
      DATA(Q)$\leftarrow$ data associated with record whose key value is KV.
6. [Set links] If KV < KEYVALUE(P), set LLINK(P)$\leftarrow Q$;
      otherwise, set RLINK(P)$\leftarrow Q$.
7. [Exit] Exit algorithm.

The average internal search path length ($\overline{P}_I$) for a random binary search tree with n nodes is $1.386\log_2 n - 1$, and the average external path length ($\overline{P}_E$) is $1.386\log_2 n$. The following relationship exists between $\overline{P}_I$ and $\overline{P}_E$ for random binary search trees

$$\overline{P}_I = (\frac{n + 1}{n}) \overline{P}_E - 1$$

The best guess for the shape of a random binary search tree is that it will not be perfectly balanced. A binary tree is *perfectly balanced* if for each node, the number of nodes in its left and right subtrees differ by at most one. Figure 4.3 illustrates a perfectly balanced binary tree. The perfectly balanced tree is an example of a restricted growth tree whose average path length is $\log_2 n - 1$. This is the shape that a tree must have to minimize P_I. The worst shape for a random binary search tree is the degenerate tree, that is, a tree constructed

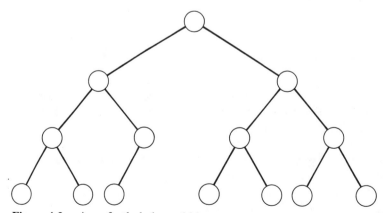

Figure 4.3.   A perfectly balanced binary tree.

when all key values arrive in ascending or descending order. Figure 4.4 shows a degenerate binary search tree. The average search path length for the degenerate tree is $O(n)$. Since the worst case for the random tree leads to the poor performance of algorithm TREE_INSERT, some consideration should be given to using a restricted growth search tree with better search characteristics.

If coefficients are ignored, the ratio of the average search path length for random trees with n nodes to the average search path length for perfectly balanced trees is

$$\frac{1.386 \log_2 n}{\log_2 n} = 1.386$$

The above ratio can be interpreted in the following manner. If key values are accessed with equal probability, then the time taken to construct a perfectly balanced tree instead of a random tree can be expected to yield a search path length that is about 39 percent shorter for the perfectly balanced tree. If r is the ratio between the frequency of accessing nodes and the frequency of inserting nodes, then the higher the value of r, the higher the payoff for maintaining a perfectly balanced tree. If r is relatively low, then maintaining a perfectly balanced tree versus a random tree does not pay off.

An insertion procedure that always restores a tree's structure to perfect balance is relatively complex; thus, a tree insertion procedure that always restores a tree's structure to perfect balance has little chance of being profitable except when the ratio of accesses to insertions is large. To overcome such strict definitions of balance and to permit simpler tree reorganization procedures at the cost of only a small deterioration in average search performance, Adel'son-Vel'skii and Landis developed the AVL tree. AVL trees are discussed in Section 4.3.3.

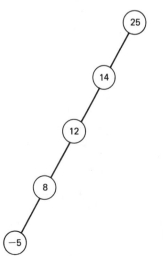

Figure 4.4. A degenerate binary search tree (a linear list).

4.3.2 Optimal Binary Search Trees

The above considerations for organizing binary search trees have been based on the assumption that each node in the tree has an equally likely chance of being accessed, that is, all key values are equally likely to occur as a search argument. This is the best assumption if there is no way to determine the frequency with which each key value will likely be a search argument. However, a few instances exist in which accurate probabilities (or frequencies) of access to individual key values can be computed. The trees constructed in these instances are almost always *static*, that is, the key values always remain the same and no insertions or deletions are made on the tree. Typical examples include the scanner of a compiler that determines for each identifier whether or not it is a keyword (or reserved word), and the assembler that translates mnemonics into their equivalent numeric opcode. In these two cases, keywords and mnemonics are considered key values. Statistics collected during the compilation and assembly of hundreds of programs can provide accurate frequencies of the use of keywords and mnemonics. If the probability of each node being accessed is known a priori, then the search tree can be organized in a way so that the total number of search steps is minimal.

The criteria for constructing binary search trees with a minimal number of search steps are as follows. A certain probability β_i of access is associated with each node i. Sometimes β_i is specified as an integral quantity that represents a frequency count or weight and not a probability; however, if desired, the probability associated with a node i can be computed from the weight by the formula

$$\beta_i = \frac{\text{WEIGHT}_i}{\sum_j \text{WEIGHT}_j}$$

The (internal) *weighted path length (WPL_I)* is the sum of the path length of each node weighted by that node's probability of access for all nodes, that is,

$$WPL_I = \sum_{i=1}^{n} \beta_i h_i \tag{4.5}$$

where h_i is the path length of node i and $\sum_{i=1}^{n} \beta_i = 1$. The goal is to minimize the weighted path length for a given probability distribution representing the probability of access of each node. The search tree for a given probability distribution may not be a perfectly balanced tree. In fact, in some cases it may turn out to be a degenerate tree. Figure 4.5 illustrates the five search trees that can be constructed from the three key values A, B, C. Note that there are $n!$ orderings of n key values but there are not necessarily $n!$ distinct binary search trees; for example, the orderings B, A, C and B, C, A produce the same search tree. If the probability of access of the nodes is $\beta_A = 2/7$, $\beta_B = 2/7$, $\beta_C = 3/7$, then the weighted path length of each of the five search trees in Figure 4.5 can be computed using (4.5) as

$$WPL_{(a)} = 1 \times 2/7 + 2 \times 2/7 + 3 \times 3/7 = 15/7$$
$$WPL_{(b)} = 1 \times 2/7 + 2 \times 3/7 + 3 \times 2/7 = 13/7$$
$$WPL_{(c)} = 1 \times 2/7 + 2 \times 2/7 + 2 \times 3/7 = 12/7$$
$$WPL_{(d)} = 1 \times 3/7 + 2 \times 2/7 + 3 \times 2/7 = 13/7$$
$$WPL_{(e)} = 1 \times 3/7 + 2 \times 2/7 + 3 \times 2/7 = 13/7$$

In this example the balanced tree (c) is the optimal arrangement, but if the probabilities of access are changed to $\beta_A = 1/7$, $\beta_B = 2/7$, $\beta_C = 4/7$, then the degenerate tree (d) has the optimal arrangement.

In practice, the problem of constructing a binary search tree with minimal search time is generalized by considering not only the probabilities with which a successful search is completed, but also the probabilities with which unsuccessful searches occur. For example, with respect to the compiler scanner mentioned above, identifiers occurring in source statements are not always keywords; in fact, their being keywords is probably the exception. Therefore, it is important to take into consideration the probability of an unsuccessful as well as successful search. Determining that a keyword is not in the keyword search tree can be considered an unsuccessful search that ends with the accessing of an extended node.

The optimum search tree problem can now be formalized in the following manner. Given n key values $KV_1, KV_2, \ldots, KV_n$ and $2n + 1$ probabilities (or weights) $\alpha_0, \alpha_1, \ldots, \alpha_n, \beta_1, \beta_2, \ldots, \beta_n$, where β_i is the probability of encountering KV_i and α_i is the probability of encountering a key value that lies between KV_i and KV_{i+1}, the problem is to determine the binary search tree that minimizes

$$WPL = \sum_{i=1}^{n} \beta_i h_i + \sum_{j=0}^{n} \alpha_j h'_j \tag{4.6}$$

where

$$\sum_{i=1}^{n} \beta_i + \sum_{j=0}^{n} \alpha_j = 1 \tag{4.7}$$

The variable h_i is the path length of the internal node i and h'_j is the path length

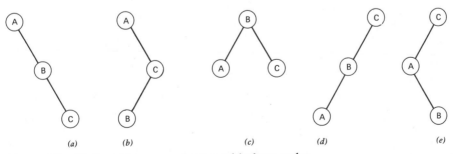

(a) (b) (c) (d) (e)

Figure 4.5. Distinct binary search trees with three nodes.

of the extended node j. When the β_i and α_j are integral weights instead of probabilities, the summation (4.7) is obviously not required to be satisfied. When the β_i and α_j are integral weights, the summation (4.7) is customarily much larger than one and in this case it is called the *weight of the tree*. Using weights instead of probabilities has the computational advantage that the *WPL* can be computed using only integer quantities, and the probabilities do not have to be computed from established frequency counts or weights.

A binary search tree whose structure yields the minimum *WPL* for a given set of key values KV_i and probabilities (or weights) β_i and α_j is called an *optimal binary search tree*. It should be noted that when the β_i and α_j are probabilities of access, the *WPL* is actually the *average weighted path length*.

The *WPL* of the tree in Figure 4.6 is

$$WPL = 3\alpha_0 + 2\beta_1 + 3\alpha_1 + \beta_2 + 4\alpha_2 + 3\beta_3 + 4\alpha_3 + 2\beta_4 + 3\alpha_4$$

The weighted path length measures the relative amount of work (or cost) required to search the tree.

In the process of constructing an optimal search tree, the number of possible configurations of n nodes grows exponentially with n. When n is large, there are approximately $4^n/(\sqrt{\pi}n^{3/2})$ binary trees. Thus, the task of determining an optimal subtree may seem rather hopeless for large n. But all subtrees of an optimal search tree are also optimal. This suggests an algorithm that starts with individual nodes as the smallest possible subtrees and systematically finds larger and larger trees. The effort (that is, the number of steps) to determine the optimal search tree is of order $O(n^2)$ and the amount of storage required is $O(n^2)$. This is unacceptable if n is very large, and it is questionable whether optimal search trees are useful for organizing even large static files. For even moderately large files, the $O(n^2)$ time and memory requirements make most algorithms for constructing optimal search trees for the general case impractical. Efficient heuristic algorithms for constructing near-optimal search trees

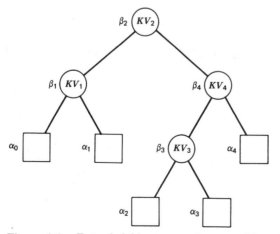

Figure 4.6. Extended binary search tree with nodes labeled with probabilities of access.

have been developed. The heuristic algorithms are good, and the reason for this is that they produce search trees that are nearly balanced, and the balanced search trees have approximately the same weighted path length as optimal search trees.

A simpler and somewhat related problem to finding optimal binary search trees is the problem of finding binary trees with minimal weight external path length. In this case, the α_j are weights and each of the weights is associated with one of the $n + 1$ external nodes in a binary tree with n internal nodes. The internal nodes in this type of binary tree do not contain any information. Note that these trees are *not* binary search trees.

Minimal weight external path length binary trees find applications in several areas. One of these applications, appropriate to discuss in this book, is determining an optimal merge pattern for $n + 1$ sorted runs using a 2-way merge. The 2-way merge is described in Chapter 7 (Sorting). For this application, weight α_j is the number of records in run R_j. Each internal node represents the result of a 2-way merge. As an example of this application, suppose $n = 3$ and the four runs $R_0 - R_3$ have the following number of records: $R_0 = 24, R_1 = 4, R_2 = 7,$ and $R_3 = 12$. The tree with minimal external weighted path length is given in Figure 4.7, and it defines the following merge pattern: merge R_1 and R_2; merge this result with R_3; and finally merge this result with R_0. Since two sorted runs with n_1 and n_2 records can be merged in time $O(n_1 + n_2)$, the merge time following the pattern of the tree in Figure 4.7 can be shown as proportional to the weighted external path length of the tree. Thus, minimizing the weighted external path length of the tree minimizes the merge time.

A simple solution to the problem of finding binary trees with minimal weighted external path length has been developed. The algorithm can be described as follows. T is a list of extended binary trees. Initially, all trees in T have only one node. For each tree, this node is an external node and its weight is one of the α_j. During the course of the algorithm, for any tree in T with root node R and a depth greater than one, the weight of R is the sum of the weights of all external nodes in R. The trees in T are maintained in sorted order on the weight of the tree. Initially, list T consists of the four extended binary trees.

The two trees with minimum weights are selected, and a new tree is created with these two trees as its left and right subtrees. The first tree with minimum weight is the left subtree, and the second tree is the right subtree. When this is done, T consists of

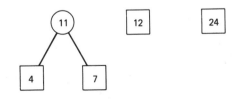

The internal node contains the value 11 that is the weight of the tree. After the two trees with minimum weights are selected again, T contains

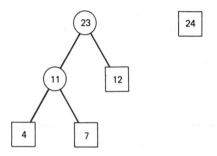

Finally, T contains the tree illustrated in Figure 4.7.

Two of the binary search trees discussed so far, perfectly balanced and optimal binary search trees, have good search characteristics. But neither is well-suited for applications requiring dynamic insertions and deletions. The algorithms for maintaining a search tree in perfectly balanced form are complex and not always profitable. The optimal search tree is practical only for constant trees having a known probability distribution for the access of nodes. Since access frequencies are usually not known with great accuracy, it may not be profitable to expend much effort on constructing an optimal search tree using inaccurate weights when there are simple algorithms for constructing trees whose performance is very near that of optimal search trees.

4.3.3   AVL Trees

The complexity of maintaining a perfectly balanced search tree and the impracticality of using optimal search trees for situations requiring dynamic binary search trees have led to the development of other alternatives for restricted growth trees. These alternatives were investigated because in a

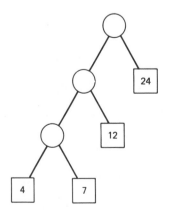

Figure 4.7.   Optimal merge pattern tree.

binary search tree, it is more realistic to assume that the tree is dynamic rather than static. One such tree is the AVL tree. The AVL tree, invented by and named after Adel'son-Vel'skii and Landis, is a restricted growth binary search tree. The AVL tree relaxes the balance criteria of the perfectly balanced search tree, thus making restructuring after insertions and deletions less complex. The average search time is only slightly larger than that of perfectly balanced search trees.

A *binary tree is balanced* (or is an AVL tree) if and only if for every node the heights of its two subtrees differ by at most 1. Figure 4.8 illustrates an AVL tree (note that this tree is not perfectly balanced). It has been shown that the height of an AVL tree with n nodes lies between $\log_2 (n + 1)$ and $1.4404\log_2 (n + 2) - 0.328$. This result guarantees that an AVL tree will never be more than 45 percent higher than a perfectly balanced tree. The average search path length for an AVL tree is $\log_2 n + c$ ($c \cong 0.25$). This means that in practice an AVL tree performs about as well as a perfectly balanced tree, and it is simpler to maintain.

A requirement for a highly dynamic tree is that insertions and deletions be performed easily while maintaining the tree within the desired class, for example, perfectly balanced, AVL, etc. The following three operations can be performed on AVL trees in $O(\log_2 n)$ units of time even in the worst case:

1. Locate a node with a given key value.
2. Insert a node with a given key value.
3. Delete a node with a given key value.

Algorithms for inserting and deleting nodes are not presented here; instead, only a brief description of the three cases that must be distinguished when a node is inserted is given.

Given a node x with left and right subtrees l and r and assuming that the new node is inserted in l, causing its height to increase by one, there are three distinct cases to consider (h_l and h_r are the height of the left and right subtrees, respectively):

1. $h_l = h_r$ and the insertion causes $h_l > h_r$ but the balance criterion is not violated.

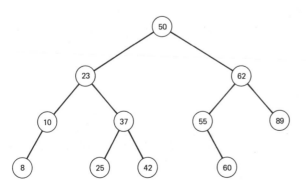

Figure 4.8. An AVL tree.

2. $h_l < h_r$ and the insertion causes $h_l = h_r$ and the balance is improved.
3. $h_l > h_r$ and the insertion causes the balance criteria to be violated and the tree with node x as the root must be rebalanced.

Node insertion consists essentially of three parts:

1. Following the search path until it is verified that the key value is not already in the tree.
2. Inserting the new node in the tree.
3. Retreating along the search path and checking the balance factor ($h_r - h_l$) at each node, rebalancing if necessary.

The rebalancing operations are performed entirely by sequences of pointer adjustments. Pointers are cyclically exchanged, resulting in either a single or double rotation of the nodes involved. In addition to pointer adjustment, the node balance factor ($h_r - h_l$) stored in each node must also be adjusted.

There are two cases that must be considered when rebalancing is required and there are two instances of each case. Case 1 is illustrated in Figure 4.9, and it involves a single rotation to the left for case 1a and a single rotation to the

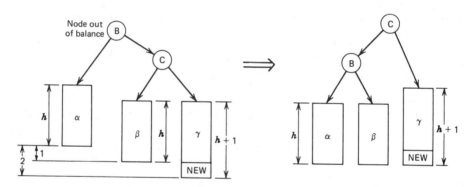

Case 1*a*

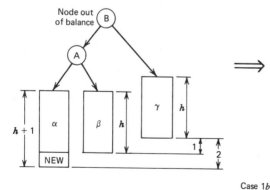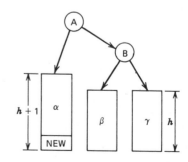

Case 1*b*

Figure 4.9.   Single rotation transformations.

right for case 1*b*. These transformations are like applying the associative law to an algebraic expression, replacing $\alpha(\beta\gamma)$ by $(\alpha\beta)\gamma$ for case 1*a* and replacing $(\alpha\beta)\gamma$ by $\alpha(\beta\gamma)$ for case 1*b*. Case 2(*a*), illustrated in Figure 4.10, involves a double rotation, first rotating (B, C) to the right, followed by rotating (A, B) to the left. Case 2*b* also involves a double rotation, first rotating (A, B) to the left, followed by rotating (B, C) to the right.

Figure 4.11 illustrates the insertion and balancing techniques for the sequence of key values 7, 8, 10, 5, 4, 6, and 9. The insertion of key value 10 into tree (*b*) results in an unbalanced tree (unbalanced to the right). Its rebalancing involves a single rotation to the left, yielding tree (*c*). The insertion of key value 6 offsets the balance of tree (*e*) and rebalancing in this case requires a double rotation—first to the left about node 5 and then to the right about node 8—giving tree (*f*). The insertion of key value 9 causes the subtree with node 8 as its root to be unbalanced. The tree is rebalanced by a double rotation about node 8.

The complexity of balancing operations indicates that AVL trees should probably be used in situations for which the number of retrievals on a tree is considerably larger than the number of insertions and deletions. Rebalancing is usually necessary once for every two insertions. Tree deletion is slightly more complicated than insertion although the rebalancing operation is essentially the

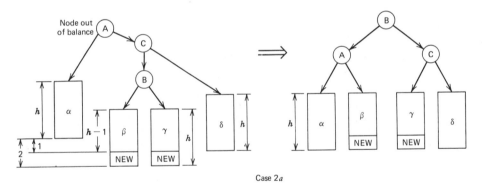

Case 2*a*

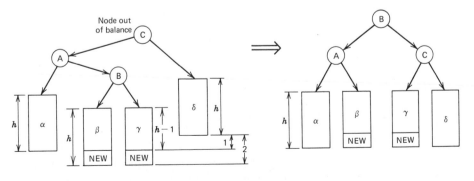

Case 2*b*

Figure 4.10. Double rotation transformations.

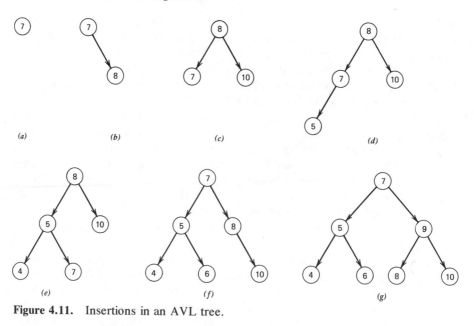

Figure 4.11.   Insertions in an AVL tree.

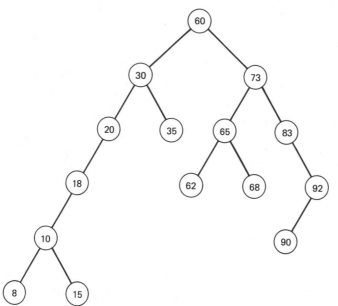

Figure 4.12.   Generalized AVL tree with $\Delta = 3$.

same as that for insertion. The deletion of a node from an AVL tree can be performed, even in the worst case, in $O(\log_2 n)$ operations. The insertion of a key value results in, at most, either a single rotation or a double rotation, but deletion may require a rotation at every node along a search path. Empirical tests show that one rotation is required for every five deletions.

If a tree is built and then used for an extended period of time before insertions and deletions are done on the tree, then AVL trees with very close to minimal retrieval time are the best bet. On the other hand, if a tree is built and seldom if ever used, then unrestricted growth trees, that is, random trees, with minimum overhead should be considered.

The concept of AVL trees has been generalized by permitting the imbalance (Δ) at nodes of the tree to take on values larger than one, while still retaining restricted growth. Generalized AVL trees offer several alternative choices that allow the programmer to trade off access time for ease of construction. Figure 4.12 illustrates a generalized AVL tree with the imbalance factor $\Delta = 3$.

4.3.4 Multidimensional Binary Search Trees

The binary search trees discussed in the previous part of this chapter are suitable only for primary key retrieval, and the position of each record (node) in a tree is determined by the value of the primary key in the record. A multidimensional binary search tree is a data structure for storage of data to be retrieved by multikey queries on secondary keys.

A multidimensional binary search tree is also referred to as a k-d tree, where k is the number of keys for each record in the tree. Each record P in a file F, represented as a k-d tree, is an ordered k-tuple $(v_0, v_1, \ldots, v_{k-1})$ of values that are key values of the record (note that there may also be data items in each record in addition to the key values). Associated with each node, though not necessarily stored as a field, is a *discriminator,* which is an integer between 0 and $k-1$, inclusive. The key values of record P are called $K_0(P), \ldots, K_{k-1}(P)$, the two pointers in each node are LOSON(P), the low son pointer, and HISON(P), the high son pointer, and DISC(P), the discriminator. The discriminator of a node is used to specify which key value in a k-tuple is used to make a branching decision at a node during a search. All nodes on any given level have the same discriminator. The root node has discriminator 0, its two sons have discriminator 1, the kth level discriminator is $k-1$, and the $(k+1)^{st}$ level discriminator is 0, that is, the discriminator j of a node at level l is $j = (l-1) \bmod k$.

The procedure for inserting a record Q in a k-d tree is also used to search for a specific record Q in the tree. For any record P in a k-d tree, let j be DISC(P); then, the traversal of the tree during searching is as follows:

1. If $K_j(Q) < K_j(P)$, then record Q is in LOSON(P).
2. If $K_j(Q) > K_j(P)$, then record Q is in HISON(P).

This traversal procedure does not take into account the possibility of the equality of key values. If the two key values $K_j(Q)$ and $K_j(P)$ are equal, then the decision must be based on the remaining key values in each record. This is done by defining a superkey of P by

$$S_j(P) = K_j(P)K_{j+1}(P) \ldots K_{k-1}(P)K_0(P) \ldots K_{j-1}(P)$$

$S_j(P)$ is the cyclical concatenation of all key values in record P, starting with K_j. Now the search procedure for record Q is:

1. If $S_j(Q) < S_j(P)$, then record Q is in LOSON(P)
2. If $S_j(Q) > S_j(P)$, then record Q is in HISON(P).
3. If $S_j(Q) = S_j(P)$, then all key values in record Q and record P are equal.

Figure 4.13 illustrates a k-d tree with k = 3. The records were inserted in the tree in the order

| 8 | A | 9 |, | 6 | Q | 3 |, | 12 | C | 7 |, | 7 | B | 9 |, | 6 | B | 14 |,

| 10 | A | 5 |, | 9 | F | 2 |, | 10 | F | 1 |, and | 9 | F | 0 |

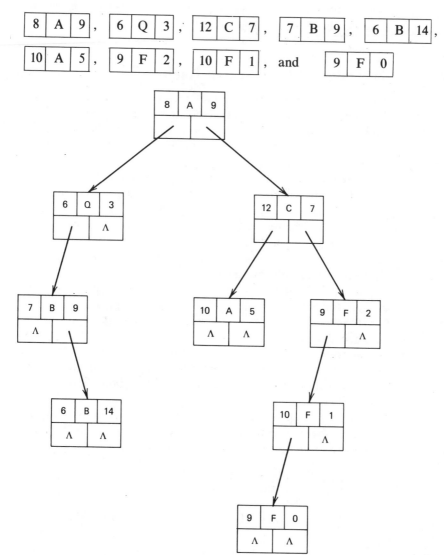

Figure 4.13.   k-d tree with $k = 3$.

The standard binary search tree is a 1-d tree. The average search path length for a random k-d search tree is approximately $1.4\log_2 n$. This is precisely the average search path length for 1-d random search trees. It has been shown that the theorems proven for 1-d binary search trees also apply to k-d trees.

The purpose of a k-d tree search is to find all records satisfying a specific query. The k-d tree is capable of answering simple queries, range queries, and Boolean queries. If the exact match Boolean query, that is, a query that asks if a specific record is in a k-d tree, is the only type of query to be specified, a k-d tree should probably not be used as the structure to store the records. Even though to a user the keys appear to be independent, they should be merged together into one superkey and the 1-d structure should be used for storage and retrieval.

A partial match query is one in which values are specified for a proper subset of keys, that is, values are specified for t keys, $t < k$. If $\{s_i\}$ and $\{v_i\}$ are sets such that the keys specified are $K_{S_1}, K_{S_2} \ldots, K_{S_t}$, and the values they must have to be a valid response to the query are $v_{S_1}, v_{S_2}, \ldots, v_{S_t}$, then a set of records for which searching is undertaken is the set of all P such that $K_{S_i} = v_{S_i}$ for $1 \le i \le t$. An example of a partial match Boolean query is the following query:

$$(K_1(P) = 10) \lor (2 \le K_3(P) \le 7 \land 0 \le K_5(P) \le 4)$$

The amount of work done in any partial match search with t keys for a tree with n nodes is $cn^{1-t/k} + d \ (t < k)$ for some small constants c and d.

The deletion of nodes (records) from a k-d tree is possible although it is rather expensive. If the node P to be deleted has descendants, then node P should be replaced with one of those descendants Q that will retain the order imposed by P. That is, all nodes in HISON(P) will be in HISON(Q) and all nodes in LOSON(P) will be in LOSON(Q). Once Q is found, it can serve as the new root and the only reorganization necessary is to delete Q from its previous position in the tree.

Random insertion in an n node k-d tree requires, on the average, $O(\log_2 n)$ time. Partial match queries with t keys can be performed in k-d trees in $O(n^{1-t/k})$ $(t < k)$ time. Deletion of the root node requires $O(n^{1-1/k})$ running time, but deletion of a random node is $O(\log_2 n)$.

An advantage of k-d trees is that they support several types of queries. The k-d trees are intended primarily for use in a 1-level store, but using secondary storage might be acceptable if there are few additions and deletions after a file is created. It is necessary for k-d trees to have some minimum number of nodes before they become useful. For example, if the deepest node in a 10-d tree is on the 6th level, four of the keys will never have been used as a discriminator while the tree was being built. A good rule of thumb is to use k-d trees only if $n > 2^{2k}$. For any application in which there is a desire to retrieve on secondary keys or to have multikey retrieval, a k-d tree is potentially applicable.

4.3.5   Binary Search Trees in Two-Level Storage

A binary search tree is one of the most flexible and best understood techniques for organizing files that can be stored entirely in internal memory while they are being processed. The main problem concerning the use of a binary search tree for organizing a large file involves allocating external storage for nodes. The most realistic model for large files must take into account the fact that the largest parts of a binary search tree must reside on an external storage device from which parts of the tree are transferred into internal memory when needed. If storage for a tree is allocated properly, large parts of it will be brought into internal memory in block transfers rather than a node at a time. The performance of the tree will be measured not in terms of the average number of comparisons required to locate a record, but in terms of the average number of block transfers.

The problem of how the nodes of a binary search tree should be allocated to pages so as to minimize the average number of accesses necessary to search a tree is discussed below. Pages are fixed size memory blocks that are the units in terms of which data are transferred between internal memory and external memory. Figure 4.14 illustrates a binary tree with seven nodes per page. Two methods for allocating storage to nodes as they are added to the tree are described. The most straightforward allocation scheme is sequential allocation. This method ignores page boundaries and allocates storage for new nodes in consecutive locations as nodes are received. Nodes on a given page are related by locality in the input sequence and not necessarily by locality in the tree.

The second method is called grouped allocation and it takes page boundaries into consideration. When a node is added to a tree, the father node to which a new node is to be linked is located. If the father node is on a partially filled page, then the new node is allocated space on this page. If the father is on a full page, then a new page is allocated to the tree and the new node is allocated at the beginning of this page. The first node allocated on a page is called the *seed node* for that page. Only nodes in a subtree of the seed node will be allocated on this page. Nodes on the same page are related by locality in the search tree; thus, fewer page accesses are necessary to search a binary search tree.

The grouped allocation scheme can result in many sparsely filled pages being allocated to a search tree. If the total size of a search tree is known or can be estimated, the grouped allocation scheme can be modified to limit the number of pages allocated. This method allocates new pages to seed nodes until there are no more pages available. Then seed nodes are allocated on partially filled pages. The pages in which seed nodes are to be planted are selected so that seed nodes are evenly distributed over partially filled pages.

If the page size for grouped allocation is p, then the average search path length $l(n, p)$ for a tree with n nodes can be estimated by

$$l(n, p) \cong \frac{1.4\log_2 n}{1.4\log_2 p} = \frac{\log_2 n}{\log_2 p} = \log_p n$$

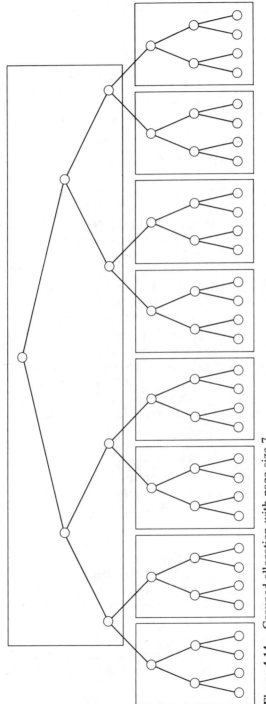

Figure 4.14. Grouped allocation with page size 7.

If n is 10^6 ($\cong 2^{20}$), the page size is 7, and only one page at a time is accessed (from a disk), then

$$l(n, p) \cong 7$$

that is, only about one-fourth as many page accesses are required as when the nodes in a tree are not allocated to pages by locality in the tree. When nodes are not grouped into pages, a binary search tree with 10^6 nodes requires on the average about 28 accesses to external memory to locate a specific node.

4.4   MULTIWAY SEARCH TREES

If each page in the binary search tree illustrated in Figure 4.14 is considered to be a single node, then a binary tree essentially becomes a multiway tree. The average search path length for a multiway tree of n nodes and a constant branching factor of s is $O(\log_s n)$. This expression for the average search path length is developed in Section 4.4.3. If 100-way branching occurs at each node, then any desired key value out of 10^6 key values can be located after examining, on the average, $\log_{100} 10^6$ ($=3$) nodes (if we assume that the root is at level one and it is kept in internal memory). If the multiway tree with 10^6 key values is allowed to grow at random in an unrestricted manner, then the average path length for the worst case is much larger than three. Thus, a scheme for restricted growth is also important in many cases for multiway search trees just as it is for binary search trees. The nodes (pages) should not be made arbitrarily large since internal memory size is limited and also since it takes longer to access a large node.

Multiway search trees afford a feasible and practical alternative to binary search trees. This is especially true when constructing and maintaining large search trees in which insertions and deletions are necessary, but in which the internal memory of a computer is not large enough or is too costly to be used for long-term storage. A storage organization requiring very few accesses to external storage to locate a record is highly desirable and the multiway search tree is a practical solution to this problem.

4.4.1   Trie Structures

A trie (pronounced try) structure is a complete m-ary tree in which each node consists of m components (a node can be considered to be an m-place vector). Typically, the components are digits or letters. Trie structures are usually used in the area of information storage and retrieval to store large synonym dictionaries (20,000–50,000 words) for the English language. Each word is a key value and the data associated with each key value is a list of synonyms. Frequently used dictionaries must be represented in a manner that allows for efficient searching.

Instead of accessing records based on a comparison between complete key values, use is made of a key value's representation as a sequence of digits or alphabetic characters. Each node on level l represents a set of key values that begin with a sequence of l characters. A node (on level l) specifies an m-way branch depending on the lth character of the key value, that is, at level l the lth character is used to determine the node to branch to on the $(l+1)$st level.

To construct a trie for a given set of n key values, the key values are placed into sorted order, and the trie is constructed one level at a time. A key value is removed from the sorted list when it becomes uniquely identified. Figure 4.15 gives an example of a trie structure (organized in table form) for the 26 English words given in Table 4.3. Figure 4.16 gives a tree view of the trie. The trie in Figure 4.15 consists of 13 nodes with each node being a vector of 27 components. Each component contains either a blank (b), the desired word, or a node number. The blank (b) is used to indicate when the node is a path end for some key value—that is, it is the terminating character for each key value.

A trie structure is searched for a key value KV in the following manner. If the contents of a table entry X corresponding to an input character of KV is not a number pointing to another node, then it is a key value. If $KV=X$, then the search procedure terminates successfully, and KV is in the table; otherwise, KV is not in the table.

It takes four levels in a trie to distinguish between ERR and ERRAND. To illustrate the use of the trie structure in Figure 4.15, the search for GOAT is traced. The letter G in node 1 indicates that the search should be continued in node 7. The entry corresponding to O in node 7 says that the search should be continued in node 12. The letter A is used to select the proper element in node 12 and this entry is used to locate the desired word GOAT.

The node vectors in Figure 4.15 are arranged according to the internal character code of the characters. Thus, a trie search is executed by using the characters of the key values as subscripts into node vectors. Since each entry in

Table 4.3

English Words Used in Constructing the Trie in Figure 4.15

ALWAYS	GOAT
BEGUN	GOTO
BURN	IF
CARVE	NONE
CHECK	OPEN
DECLARE	PROOF
DOOM	PUT
ERR	RUN
ERRAND	STOP
FLOW	THEN
FORMAT	TO
FREE	WHILE
GO	WRITE

Node Number

	1	2	3	4	5	6	7	8	9	10	11	12	13
A	ALWAYS		CARVE									GO	ERR
B	2											GOAT	ERRAND
C	3												
D	4												
E	5	BEGUN		DECLARE									
F	6												
G	7												
H	IF		CHECK						THEN	WHILE			
I													
J													
K													
L						FLOW							

112

M											
N	NONE										
O	OPEN	DOOM		FORMAT		TO				GOTO	
P	8										
Q											
R	RUN		11	FREE		PROOF		WRITE	13		
S	STOP										
T	9										
U		BURN				PUT					
V											
W	10										
X											
Y											
Z											

Figure 4.15. Trie structure in table form for the English words in Table 4.3.

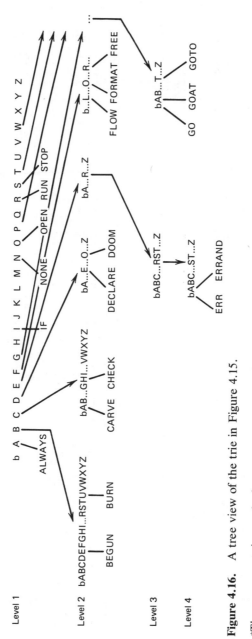
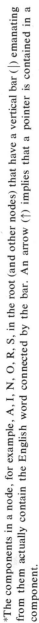

Figure 4.16. A tree view of the trie in Figure 4.15.

*The components in a node, for example, A, I, N, O, R, S, in the root (and other nodes) that have a vertical bar (|) emanating from them actually contain the English word connected by the bar. An arrow (↑) implies that a pointer is contained in a component.

a node component in the trie in Figure 4.15 is either a pointer or a complete key value, this particular organization of the trie structure means that entries in a node vector may be of variable length. Also, a table representation of a trie wastes memory space since many table entries are empty, especially after the first few levels of the trie structure. Memory space can be conserved at the expense of running time if a linked list is used for each node vector since most of the entries in the vectors tend to be empty. This amounts to replacing the trie of Figure 4.15 by the forest of trees in Figure 4.17. Searching in such a forest proceeds by finding a root that matches the first character, then finding the son node of that root that matches the second character, etc.

The tree branching does not have to stop as indicated in the forest in Figure 4.17. Instead, each key value can be represented, character by character, until the end-of-key value delimiter (b) is reached. If so, the E tree in Figure 4.17 is represented as illustrated in Figure 4.18. This representation requires more storage but makes the processing of variable length key values easy.

The average search time for the trie in Figure 4.15 is $O(\log_m n)$, where n is the number of key values and m is the number of components in each node. On the other hand, the average search time for a binary search tree with n key values is $O(\log_2 n)$. The nodes in the trie in Figure 4.15 are sparsely filled after

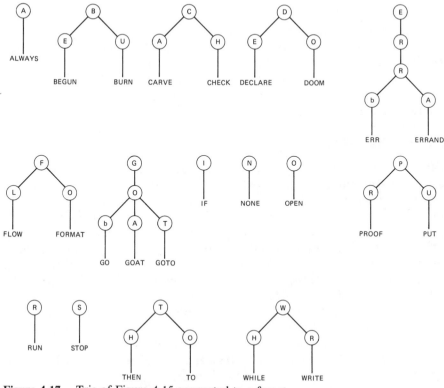

Figure 4.17. Trie of Figure 4.15 converted to a forest.

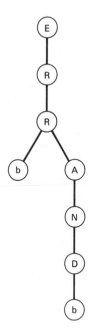

Figure 4.18. Character by character tree representation of key values ERR and ERRAND.

the first two levels. Thus, in order to conserve storage space and to take advantage of the search time characteristics of the trie at the top levels of the tree, a trie is used for the first few characters of a key value and then some other technique is used for distinguishing the rest of the key value. This idea usually decreases the number of trie nodes without substantially changing the running time. When compared with a binary search tree, a trie requires more storage, but searching is much faster.

4.4.1.1 The C-Trie

A trie structure, called a compressed trie (C-trie), has the same underlying m-ary tree structure as a trie, but the components in a node are only one bit long. When a component bit of a node is set, the bit indicates that one or more key values pass through the node. The retrieval of a key value is made possible by adding one field to each node that gives the number of nonzero bits to the left of a node on its level. A node on level l in a C-trie has the structure illustrated in Figure 4.19. U is a one bit field, and if $U = 0$, then a node is an internal node. If $U = 1$, then a node is a leaf and the fields BKC contain the suffix of the key value. B is a one-bit field, and it is set to one if one of the key values passing through the node terminates at level l. B is needed since a key value X may be a proper prefix of another key value Y. K is an $(m-1)$ bit field with each bit corresponding to a field in a node of the trie. C is a field with length less than or equal to $\log_2 n$ bits. It gives the number of nonzero bits in the K fields in nodes on level l to the left of a node.

Since each component in a node is only one bit long, a key value, once it is uniquely identified, can no longer be stored in a component. For this reason the

U	B	K	C
1	1	$m-1$	$\leqslant \lceil \log_2 n \rceil$

Figure 4.19. Structure of a node in a C-trie.

path is prolonged by one level. On this last level, the U bit is set to one and the suffix is stored in the BKC fields of the node. If the suffix cannot be stored entirely in a node of $m + \lceil \log_2 n \rceil$ * bits, then the K field holds part of the suffix and the C field points to an auxiliary table containing the remainder of the suffix. A prefix does not have to be stored since it is implicitly defined by the path from the root of a C-trie to a terminal node containing the suffix. Part of the trie structure in Figure 4.15 is represented as a C-trie in Figure 4.20. The links represented in Figure 4.20 are not explicitly present since the components are only one bit long; the links are there only for readability purposes.

C-tries are constructed in basically the same way as tries. The n key values are given as a sorted list. The tree is constructed one level at a time. The result of the construction process is a sequence of nodes stored as a continuous bit string. Each node, consisting of $m + \log_2 n$ bits, is an addressable entity.

Before an algorithm for searching for a key value in a C-trie is given, some variables and functions must be defined. LEVEL(i) contains the base address of nodes on level i and P is a pointer to a node. The functions $U(P), B(P), K(P)$, $C(P)$, and $BKC(P)$ return the values of the fields described in Figure 4.19 and NLEFT(P, x_i) returns the number of 1-bits to the left of and including the x_i^{th} bit in $K(P)$. The x_i^{th} field in $K(P)$ is referred to as $K(P, x_i)$. A key value X is assumed to be written as the string $X = X_1 X_2 X_3 \ldots X_k$, and x_i is the bit in $K(P)$ that corresponds to X_i on level i. An algorithm for searching for a key value in a C-trie is given below.

Algorithm SEARCH-TRIE

1. $i \leftarrow 1, P \leftarrow$ LEVEL($i-1$) + 1 [P points to the root node].
2. If $U(P) = 1$, then the search terminates successfully
   if $BKC(P) = X_i \ldots X_k$, otherwise unsuccessfully.
3. If $K(P, x_i) = 0$, then the search terminates unsuccessfully.
4. If $x_i = 0$, then the search terminates successfully.
5. $P \leftarrow C(P)$ + NLEFT(P, x_i) + LEVEL(i).
6. $i \leftarrow i+1$ and go to Step 2.

The search time for a C-trie is of the order $\log_m n$, and the storage requirement is of the order $n \times (m + \log_2 n)$ bits.

A C-trie structure allows the storage of a large number of key values in internal memory. When compared to a trie, the memory requirements of a C-trie are, in general, smaller by an order of magnitude while the retrieval time is about the same. C-tries are not suitable for rapidly and constantly changing

*$\lceil \rceil$ denotes the ceiling function.

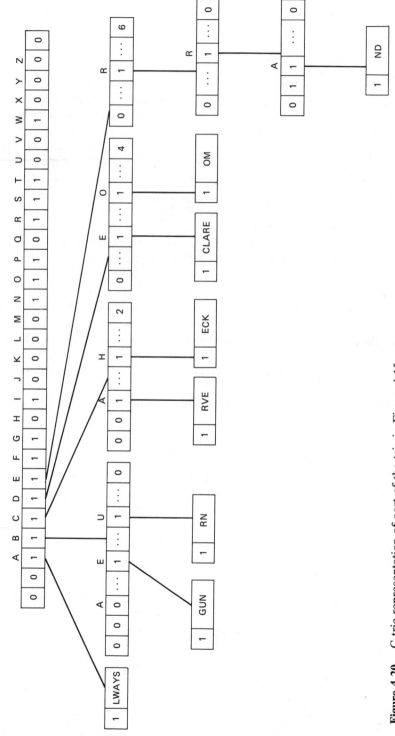

Figure 4.20. C-trie representation of part of the trie in Figure 4.15.

118

files. They are best suited for static files in which changes may be batched. If the updates are few, then these changes might be incorporated into an existing C-trie. Since no links are actually employed by this structure, updates imply that nodes may have to be moved about. Therefore, it may probably be best to reconstruct the entire C-trie.

4.4.2 B-trees

The B-tree is a restricted growth multiway search tree. A B-tree of order m is a tree that satisfies the following properties:

1. Every node has $\leq m$ sons.
2. Every node, except the root and the terminal nodes, has $\geq \lceil m/2 \rceil$ sons.
3. The root has at least 2 sons unless it is a terminal node.
4. All terminal nodes appear on the same level and carry no information.
5. An internal node with k sons contains $k-1$ key values.

For a B-tree of order 5, all nodes except the root and the terminal nodes have between $\lceil 5/2 \rceil = 3$ and 5 sons so they contain 2, 3, or 4 key values. A root is allowed to contain from 1 to 4 key values. All key values in each node appear in increasing order from left to right, and the number of sons of each node is exactly one greater than the number of key values in each node. Figure 4.21 illustrates a B-tree of order 5. The terminal nodes in Figure 4.21 contain no information, and in practice they do not actually appear in a tree; they are instead represented by null pointers.

A node that contains j key values and $j + 1$ pointers can be represented as

$$\boxed{P_0 \ K_1 \ P_1 \ K_2 \ P_2 \ K_3 \ldots P_{j-1} \ K_j \ P_j}$$

where $K_1 < K_2 < K_3 < \ldots < K_{j-1} < K_j$, $1 \leq j < m$, and P_i points to a subtree holding key values between K_i and K_{i+1}.

Searching a B-tree for a specified key value is as follows. A node, starting with the root node, is brought into internal memory and searched, possibly using a binary search for large j, for the given argument key value among the key values $K_1, K_2, \ldots, K_j$. If the search is successful, then the desired key value is located, but if the search is unsuccessful because the argument key value lies between K_i and K_{i+1}, then the node pointed to by P_i is retrieved and the search continued. The pointer P_0 is used if an argument key value precedes K_1, and P_j is used if an argument key value follows K_j in sorted order. If $P_i = \Lambda$, the search is unsuccessful.

4.4.2.1 *Updating B-trees*

The insertion process for B-trees is relatively simple; each terminal node corresponds to a place where a new key value may be inserted. If the new key value 258 is inserted into the B-tree in Figure 4.21, then the node

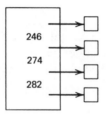

is changed to

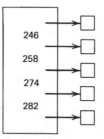

If the key value 80 is to be inserted, there is no room since the node

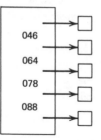

on level 3, where key value 80 should be placed, is already full, that is, it already has four key values and five pointers. This problem can be handled by splitting the node into which key value 80 should be placed into two parts with two key values in each part, and passing key value 78 up to its father node. That is,

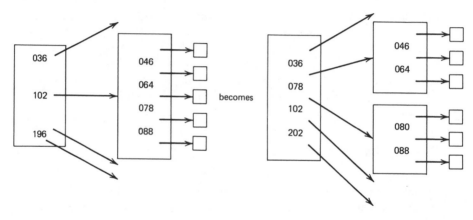

becomes

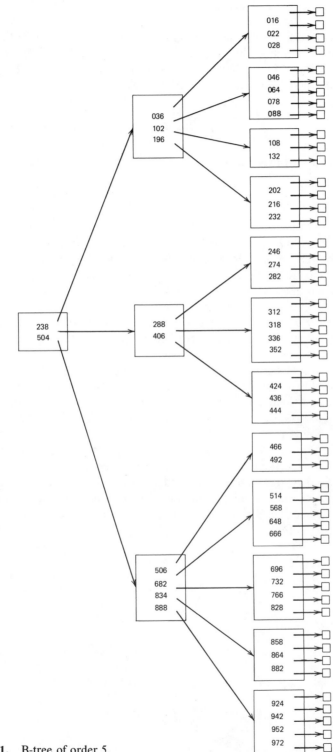

Figure 4.21. B-tree of order 5.

In general, a key value inserted into a B-tree of order m with the terminal nodes at level l is placed in an appropriate node on level $l-1$. If this node now contains m key values, then it must be split into two distinct nodes. For example, if a node after the insertion of a new key value looks like

$$P_0 \ K_1 \ P_1 \ K_2 \ P_2 \ldots P_{m-1} K_m \ P_m$$

then it is split into two nodes

$$P_0 \ K_1 \ P_1 \ K_2 \ldots K_{\lceil m/2 \rceil -1} \ P_{\lceil m/2 \rceil -1} \qquad P_{\lceil m/2 \rceil} \ K_{\lceil m/2 \rceil +1} \ P_{\lceil m/2 \rceil +1} \ldots K_m \ P_m$$

and the key value $K_{\lceil m/2 \rceil}$ is inserted into the father of the original node. This insertion may cause a father node to contain m key values, and if so, it is split in the manner illustrated above. If a root node must be split (a root has no father), then a new root node is created containing the single key value $K_{\lceil m/2 \rceil}$. The tree becomes one level taller in this case. Thus, a B-tree grows upward from the top instead of downward from the bottom. The procedure described above for inserting new key values into a B-tree is exactly the procedure used to create a B-tree.

The deletion of a key value from a B-tree is more complicated than inserting a new key value into a B-tree. The deletion of a key value on level $l-1$ simply causes it to be erased from a node. When this erasing makes a node too empty (that is, underflow occurs), the right (or left) brother is examined and key values are moved from the brother until both nodes have approximately the same number of key values. The key values are not moved directly from the brother to the underflowed node; instead, the preceding key value in the parent node is moved to the underflowed node and the preceding key value in the brother replaces the key value in the father node. For example, the deletion of key value 108 in the B-tree in Figure 4.21 causes the following changes to occur.

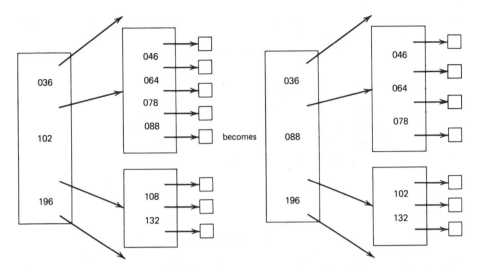

A delete operation that results in underflow fails only if the brother is minimally full. But in this case, the two nodes can be collapsed into one (together with one key value from their father). This collapsing may cause the father to underflow (why?).

When a key value to be deleted is not on level $l-1$, it is replaced by its successor and the successor is deleted. For example, if key value 682 in Figure 4.21 is deleted, it is replaced by key value 696 and key value 696 is deleted from the node where it resides, that is,

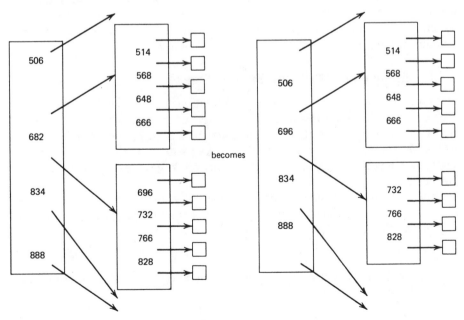

The movement of a successor key value to its father node during a delete operation like the one just illustrated may cause the successor key value's original node to underflow. This problem can be solved as described above.

4.4.2.2 B-tree Search Characteristics

The effectiveness of a B-tree search is determined by the shape of the tree, and the shape of the tree is determined by the order, m. When m is small, a tree is tall and narrow, and when m is large, a tree is short and bushy. The maximum number of nodes, K, that must be accessed during a B-tree search is

$$K \leq 1 + \log_{\lceil m/2 \rceil} \left(\frac{n+1}{2} \right) \tag{4.8}$$

where m is the order and n is the number of key values in a tree. The derivation of the expression (4.8) is left as an exercise. The right side of expression (4.8) is also a bound on the number of levels in a B-tree with n key values. A B-tree of order 256 containing 100,000 key values has a maximum search length of 4.

The above bound on the number of levels in a B-tree indicates that it is preferable to use a large value for m. In fact, if $m = n + 1$, then only one level exists in a tree; this choice of m, however, is not reasonable if a tree is too large to fit in internal memory. When a value for m is selected, the primary objective is to minimize the total amount of time required to search a B-tree for a key value KV. This time has two components: (1) the time required to access a node in external memory, and (2) the time required to search this node, in internal memory, for KV. It turns out that there is a value of m, $\overline{m}$ (see Figure 4.22), for which the search time is a minimum. For values of m exceeding $\overline{m}$, the total amount of time required to search a B-tree increases.

4.4.3 Analysis of Multiway Search Trees

With multiway search trees an important relationship exists between a branching factor s of the nodes in a tree and the height of the tree. The branch factor is the number of branches that can emanate from nodes. The branch factor is usually either the same as the number of key values that can be placed in a node, or it may be one greater than the number of key values (this is the case for B-trees).

The following analysis assumes, for simplicity, that each node has branching factor s, and that the number of key values per node is also s. The number of key values that can be placed in a tree of height h is

$$s + s^2 + s^3 + \ldots + s^h \tag{4.9}$$

The height h can be easily determined by equating expression (4.9) to n and solving for h, that is,

$$n = s + s^2 + s^3 + \ldots + s^h \tag{4.10}$$

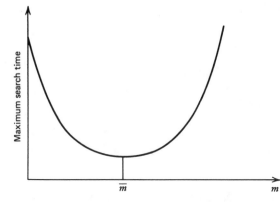

Figure 4.22. Maximum search time versus order *(m)*

If the formula for the sum of a geometric series is used, (4.10) can be rewritten as

$$n = (s^h - 1)(\frac{s}{s-1}) \qquad (4.11)$$

Expression (4.11) can be rewritten as

$$s^h = 1 + (\frac{s-1}{s})\, n \qquad (4.12)$$

The height, h, can be written as a function of n and s by taking the logarithm of both sides of (4.12) with respect to s, that is,

$$h = \log_s[1 + (\frac{s-1}{s})\, n] \qquad (4.13)$$

When s is reasonably large, that is, when $(s-1)/s$ approaches the value 1, (4.13) can be written as

$$h \cong \log_s(n+1) \qquad (4.14)$$

or the height is $O(\log_s n)$.

Expression (4.14) reveals that as the value of s increases, the height of a tree (for constant n) decreases; however, larger nodes require more time to be moved into internal memory from external memory. As s decreases, the height of a tree increases, thus, more nodes must be accessed to locate the desired node. When $n = 2^{21}$ and $s = 2^7$, h is approximately 3; on the other hand, when $s = 2^3$, h is approximately 7.

EXERCISES

1. Show that for a given n, the number N of binary trees with differing shapes that can be formed, each containing n nodes, is given by

$$\frac{4^n}{n^{3/2}\sqrt{\pi}} + O(4^n n^{-5/2})$$

2. In a tree with n internal nodes and $n + 1$ extended (or external nodes), prove that

$$P_E = P_I + 2n$$

Assume that the root of a tree is at level 0.

3. Show that the average search path length for a binary search tree created with random input (n key values) is given by

$$1.386\log_2 n$$

4. Show that the search time for an arbitary B-tree of order m with n keys is less than or equal to

$$1 + \log_{\lceil m/2 \rceil} (\frac{n + 1}{2})$$

5. Develop an algorithm for deleting a key value X from an AVL tree. Derive the time complexity for the algorithm.

6. Develop an algorithm for deleting a key value X from a B-tree of order m.

7. Develop an algorithm for inserting a key value X into a perfectly balanced binary search tree. Derive the time complexity for this operation.

8. Shown below is a sequence of key values that are to be stored in a B-tree of order 5. Draw the B-tree that exists at each point in the sequence where a semicolon appears. For example, draw the B-tree that exists after the key 32 has been inserted, etc.

    25 45 24 38 32; 8 27 46 13; 42 5 22 18; 26 7 15 35; 20 30 10 28;

9. Draw the k-d tree (when $k = 2$) that results from inserting the following key values in order from left to right.

    (5, F) (3, G) (10, F) (10, B) (1, Z) (3, A) (4, F) (6 A)

10. Given the B-tree of order 5

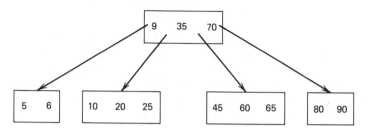

(a) Draw the B-tree that results when the key values 15, 30, 40, and 50 have been inserted (show the tree after each insertion).

(b) Using the original B-tree (before step (a)), draw the B-tree that results when the key values 20, 90, 5, and 60 are deleted in that order (show the tree after each deletion).

11. In Section 4.3.2 it was suggested that the merge time utilizing the merge pattern suggested by an optimal merge pattern tree can be shown as

proportional to the weighted external path length of the tree. Show this result.

12. Repeat Exercise 8 for an AVL tree.
13. Write an algorithm to insert a key value X into a trie. Assume that the key value is a string of alphabetic characters.
14. Some of the references at the end of this chapter discuss heuristic algorithms for constructing near-optimal binary search trees. Write a program in an appropriate programming language to implement one of these algorithms and then test it using the data in Exercise 8.
15. By utilizing algorithm SEARCH_TRIE in Section 4.4.1.1, develop an algorithm to create a C-trie. Test the algorithm using the input in Table 4.3.

REFERENCES

4.1 Adel'son-Vel'skii, G.M. and Landis, E.M. "An Algorithm for the Organization of Information," *Dokl. Acad. Nauk SSSR Math.,* Vol 146, No. 2, 1962, pp. 263–266.

The authors introduce the AVL tree as a restricted growth binary search tree that can be practically used in situations requiring dynamic trees. They derive the expression given in Section 4.3.3 for the expected height of an AVL tree.

4.2 Bayer, R. and McCreight, E. "Organization and Maintenance of Large Ordered Indexes," *Acta Informatica 1,* 1972, pp. 173–189.

This paper introduces the B-tree as a way of organizing indexes for files.

4.3 Bentley, J.L. "Multidimensional Binary Search Trees Used for Associative Searching," *Commun. ACM,* Vol. 18, No. 9, September 1975, pp. 509–517.

The k-d tree as a data structure for storage of data to be retrieved by associative searches is described and analyzed. The k-d tree is shown to be suitable for storing data to be retrieved using multikey queries. A recursive search algorithm for finding all records satisfying a partial match query and a deletion algorithm are given.

4.4 Foster, C. C. "A Generalization of AVL Trees," *Commun. ACM,* Vol. 16, No. 8, August 1973, pp. 513–517.

Generalized AVL trees with an imbalance factor greater than one are described and analyzed.

4.5 Knuth, D.E. "Optimum Binary Search Trees," *Acta Informatica 1,* No. 1, 1971, pp. 14–25.

An algorithm for creating optimal binary search trees is given.

4.6   Muntz, R. and Uzgalis, R. "Dynamic Storage Allocation for Binary Search Trees in a Two-Level Memory," *Proceedings of 4th Princeton Conference*, Princeton, New Jersey, 1970.

This paper describes two methods for allocating external storage for nodes in a binary search tree.

4.7   Knuth, D.E. *Sorting and Searching*, Vol. III, Addison-Wesley, Reading, Massachusetts, 1973, 721 pages.

This book provides an in-depth look at the analysis of a number of tree searching techniques. It is an excellent reference for this chapter.

4.8   Huffman, D.A. "A Method for the Construction of Minimum-Redundancy Codes," *Proceedings of IRE*, Vol. 40, pp. 1098–1101.

This paper gives a simple algorithm for generating binary trees with minimal weighted external path length.

4.9   Horowitz, E. and Sahni, S. *Fundamentals of Data Structures*, Computer Science Press, Inc., 1976, 564 pages.

Good book that analyzes various algorithms for tree searching and sorting. In addition, it briefly covers file organizations and file searching and updating.

4.10   Nievergelt, J. "Binary Search Trees and File Organization," *ACM Computing Surveys*, Vol. 6, September 1974, pp. 195–207.

This paper advocates the use of binary search trees for organizing files. The time and space complexities for binary trees are compared with other structures that can be used to organize files.

4.11   Sussenguth, E.H. "Use of Tree Structures for Processing Files," *Commun. ACM*, Vol. 6, No. 5, May 1963, pp. 272–279.

Paper shows that a file may be searched and updated with times proportional to $s \log_s N$, where N is the number of records and s is the branch factor of nodes in the tree.

4.12   Fredkin, E. "Trie Memory," *Commun. ACM*, Vol. 3, No. 9, September 1960, pp. 490–499.

Trie memory is described as a paradigm for organizing information storage and retrieval systems.

4.13   Maly K. "Compressed Tries," *Commun. ACM*, Vol. 19, No. 7, July 1976, pp. 409–415.

Algorithms for constructing C-tries and searching C-tries are given.

Algorithm SEARCH_TRIE in this chapter was taken from this paper.

4.14 Hibbard, T.N. "Some Combinatorial Properties of Certain Trees with Applications to Searching and Sorting," *Acta Informatica*, 1961, pp. 13−28.

A classic paper that introduces the binary search tree and develops the expression $1.386\log_2 (n+1)$ as the average search path length for the binary search tree.

List-Structured File Organizations

5.1 INTRODUCTION

With the exception of the k-dimensional binary search tree, the file organizations described in Chapters 3 and 4 are suitable only for primary key retrieval. There are numerous applications in the general area of information retrieval that require the capability to retrieve records based on the value of more than one data item in a record. These data items in the record are designated as keys, and records may be retrieved by specifying values for one or more of the keys. Unlike primary key values, these key values usually do not uniquely identify a record. Such keys are referred to as *secondary keys,* and retrieval using these keys is called *secondary key retrieval.* Typical examples of secondary keys that appear in files, such as personnel files, are DEPARTMENT, SALARY, AGE, etc.

Secondary key retrieval may be typified in the following manner. The number of records in a file is usually large, and the number of records having a particular key value may be quite large. A secondary key retrieval request formulated as a Boolean query may retrieve only a small portion of the records actually examined. In fact, when Boolean queries are involved, the search time to answer the query may bear no relationship to the number of records satisfying the query. Therefore, a file on which secondary key retrievals are to be made should be organized to minimize the search effort in answering the query. The list-structured file organizations described in this chapter have been used successfully in several sytems that require secondary key retrieval.

While lists are general data structures capable of structuring data in various ways, they have some inherent disadvantages—namely, the space overhead for storing pointers and the time overhead incurred while performing read operations to traverse lengthy lists. The lists may run from track to track and cylinder to cylinder (on disks) and considerable access time may be consumed in traversing them. Fortunately, the effect of these problems is reduced by some of the list-structured file organizations described in this chapter.

5.2 SECONDARY KEY RETRIEVAL

Secondary key retrieval queries may be of the three types of queries: simple, range, or Boolean, described in Section 3.2. Normally, queries are formulated as Boolean expressions. It is well known that any Boolean expression can be expressed in disjunctive normal form,* that is, as a sum of products of terms. Thus, each Boolean query, Q, can be expressed in the form

$$Q = T_1 \vee T_2 \vee \cdots \vee T_n \, (\text{or } Q = \bigvee_{i=1}^{n} T_i)$$

Each T_i is a product (also called a conjunct) of terms of the form

$$T_i = T_{i_1} \wedge T_{i_2} \wedge \cdots \wedge T_{i_m} \, (\text{or } T_i = \bigwedge_{j=1}^{m} T_{ij})$$

where each T_{ij} is either a simple query or a range query, that is, each T_{ij} is a key, key value pair connected by one of the operators: $=, <, \leq, >,$ or $\geq$. Q can now be written as

$$Q = \bigvee_{i=1}^{n} (\bigwedge_{j=1}^{m} T_{ij})$$

Conceptually, a query Q is satisfied (answered) in the following manner. Let L_{ij} be the list of records (or list of record addresses) that satisfy T_{ij}, L_i the list of records that satisfy T_i, and L the list of records that satisfy Q. Then,

$$L_i = \bigcap_{j=1}^{m} L_{ij},$$

and

$$L = \bigcup_{i=1}^{n} L_i.$$

If these two expressions are combined, then L can be expressed as

$$L = \bigcup_{i=1}^{n} (\bigcap_{j=1}^{m} L_{ij}). \tag{5.1}$$

If L is a list of record addresses (instead of records), then the records that satisfy Q are the records whose addresses are in L. The final step then in answering the query Q is to retrieve the records whose addresses are in L and present them to the programmer who formulated the query.

---

*This can be done using DeMorgan's laws.

The above procedure for determining the records that satisfy a query is essentially the way that it is done for the inverted file organization described in Section 5.7. The remainder of this section gives some examples of queries and suggests that through the use of indexes and proper file organization, it is possible to efficiently determine the list of records L_{ij} that satisfy a term T_{ij}.

A student using an on-line library retrieval system might formulate the Boolean query

$$\text{SUBJECT} = \text{'PROGRAMMING'} \wedge \text{AUTHOR} = \text{'WIRTH'} \quad \text{(Q5.1)}$$

The student, in formulating this query, wants the shelf numbers for all books about programming written by Wirth. SUBJECT and AUTHOR are keys and 'PROGRAMMING' and 'WIRTH' are key values. The negation symbol ($\neg$) should be used with caution in queries, especially in purely disjunctive queries. For example, AUTHOR $= \neg$'WIRTH' causes the shelf numbers for all books except a few to be returned.*

To satisfy query (Q5.1), the retrieval system must be able to determine the list of all books on programming, the list of all books written by Wirth, and then select the books common to both lists. The set of books that satisfy query Q5.1 is a small percentage of all books in the library. Files designed for secondary key retrieval should be carefully organized to minimize the time required to answer queries.

To reduce the search time required to determine the list of record(s) that contain a specified key value, an index for the key can be provided. There may be an entry in an index for each corresponding key value in a file. Each index entry contains a key value and a pointer to the list of records having that key value (see Figure 5.1). When an index exists for a key, a file is said to be *indexed* on that key. A file indexed on every key value that a key has is said to be *fully indexed* on that key, and the index in this case is referred to as a *dense index*. A file indexed on only some of the key values that a key has is said to be *partially indexed* on that key, and the index in this case is called a *sparse index*. A secondary key index is often dense, while a primary key index need not be dense if the records are laid out in the sequence of the primary key values. The indexed sequential file organization is an example of a primary key retrieval file organization that has a sparse index. The collection of indexes for a file is often referred to as a *directory* for the file.

A file may be searched on a key, using sequential searching, without an index existing for the key. Indexing is a search technique for reducing the effort required to answer a query. An interesting question then is on which keys should a file be indexed. A basic premise is that secondary key indexes should exist only for those keys that are frequently referenced in queries and require minimum search times. If there are several keys on which a large file is to be indexed and each key has many key values, the space occupied by a directory

---

*Retrieval systems may provide presearch statistics that give the user an indication of the number of records satisfying a query before presenting them to him. The user may then decide to reformulate the query to reduce the number or select only a few of the possible records.

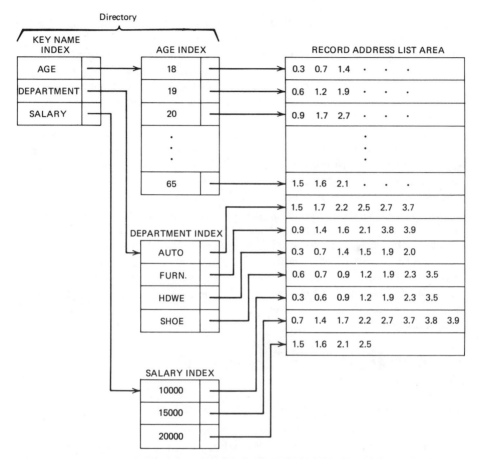

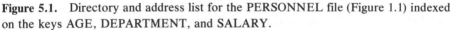

Figure 5.1. Directory and address list for the PERSONNEL file (Figure 1.1) indexed on the keys AGE, DEPARTMENT, and SALARY.

can become very large. In fact, a directory can occupy more space than the data records, and the directory itself may be organized as a file. The selection of keys for indexing is discussed more fully in Section 5.10.

An index can be organized as a sequential list if the number of distinct key values is small, or as one of the tree structures, for example, the B-tree described in Chapter 4, if the number of key values is relatively large. When an index is organized as a sequential list, it can be searched using the binary search method even if the index cannot be kept entirely in internal memory. A directory is normally organized as a multilevel structure to facilitate searching. A directory and record address list for the PERSONNEL file defined in Figure 1.1 is illustrated in Figure 5.1. In this example, the file is indexed on the AGE, DEPARTMENT, and SALARY keys. The directory in Figure 5.1 is organized as a two-level structure, and if the separate record address list area is considered part of the directory, as it sometimes is, then the directory is a three-level structure.

Each entry in the first level index in Figure 5.1 contains the name of a key on which the file is indexed and a pointer to the corresponding index. Since the number of keys on which a file is indexed is normally small, this index can be stored sequentially as an ordered list. Because a directory is frequently used, the first level (root level) should be kept in fast storage for efficient accessing. The only purpose of the key name index is to locate the index corresponding to the key of a (key, key value) pair specified in a query. Each entry in the second level indexes, for example, the DEPARTMENT index, contains a key value and a pointer to the list of records having the key value. A list of records can be represented as a list of record addresses as illustrated in Figure 5.1, or a list of records can be a linked list of records with the record addresses in the record address list in Figure 5.1 embedded in the records.

The requirement to maintain a directory for the purpose of achieving random access imposes an overhead in both space and time. A directory is usually sufficiently large to require storage in external memory. Thus, before data record accesses can be done, one or more index records may have to be accessed. In addition, updating usually requires that one or more index entries be updated. Regardless of the space and time overhead, the overall efficiency gained by using indexes in secondary key retrieval usually more than offsets the overhead.

5.3 GENERALIZED FILE ORGANIZATION

A generalized file organization is a multilevel structure consisting of a set of indexes and a data record area. Access is made to a data record in a generalized file via a series of intermediate accesses to indexes, each of which represents a different level in an access path, followed by one or more accesses to the data record area. Although more than one access to a data record area may be required to access a desired data record, the records in this area are all considered to be on the same level. In fact, they are considered to be the terminal elements in a file. The list-structured file organizations, especially the multilist, inverted, and cellular multilist, can be described very nicely in the context of the generalized file organization.

The process of answering queries and updating for generalized files can be described with the aid of two functions: DS (Directory Search) and FS (File Search). The DS function traverses a directory and the FS function is used to traverse a list of data records. The two functions, DS and FS, are introduced here for a specific purpose, namely to facilitate subsequent discussions on query processing and updating. Neither function is used explicitly by a programmer during query formulation or update specification; instead, they are considered system functions that are invoked during the processing of a query or an update operation. What this really means is that a process, called the query processor, takes a programmer-formulated query and translates it into a sequence of references to the functions, DS and FS, that, when executed, determine the records satisfying the query. In addition to the DS and FS functions, the query processor also has available other procedures, such as INTERSECT and UNION, for performing the intersection and union of lists, respectively. Sophisticated query processors may actually optimize a programmer's query in an attempt to reduce the search time to answer the query.

5.3.1 The DS Function

The DS function has two uses, both of which involve traversing a directory. First, for query processing, DS decodes a key value in the proper index and produces the address of the list of data records indexed by the key value. In this case the function DS is written symbolically as

$$y = DS(K, KV) \tag{5.2}$$

where K is a key and KV is a key value of key K, and y is the address of the list of records indexed by KV. If KV is not in the index associated with key K, then DS returns a coded status value indicating this, or if the file is not indexed on the key K, then DS returns another coded status value indicating that the query formulated by the programmer is invalid.

The second use of DS is in directory updating. In this case, it is used to create an index entry in an index. This may involve adding a new key value to the index and/or initializing or modifying the pointer to a list of records in an index entry. In this case, the function DS is written symbolically as

$$DS(K, KV) = y \tag{5.3}$$

When (5.2) is evaluated with respect to Figure 5.1, the value of DS (DEPARTMENT, 'FURN') is the address of the list of records in the record address list having 'FURN' as a key value. The value of DS(SALARY, 15000) with respect to Figure 5.5 is 0.7. The result of executing DS(DEPARTMENT, 'FURN') = 1.4 with respect to Figure 5.5 is that the pointer value in the 'FURN' index entry is modified to 1.4.

5.3.2 The FS Function

Like the DS function, the FS function has two uses. For query processing, FS is used in the following manner:

$$y = FS(K, KV, A) \tag{5.4}$$

where KV is a key value of key K in the data record whose address is A, and y is the address of the next record in the list indexed by KV. It may not be apparent at this point why K is needed as a parameter in the FS parameter list, but it will become apparent later (in Section 5.6).

A data record is said to be retrieved only if its address, A, has been used by FS for producing a pointer y. The value of y in expression (5.4) with respect to Figure 5.5 for FS(DEPARTMENT, 'FURN', 0.9) is 1.4 and for FS(DEPARTMENT, 'FURN', 1.4) it is 1.6. With respect to Figure 5.1,

FS(DEPARTMENT, 'AUTO', 1.7) has value 2.2 and FS(DEPARTMENT, 'AUTO', 2.2) has value 2.5. As suggested by the above examples, FS can be used to traverse and access a list of data records. When the value of FS is null (or zero), the end of a list has been reached.

FS can also be used during updating to insert a record into the list of records indexed by KV. In this case FS is written symbolically as

$$FS(K, KV, A) = y \qquad (5.5)$$

The logical interpretation of (5.5) is that the record whose address is y is inserted into the list of data records indexed by KV following the record with address A. The physical interpretation of (5.5) depends on the representation of the list of records indexed by KV.

5.4 UPDATING LIST-STRUCTURED FILES

All of the list-structured files have much in common with respect to updating; in the interests of not repeating redundant information for each file organization described in this chapter, all the relevant information is factored out and provided in this section. The description of each file organization still includes updating, but little of the material presented here is repeated. Updating files organized for secondary key retrieval is somewhat different and in some respects more complex than it is for files organized for primary key retrieval. There are two basic reasons for this:

1. A record may be a member of several lists.
2. Files appropriate for secondary key retrieval are frequently used in large on-line real-time retrieval systems with critical response time considerations.

While the comments in this section are directed primarily at the file organizations described in this chapter, some of them are also appropriate for the file organizations described in Chapters 3 and 4. Some update operations such as insertion require that external memory space be allocated, and other update operations such as deletion and some insertions cause memory space to become available for recovery (or reclamation). The allocation and recovery of storage space is referred to as *space maintenance*. Space maintenance is a side-effect of updating, and it is one of the topics discussed in Chapter 7.

A few comments on space maintenance with respect to when it is done, however, are appropriate here. These comments are directed at space recovery and not space allocation since there is no decision to make on when space should be allocated; it must be done immediately. The time at which space reclamation is performed depends on the environment, real-time or batched, in which files are being used. If updates are batched, then it may be appropriate to perform space reclamation while updating is in progress. However, if updating must be done in a real-time environment, then space recovery is almost sure to be deferred until a later time, such as at file reorganization time, or in background mode.

Exactly when and how updates are performed also depends on the environment. In some cases it may be feasible to batch updates, even in on-line systems, and in other cases the time lapse required to collect a batch of updates cannot be tolerated because updates must be done immediately. In real-time airline and hotel reservation systems, the updates must be done immediately to reflect the availability of seats on flights or rooms in hotels.

The time at which some updates, such as deletions, are performed depends on how much time is available for doing them. Deletion removes a record from consideration as a record for satisfying a subsequent query. One way to delete a record from a list is to mark it as being deleted and leave the record physically in the list. Logically, a deleted record is not a member of a list. If a list is a linked list, then a marked record is used during a traversal of the list for query processing.

Marking a record as being deleted requires less time than physically deleting a record from a file. Thus, marking is especially appropriate for updating (deleting) in on-line real-time systems. Physically deleting a record requires that pointers be modified to exclude the deleted record (in a linked list) or moving records to assume the space formerly occupied by the deleted record (in a sequential list). When a deletion operation physically removes a record from a list, the number of records remaining in the list is the same with respect to its logical and physical organization.

Regardless of how deletions are performed, the space occupied by deleted records must eventually be recovered. For volatile files, the overhead incurred by leaving deleted records in files can be costly in terms of both storage space and retrieval time. Performance can usually be improved by periodically performing space maintenance at file reorganization time.

The updates that can be made on files organized for secondary key retrieval include:

1. Whole record deletion.
2. Key value deletion (from an existing record).
3. Whole record addition (insertion).
4. Key value addition (to an existing record).
5. Alteration (or modification) of nonkey data items.

Whole record deletion causes a record to be removed from consideration as a record for satisfying a query. Key value deletion deletes a key value from an existing record. This is essentially equivalent to removing a record from the list indexed by a key value. Whole record addition causes a record to be inserted into all the lists indexed by the key values present in the record. Key value addition causes a key value to be added to an existing record. This update results in the record being inserted into the list indexed by the new key value. Record modification occurs when nonkey data item values are altered in an existing record. Record modification does not include key value alteration since key value alteration is essentially equivalent to key value deletion followed by key value addition.

The update operations that involve altering a record, such as adding a new key value, altering data items, etc., can cause the size of the record to increase or decrease. The record to be altered is brought from external memory into internal memory for the modifications to be made. After the updates are made, it is rewritten (restored) back to external memory. If the updated record has increased in length, then it may not be possible to place it at the same address that it resided in prior to updating. If the updated record must be relocated, then space is allocated for it and it is rewritten at the new address. When rewriting results in relocation, the system essentially performs a replacement operation. A replacement is semantically equivalent to a deletion of the original record, followed by an insertion of the updated record. One solution to the problem caused when a data record grows in size because of updating is to initially allocate 10-15 percent more space for each record than is actually needed at file load time. When an updated record decreases in length, it may be rewritten in its original position, or it may be handled exactly like records that increase in size. When an updated record does not change in size, then it can be rewritten to its original position.

5.5 RING-STRUCTURED FILES

A ring is a linear list in which the pointer in the last record points back to the first record called the starting record of the ring. In a ring structure one can start at an arbitrary record in the ring with every other record in the ring then becoming accessible. A specially designated starting record is necessary to prevent the possibility of an infinite loop resulting during processing, for example, when copying a file. A starting record can be designated by placing a special symbol in it. Each record in the ring structure in Figure 5.2a has a special data item for designating the starting record. The value of the data item is '$' for the starting record and 'b' (blank) otherwise. If the starting record in Figure 5.2a is deleted, then the next record becomes the designated starting record and the pointer in the last record must be updated to point to the new starting record.

Another way to designate a starting record of a ring is to define each ring with a record called the head record (or head of the ring). The head record does not contain data; it is used primarily to point to the first data record in the ring. Figure 5.2b illustrates a ring with a head record. The advantages of having a ring head is that a ring is never empty, and when the first data record of the ring is deleted, only the pointer in the ring head is updated to point to the new first data record. The pointer in the last record does not have to be updated because it already points to the ring head. Using a ring head to designate the starting point of a ring can simplify ring updating. In addition, since the data portion of the ring head record is not used to store data, it can be used for other purposes such as maintaining a count of the number of data records in the ring, holding a

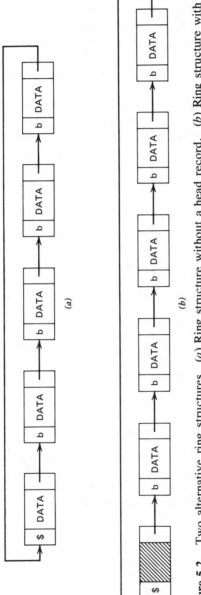

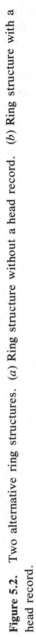

Figure 5.2. Two alternative ring structures. (a) Ring structure without a head record. (b) Ring structure with a head record.

pointer to the last record in the ring, or holding information about the ring such as the data item on which the ring is sorted.

As was mentioned earlier, one of the primary advantages of a ring structure is that any record can be accessed starting at any point. In some instances when a ring is entered, it may be desirable to obtain the information in the ring head quickly without traversing the records that lie between the point of entry and the head. Direct access to the head of the ring can be provided by means of an additional pointer in each record that points directly to the head. If this organization is necessary, then it is important to have an explicit ring head record as illustrated in Figure 5.3; otherwise, the overhead for updating all of the pointers to the starting record (as in Figure 5.2a) can be enormous when the starting record is deleted.

A ring structure that is more powerful than the simple ring structure described above can be utilized. This type of ring structure, called a multiple ring structure, permits multiple rings to pass through a record with the records in each ring logically related. The structure in Figure 5.4 is an example of such a ring structure. This type of ring is versatile since it provides the capability to retrieve and process all the records in any one ring while branching off at any of the records to retrieve and process other records that are logically related. The structure in Figure 5.4 has two major rings, and it can be entered using either of the keys DEPARTMENT or SALARY. Although a ring structure is not particularly well-suited for real-time secondary key retrieval, it can be used in batched environments. Its primary disadvantage is that the number of operations required to locate a record may be larger than is acceptable. The ring in Figure 5.4 can be used to answer queries like

DEPARTMENT = 'SHOE',
SALARY = 15000, or
DEPARTMENT = 'SHOE' ∧ SALARY = 20000.

Since ring structures like the one illustrated in Figure 5.4 typically have more than one ring passing through a record, a tag field is usually associated with each pointer to specify in which rings a record is an element.

An important use of ring structures is to represent classifications of data. All records having the same classification belong to the same ring. Associated with

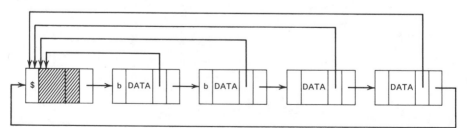

Figure 5.3.   Ring structure with a head record and a special pointer in each record pointing to the head.

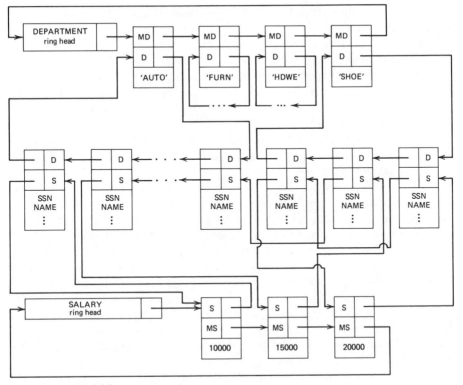

Figure 5.4. Multiring structure.*

each record within a class may be a subclass, and this subclass is represented by a ring of records. A classification scheme may be hierarchic; if so, the ring structure representing the classification scheme is referred to as a hierarchical ring structure. Searching a hierarchical ring-structured file can be performed by starting with the highest level ring. The ring structure in Figure 5.4 is not considered purely hierarchical even though it has some of the characteristics of a hierarchical ring.

One of the disadvantages of ring files is that they can take a long time to search. If there are *n* records in a file and every record has an equal probability of being accessed, then the average number of records accessed to find a desired record is $O(n)$.

5.5.1 Updating Ring-Structured Files

The complexity of updating ring structures varies with the representation selected for a ring; as always, the proper choice of representation depends on

---

*The tag values MD, MS, D, and S are used to designate the major department, major salary, department subring, and salary subring, respectively.

the type of insertions, deletions, and traversals that are needed in a given problem environment.

Inserting a new record into the middle of a ring is usually relatively simple. Insertion, however, can be complex in the following case: a ring does not have a head record and the inserted record replaces the first data record in the ring and each record in the ring has an explicit pointer to the starting record. In this case, the entire ring must be traversed to update all of the pointers to the starting record.

When a record is deleted from a ring, neither its predecessor record nor the head (or starting record) of the ring has to be specified since the predecessor record can be found from any point in the ring by traversing the structure (the assumption here is that the ring is represented as a singly linked list). Deletion performed by traversing a structure and searching for the predecessor record requires that the address of the record to be deleted be saved and compared with the address of the succeeding records accessed. In this case, the entire ring must be traversed for each deletion. If the address of the head or starting record is known, or even better, if the address of the predecessor record is known, then the delete operation can be performed with little (or no) traversing to locate the predecessor record. However, in some instances, for example, when the ring is part of a multiple ring structure, the programmer may not have this information available when the delete operation is issued. The deletion operation is simplified considerably when a ring is represented as a doubly linked list since traversing is not required to locate the predecessor record. For rings without heads and with each record in the ring having a pointer to the starting record, deletion of the starting record causes each pointer to it to be updated. Altering the value of data item(s) in a record poses no particular problems.

5.6   THE MULTILIST FILE ORGANIZATION

The multilist file organization consists of a directory containing one or more indexes and a data record area. An index entry for a key value consists of three pieces of data:

1. The key value.
2. A pointer to the list of records containing the key value.
3. The number of records in the list, that is, the list length.

Rather than storing the pointers to data records separately as is illustrated in Figure 5.1, the multilist organization stores the pointers within the data records. Thus, the multilist organization is obtained by merging record address lists, like those illustrated in Figure 5.1, with data records in a data record area. For long lists, the amount of time required to determine the addresses of records (and hence the records) that satisfy a query can be considerable because the data records themselves must be accessed rather than a compact list of record addresses like those illustrated in Figure 5.1.

Figure 5.5 illustrates a multilist file indexed on the DEPARTMENT and SALARY keys. The data record area of this file is divided into four distinct areas called cells. The cells are numbered 0, 1, 2, and 3, and the address of each data record is written in the qualified notation, cell.record-number. For example, the record with address 1.5 is record number 5 in cell 1. A cell can be a track, cylinder, volume or any other zone delimited by a natural hardware boundary. The concept of cell is important because it can be used to decrease the response time for queries, especially conjunctive queries, against multilist files. The cellular multilist file organization discussed in Section 5.8 is designed to take advantage of the cell concept for reducing the response time.

Each data record in a multilist file can be viewed, logically, as consisting of two parts. One part consists of one or more key/key value/pointer triples; the pointer points to another record containing the same key/key value pair. The other part of a record contains the values of the nonkey data items, if any. The format of a multilist data record can be expressed more precisely. Let a multilist file be indexed on n distinct keys, K_i, $1 \leq i \leq n$, with each key K_i having m_i distinct key values, KV_{ij}, $1 \leq j \leq m_i$. Each pair K_i/KV_{ij} is distinct. Each data record in a multilist file is composed of one or more triples of the form $K_i/KV_{ij}/P$ and zero or more nonkey data item values. P is a pointer to another data record containing a K_i/KV_{ij} pair. A data record has a triple for each list of which the record is a member, that is, if a record is a member of 5 lists, then it contains 5 triples. Record 0.6 in Figure 5.5 has the format

DEPARTMENT/SHOE/0.7	SALARY/10000/0.9	Nonkey data item values

while record 1.5 in Figure 5.5 has the format

DEPARTMENT/ AUTO/1.7	DEPARTMENT/ HDWE/1.9	SALARY/ 20000/1.6	Nonkey data item values

The two record examples given above illustrate an important characteristic of multilist files (and, in general, of other secondary key retrieval file organizations): the records may be variable in length. The reasons for this are clear. The number of key/key value/pointer triples per record can vary, and the lengths of the key names (and possibly the lengths of the key values) can vary. The pointer element in each triple is normally fixed in length. In order to handle variable length records, it is customary to place a header on each data record. The header is essentially a table of contents that describes a record. For example, for multilist files, a data record header may contain: (1) the number of key/key value/pointer triples, (2) a fixed-length element for each triple containing the amount of space occupied by the triple, the length of the key name in the triple, and possibly the length of the key value in the triple, and (3) a fixed-length element for each nonkey data item specifying the length of its value. If the key names and key values are fixed in length, then the header may contain only the number of triples and their lengths. The contents and format of

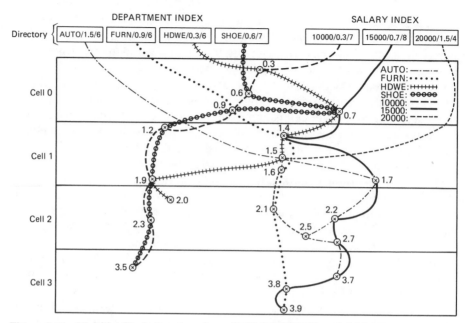

Figure 5.5. Multilist file indexed on keys DEPARTMENT and SALARY.*

a header may vary depending on the file designer's requirements and preferences.

When the header contains the information suggested above, it has the format illustrated in Figure 5.6. If each key value occupies four bytes of storage and each pointer occupies six bytes of storage then record 0.6 in Figure 5.5 has the form

2	20/10/4	16/6/4	DEPARTMENT/ SHOE/0.7	SALARY/ 10000/0.9	Nonkey data item values

It may be desirable to code each key name in a data record instead of placing the entire key name in a triple. This can result in considerable savings in storage space since a code is short and has the additional advantage that it is fixed in length. If a code is used in place of an actual key name, it may be desirable to place it in a data record header rather than a triple.

In some systems, key names are omitted or implied, and only key values are stored in data records. However, in this book key names are assumed to be included in data records. It should be noted that a system that stores only key values and not key/key value pairs will operate less efficiently since some longer list searches may result. In addition, the key values KV_{ij} are not necessarily distinct for distinct keys. That is, two keys K_1 and K_2 may have key

*The records in these multilists happen to be ordered on their address; however, in general, the multilists are unordered.

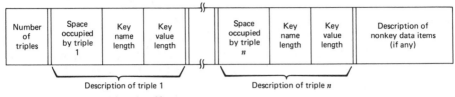

Description of triple 1   Description of triple *n*

Figure 5.6.   Record header format.

values that are identical. Some of these problems can be avoided by fixing the format of data records so that key names are implied by the position of their corresponding key values. This can be done easily if each key has only one key value per record (record 1.5 illustrated above does not fit this format). A system that stores only key values and does not require key names in queries has an added degree of flexibility because the programmer may want to see all records with a given key value regardless of its key name. In this case the key value would have to be decoded in every index and all lists indexed by that value traversed.

5.6.1 Answering Queries

The techniques developed for answering queries try to minimize the number of records that must actually be accessed and examined. This is especially important for the multilist organization since lengthy lists must sometimes be traversed to access records. Some examples are given below to illustrate query processing for multilist files. These examples are based on the multilist file illustrated in Figure 5.5.

A query to retrieve the records of all employees that work in an 'AUTO' department and have a salary of 15,000 dollars is formulated as

$$\text{DEPARTMENT} = \text{'AUTO'} \wedge \text{SALARY} = 15000 \qquad (Q5.2)$$

Query Q5.2 is an example of a conjunctive query, that is, a product of terms. In order to answer this query, the query processor decodes the two key values in the proper indexes by evaluating DS(DEPARTMENT, 'AUTO') and DS(SALARY, 15000). The index entries for 'AUTO' and 15000 are examined to determine their associated list lengths. Since Q5.2 is a conjunctive query, only the records common to both lists satisfy the query. Thus, it makes sense to examine only the records in the shortest list since this results in fewer accesses to external memory. Since the 'AUTO' list is the shortest (6 records versus 8 records), the records in it are moved into internal memory by the repeated use of the FS function, and each is examined for the occurrence of the key value 15000. The records with addresses 1.7, 2.2, 2.7, and 3.7 in Figure 5.5 contain both of the key values, 'AUTO' and 15000; thus, they are the records that satisfy query Q5.2.

The process of examining the accessed records for the occurrence of the other key value is essentially the function performed by the INTERSECT procedure for a conjunctive query against a multilist file. The algorithm for answering conjunctive queries against multilist files with more than two terms in the product is a direct extension of the above procedure.

A point that is worth repeating is that the algorithm for determining which records satisfy Q5.2 deviates from the general procedure implied by formula (5.1) in Section 5.2. This deviation is caused by a desire to keep the query processing time (or response time) as low as possible. The specific algorithm for processing queries depends on the file organization used.

When a disjunctive query such as Q5.3

$$\text{DEPARTMENT} = \text{`AUTO'} \ \lor \ \text{SALARY} = 15000 \qquad \text{(Q5.3)}$$

is formulated, all records that have one or both of the specified key values satisfy the query. The most straightforward way to determine which records satisfy this query is to follow the procedure implied by formula (5.1), that is, to access all records in the 'AUTO' list, access all records in the 15000 list, and then merge the two lists using the UNION procedure. When this method is used, 14 records (6 in the 'AUTO' list and 8 in the 15000 list) are accessed and examined. There are 10 distinct records that satisfy Q5.3, and four records are retrieved twice.

5.6.1.1 Avoiding Redundant Record Accessing

When the lists corresponding to the key values in a disjunctive query have no records in common, the simple technique described above accesses the minimum number of records, but when the lists have records in common, redundant record accessing occurs. An algorithm with a relatively low CPU time requirement exists for avoiding redundant record accessing. This algorithm is described below.

The algorithm for avoiding redundant record accessing when answering disjunctive queries is described first in general terms and then applied to query Q5.3. The multilists that must be traced to answer a disjunctive query are assumed to be indexed by the key values $KV_1, KV_2, \ldots, KV_n$. The algorithm begins by accessing all records in the KV_1 list. After a record, identified as y, is brought into internal memory, it is examined to determine if this record contains any of the other key values $KV_2, \ldots, KV_n$. For each KV_i, $i \geq 2$, contained in record y, an entry (key name, KV_i, y, w) is stored in an internal table, referred to as TABLE. This entry indicates that record y in the KV_i list has already been examined and record w is the immediate successor of record y in the KV_i list. After all records in the KV_1 list are accessed, the records in the KV_2 list are accessed; then, the records in the KV_3 list are accessed, etc. Before any record, identified by address x, in the KV_2 list is accessed, TABLE is searched for entry (key name, KV_2, x, w) for any w. Actually, at the most only one such entry in TABLE eixsts since (key name, KV_2, x, w) indicates that record w is the immediate (and unique) successor of record x in the KV_2 list. Thus, during the search only the key name, KV_2, and x need be compared. If

KEYNAME	KEYVALUE	y	w
SALARY	15000	1.7	2.2
SALARY	15000	2.2	2.7
SALARY	15000	2.7	3.7
SALARY	15000	3.7	3.8

Figure 5.7. The contents of TABLE after the 'AUTO' list in query Q5.3 is traversed.

such an entry is found in TABLE, record x does not have to be accessed again and record w becomes the next record to be considered for retrieval. The savings in record access time using this algorithm can be significant when the lists indexed by the key values in a disjunctive query have several records in common.

When the above algorithm for avoiding redundant record accessing is applied to the disjunctive query Q5.3, only ten records are accessed. The list indexed by 'AUTO' is accessed first. The contents of TABLE, after accessing the 'AUTO' list, is illustrated in Figure 5.7.

The internal table, TABLE, can be maintained in various ways. For instance, TABLE can be described as a two-dimensional array in which each element, TABLE(i, j), stores a 2-tuple (y, w) instead of a 4-tuple (key name, KV_i, y, w). Each key name/KV_i pair is unique and row i in TABLE holds the 2-tuples (y, w) that have been placed there during traversal of the KV_1, . . . , KV_{i-1} lists. The entries in each row i can be sorted on y to facilitate fast look-up when the list corresponding to KV_i is being accessed. After KV_i is accessed, the row corresponding to KV_{i+1} is sorted and then the list accessed. Row i can be discarded after the KV_i list has been accessed.

The sorting process in the algorithm is conducted at most once for each of the $n-1$ rows in TABLE. If N_i is the number of records containing KV_i and an $O(N_i \log N_i)$ sorting algorithm, for example, the quicksort algorithm is used, then the algorithm's time complexity is $O(\sum_i N_i \log N_i)$. This is a relatively low time requirement compared to that for accessing records in external memory so the algorithm is worthwhile to run. The space requirement for TABLE is $O(\sum_{i=2}^{n} N_i)$.

5.6.1.2 Traversing Multilists in Parallel

Another algorithm for processing disjunctive queries against multilist files can also be formulated. While the two algorithms described earlier for processing disjunctive queries traverse one list at a time, the algorithm described below traverses all lists in parallel. The algorithm can be described in the following manner. Let a disjunctive query be of the form

$$T_1 \lor T_2 \lor \ldots \lor T_n \qquad (Q5.4)$$

where each term T_i is of the form "key = key value." The key value in each T_i is denoted by KV_i. Each KV_i is decoded in the proper directory using the DS function, and the address of the head of the list of data records indexed by KV_i is designated by a_i, that is,

$$a_i = \text{DS(Key, } KV_i)$$

Let σ_0 be the set of head of list addresses, that is,

$$\sigma_0 = \{a_1, a_2, \ldots, a_n\}$$

where $a_1 < a_2 < \ldots < a_n$ and the a_i are distinct. Next, select the smallest address x ($x = \min\{a_1, a_2, \ldots, a_n\}$) in σ_0 and flag it as having been used in an evaluation of the function FS. Retrieve record x. Since record x contains one of the KV_i, it satisfies Q5.4. Record x also contains pointer y to another record in the list indexed by KV_i. The newly obtained address y is merged into σ_0, creating a new set σ_1. Record x is also checked for other key/key value pairs occurring in the query and their corresponding pointers merged into σ_1. This algorithm continues with new sets of addresses $\sigma_j, j \geq 2$ being created in the same manner that σ_1 was created, and it terminates when all addresses in some $\sigma_j, j \geq 0$ have been flagged as retrieved.

For a movable head disk, this algorithm performs extremely well when:

1. The disk is a dedicated device.
2. Multilists are ordered on record addresses.

In this case, an access mechanism makes a single pass over a disk in one direction accessing all lists in parallel, thereby keeping the seek time for retrieving all records satisfying a query to a minimum. But if the lists are unordered, it may not be possible to access all records in a single unidirectional pass over a disk; thus, the seek time to access all records may be larger than actually necessary.

Other more efficient algorithms for tracing unordered (and ordered) multilists in parallel have been developed (see the reference list at the end of this chapter). These algorithms attempt to minimize the total amount of seek time involved in accessing the records that satisfy a query. If the disk on which the records reside is a shared device, as it typically is, then any effort to minimize the seek time for record accessing could be nullified by interfering processes that compete for the same device. However, since the degree of sharing is difficult to predict, during the period of time in which a particular process is not competing with others for a disk, the seek action involved in record accessing can be reduced. The same thing cannot be said in every case for the algorithm presented earlier in this section unless the lists are ordered on record addresses.

Ordered multilists require more time to update and are therefore impractical for most situations in which real-time updating must be performed.

5.6.1.3   *Query Costs*

The cost to process a query for the multilist organization is the cost to decode all key values in the query plus the cost to retrieve data records. The cost is measured in terms of the time required to decode key values, retrieve records, etc. These costs can be minimized by properly organizing a directory and by avoiding redundant record accessing. The multilist organization provides a seemingly satisfactory solution for simple and range queries and for Boolean queries of the strictly disjunctive type like Q5.3 and Q5.4 (provided redundant accessing of records is avoided). But when Boolean queries of the conjunctive type such as Q5.2 are involved, the search time may bear no relation to the number of records satisfying the query. The cost of query processing for conjunctive queries is analyzed below in an informal manner for the multilist organization and is then related to the query cost for the inverted organization. A more formal discussion on the relationship of the query cost for conjunctive queries for the two organizations is presented in Section 5.7.2.1.

5.6.1.3.1   **Query Cost for Conjunctive Queries**   When the list lengths associated with key values in the terms in a product are small, the cost for query processing is less for the multilist organization than for the inverted organization. The reason for this is outlined below, with references back to Section 5.2 and formula (5.1). Assume lists L_{i_j}, $1 \leqslant j \leqslant m$, each having length denoted by length(L_{i_j}) correspond to the terms in a product T_i. If these lengths are small, then the difference between length(L_{i_j}) and length(L_i) will be relatively small. The number of records y ($= \min(\text{length}(L_{i_1})$, length($L_{i_2}$), $\ldots$, length(L_{i_m}))) actually accessed is only slightly larger than the number of records, length(L_i), that satisfy the product T_i. As will be described in Section 5.7.2.1, the query cost for the inverted organization includes a cost for accessing the inverted lists (see Figure 5.1) indexed by the key values in each term T_{i_j}. Thus, if y is only slightly larger than length(L_i), the cost to access the inverted lists is larger than the cost to access the $(y - \text{length}(L_i))$ records that do not satisfy the query. If this difference in cost is designated by C ($C \geqslant 0$), then the query cost for the multilist organization, designated by Q_{CM}, can be related to the query cost for the inverted organization, denoted by Q_{CI}, by the formula

$$Q_{CM} = Q_{CI} - C \qquad (5.6)$$

On the other hand, when the length(L_{i_j}) is large, the difference, $(y - \text{length}(L_i))$, is in practice usually large and

$$Q_{CI} = Q_{CM} - C \qquad (5.7)$$

Formula (5.7) is interpreted to mean that for long lists, the cost for query processing for an inverted organization is less than for the multilist organization. The analysis of query costs is the basis for the development of the hybrid list organizations described in Section 5.9.

5.6.2 Updating Multilist Files

Lists can be ordered or unordered. Adding a record to an ordered list requires that it be inserted in a specific position. On the other hand, adding a record to an unordered list allows it to be inserted at the head of the list, thus avoiding the need to traverse the list. Unordered lists may be periodically reorganized, and the pointer linkages between newly added records can be reconnected to lessen the access time to retrieve records. No such reorganization is possible on an ordered list.

5.6.2.1 Whole Record Addition

A whole record may be added to a multilist file or a new key value may be added to an existing record. Regardless of the type of addition, one or more of the indexes are also updated. The assumption made here is that indexes are organized as one of the tree structures, for example, the B-tree, described in Chapter 4. Hence, updating an index is considered essentially the same as updating a tree structure. Whole record addition is handled relatively easily in multilist files. When the lists are not ordered, a new record can be placed at the logical head of each list of which it is to be a member. If there are n key values, $KV_1, KV_2, \ldots, KV_n$, in a new record, then whole record addition is performed in the following manner (the record to be inserted has already been assigned storage at address x).

Algorithm ADD_MRECORD

1. [Initialize] $i \leftarrow 1$.
2. [Decode KV_i in the proper index] $a_i \leftarrow$ DS(Key, KV_i). If a_i is a valid pointer (possibly even null), then go to Step 3; otherwise, DS(Key, KV_i) $\leftarrow x$ and go to Step 5.
3. [Insert record x at the head of the list indexed by KV_i] DS(Key, KV_i) $\leftarrow x$; FS(Key, KV_i, x) $\leftarrow a_i$.
4. [Update the list length] length(KV_i) $\leftarrow$ length(KV_i) + 1.
5. [Test] $i \leftarrow i+1$; if $i \leq n$, then go to Step 2; otherwise, Exit.

Step 2 of Algorithm ADD_MRECORD should be discussed. In Section 5.3 it was explained that the value of DS(K, KV) for a KV not in the index of key K is a coded value that is not a valid pointer. Thus, if the value of a_i in Step 2 is this coded value, then DS(Key, KV_i) $\leftarrow x$ is executed. This creates an index entry for KV_i and assigns x as the value of the pointer (to list head) element in the index entry.

5.6.2.2 Key Value Addition

Key values may be added to an existing record; this can happen when an employee who works in the 'AUTO' department begins splitting his work time between the 'AUTO' and 'SHOE' departments. The employee's record must be updated by adding the key value 'SHOE' to his record. Adding a new key value to a record implies that the record must be added to the list of records indexed by the new key value. Algorithm ADD_MRECORD can essentially be used to add one or more key values to a record. Steps 2, 3, and 4 of the algorithm are repeated for each key value added to a record.

5.6.2.3 Key Value and Whole Record Deletion

Deleting a key value, KV, from a record with address x is essentially equivalent to deleting the record from the list indexed by KV. Key value deletion can be done using Algorithm DELETE_MKEY.

Algorithm DELETE_MKEY

1. [Decode KV in the proper index] $a \leftarrow DS(Key, KV)$.
2. [Delete record x] Delete record x from the list whose head has address a.
3. [Update list length] length$(KV) \leftarrow$ length$(KV) - 1$.

The delete operation in Step 2 of Algorithm DELETE_MKEY can be a physical or logical deletion. Physical deletion is accomplished by traversing the list indexed by KV and physically removing record x from the list by adjusting pointers. If this is the form of the delete, then whole record deletion can be performed by using Algorithm DELETE_MKEY repeatedly, once for each key value in the deleted record. When deletion implies physically removing a record from list(s) and the retrieval system performs real-time updating and retrieval, then bi-directional lists should be considered for representing the multilists. With bi-directional lists, a record can be deleted without traversing the list to locate its predecessor record. Record deletion can be performed more rapidly with bi-directional lists, but there is the storage overhead of an additional pointer element for each key value in a record.

It may not be feasible to physically delete records by adjusting pointers, especially for retrieval systems operating in real-time environments that require low response times for both updating and query processing. An alternative method mentioned in Section 5.4 is to logically delete records by marking. Marking can be done very quickly, and it is particularly appropriate for real-time environments. One question that arises when marking is used is whether the list length should be decreased when a record is deleted from a list. That is, should a list length reflect the logical list length or the physical list length? This question is particularly important for multilist files since marked records must be accessed during query processing even though they can never

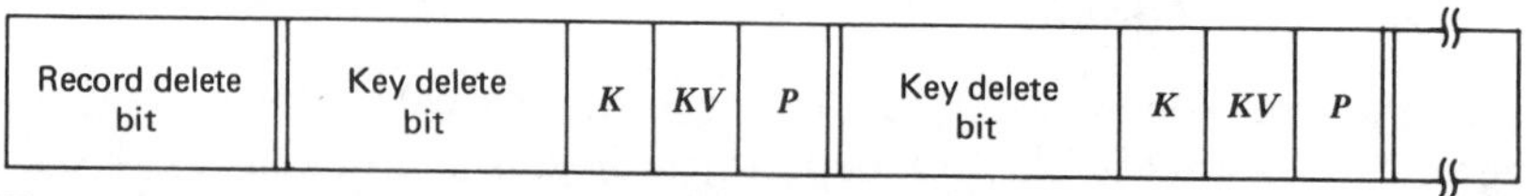

Figure 5.8. Format of multilist data records when marking is used to delete records and key values.

be members of the list of record(s) that satisfy a query. For this reason, maintaining a physical rather than a logical list length is probably more appropriate for multilists. Thus, when key values and/or whole records are deleted by marking and a list length entry in an index reflects the physical list length, Step 3 in Algorithm DELETE_MKEY is omitted.

When a file has many records that are marked, performance, with respect to query processing, may be degraded considerably. Periodic file reorganization is necessary to physically remove marked records. When marking is used in multilist files, each data record has the format illustrated in Figure 5.8. A record is logically deleted from all lists of which it is a member by setting the record delete bit, and a key value is deleted by setting the appropriate key delete bit.

The cost of an update from the multilist organization depends on:

1. The cost to decode and/or modify one or more index entries.
2. The cost to update the affected record(s).

5.7 THE INVERTED FILE ORGANIZATION

With multilist files, records containing the same key value are linked together with pointers kept in the individual records. In the case of inverted files, the pointers are removed from the individual records and kept in a separate list, called an inverted list. The process of removing the pointers from the records and placing them in a separate list is referred to as inverting the list. The variable length inverted lists of pointers corresponding to key values can be kept in the index itself as illustrated in Figure 5.9, or they can be kept in a separate record address list area as illustrated in Figure 5.10. Hence, an inverted file can consist of two components (a directory and a data record area) or three components (a directory, a record address list area, and a data record area). Each component of an inverted file may be organized as an individual file.

5.7.1 Inverted File Directories

When the organization in Figure 5.9 is used for an inverted file, the index entries are variable in length and index maintenance becomes more complex than for the organization in Figure 5.10 with its fixed-length index entries. However, there is an advantage to the organization in Figure 5.9. When a key value is decoded in an index, the record address list is immediately available and no additional access is required to move it into internal memory. The organization in Figure 5.10 requires an additional access to retrieve a record

DEPARTMENT INDEX

AUTO	1.5	1.7	2.2	2.5	2.7	3.7	
FURN	0.9	1.4	1.6	2.1	3.8	3.9	
HDWE	0.3	0.7	1.4	1.5	1.9	2.0	
SHOE	0.6	0.7	0.9	1.2	1.9	2.3	3.5

SALARY INDEX

10000	0.3	0.6	0.9	1.2	1.9	2.3	3.5	
15000	0.7	1.4	1.7	2.2	2.7	3.7	3.8	3.9
20000	1.5	1.6	2.1	2.5				

Figure 5.9.   Inverted lists for the data records in Figure 5.5. with the lists maintained in the index itself.

address list after a key value is decoded in an index. On the other hand, the index entries in Figure 5.10 are small and fixed in size; thus, more index entries can be packed per node than in Figure 5.9. This will usually allow the decoding process to be done more quickly since the index will usually have fewer levels in it (if we assume it is organized as a tree) and fewer accesses will have to be made to external memory. Since a directory is frequently used, it is important to keep it as small as possible so that: (1) updating can be performed quickly and easily, and (2) it can possibly be kept, in its entirety, on a fast storage device such as drum or large core storage. For the remainder of this book the organization in Figure 5.10 is assumed for inverted files.

DEPARTMENT INDEX   RECORD ADDRESS LIST AREA

AUTO	→	1.5	1.7	2.2	2.5	2.7	3.7	
FURN	→	0.9	1.4	1.6	2.1	3.8	3.9	
HDWE	→	0.3	0.7	1.4	1.5	1.9	2.0	
SHOE	→	0.6	0.7	0.9	1.2	1.9	2.3	3.5

SALARY INDEX

10000	→	0.3	0.6	0.9	1.2	1.9	2.3	3.5	
15000	→	0.7	1.4	1.7	2.2	2.7	3.7	3.8	3.9
20000	→	1.5	1.6	2.1	2.5				

Figure 5.10.   Inverted lists for the data records in Figure 5.5 with the lists in a separate area.

If inverted lists are kept in the directory (Figure 5.9), then an inverted file will have a much larger directory than the corresponding multilist file. But the total memory space required for the inverted file is no greater than that for the multilist file because the pointers are not kept in the data records. When the inverted lists are not kept in the directory (Figure 5.10), the directory for an inverted file is essentially the same with respect to organization and size as for a corresponding multilist file. The total memory space for the two file organizations is essentially the same, given the same set of data records. An inverted file may require less storage space than the corresponding multilist file if key, key value pairs are not kept in the data records themselves. Not including these pairs is feasible if a file is printed infrequently. Printing an inverted file with the key values removed from the data records requires that each record have its key values restored prior to output. In practice, it is common for key values to be kept in records.

The size of a directory and a record address list area can be controlled by limiting the number of data items on which a file is inverted. A partially inverted file stores the record addresses associated with all values of certain but not all data items. A completely inverted file is one in which every data item is treated as a key and the record addresses associated with every key value are stored in inverted lists. In some cases it may be best to combine an inverted organization (or a multilist organization) with a sequential or direct organization. In this way records are inverted on only one or two keys rather than all keys. Directories become smaller and it is still possible to access all records in a file.

5.7.2   Answering Queries

The inverted file organization permits rapid access to records based on any key. However, updating an inverted file is difficult because the inverted lists must be updated. For this reason, the inverted organization is most useful for retrieval when the update volume is relatively low compared to the query volume, or when updates can be batched. The inverted organization is appropriate for many applications; among these are document retrieval systems in which descriptor files are organized as inverted files. In addition, several data management systems have been designed around the inverted organization. Most inverted file systems in commercial use are of the partially inverted type.

Since the pointers to records indexed by a key value are maintained in an inverted list rather than in the data records, the records that satisfy a conjunctive query like

$$\text{DEPARTMENT} = \text{'AUTO'} \land \text{SALARY} = 15000 \qquad (Q5.5)$$

can be determined by accessing and manipulating the inverted (and ordered) lists of record addresses prior to accessing any data records. With this advantage comes a slight disadvantage: the inverted organization requires a working area in internal memory to perform the logic processing, that is, list intersection and list merging (union). Query Q5.5 is answered with respect to Figure 5.10 in the following manner. The key values 'AUTO' and 15000 are decoded by executing

$$a_1 \leftarrow DS(DEPARTMENT, \text{ 'AUTO'})$$

$$a_2 \leftarrow DS(SALARY, 15000)$$

where a_1 and a_2 are pointers to the inverted lists for key values 'AUTO' and 15000, respectively. The two inverted lists pointed to by a_1 and a_2 are moved into internal memory. The intersection of the two lists is performed by procedure INTERSECT. The addresses in the intersection list, that is, addresses 1.7, 2.2, 2.7, and 3.7, are the addresses of the records that satisfy query Q5.5. These four records are retrieved and presented to the programmer.

In order to speed up the intersection of inverted lists, each index entry can be augmented with a count giving the length of the related inverted list. This count can be used to select the shortest lists to intersect first. List intersection on three or more ordered lists can be performed more quickly when the intersection process begins with the shortest lists. The intersection of two lists almost always produces a list shorter than either of the two involved in the intersection. Since inverted lists are ordered, the INTERSECT procedure will probably not need to compare all the addresses in each pair of lists. For example, when the lists associated with key values 'HDWE' and 'SHOE' are intersected, there is no need to compare record address 2.0 in the 'HDWE' list with an address after 2.3 in the 'SHOE' list since they all follow address 2.3 in order and none of them can match 2.0.

When query Q5.6 is processed,

$$\text{SALARY} = 15000 \land \text{DEPARTMENT} = \text{ 'AUTO'} \land \text{DEPARTMENT} = \\ \text{ 'HDWE'} \qquad \qquad (Q5.6)$$

the two inverted lists corresponding to 'AUTO' and 'HDWE' are intersected first since they are the shortest of the three lists. Address 1.5 is the only address in the intersection list. When this list is intersected with the 15000 list, there are no records in the resulting intersection list. Thus, there are no records satisfying Q5.6. The important thing to note here is that the intersection of the list containing address 1.5 and the 15000 list terminates after 1.5 is compared with 1.7. Selecting the shortest lists first for intersection *does not always* result in the fewest number of comparisons. But since it is impossible to determine the order in which intersections should be done to produce the fewest number of comparisons without actually first performing the intersections, the selection of the shortest lists first, in general, results in fewer comparisons. Regardless of how list intersection is performed, the list of records that satisfy a query is the same.

The inverted file organization facilitates the answering of conjunctive queries like Q5.5 and Q5.6 since only the data records that actually satisfy a query are retrieved. This usually results in much lower response times for conjunctive queries than is possible with multilist files, especially when the multilists are lengthy. The inverted organization loses most of its advantage over the multilist organization for disjunctive queries, especially when redundant record accessing is avoided for the multilist organization. Inverted files are practical for use in real-time retrieval systems requiring low response times for query processing; however, the lower response times (lower than for multilist files) are attained at the expense of storage space (for the logical processing of inverted lists) and update time.

5.7.2.1 Query Costs

The cost to process a query against an inverted file is the sum of:

1. The cost to decode all key values in the query.
2. The cost to access all inverted lists, one per key value.
3. The cost to logically process the inverted lists.
4. The cost to retrieve the data records that satisfy the query.

In Section 5.6.1.3 an informal argument was given for showing that the query costs for conjunctive queries with short lists are less for the multilist organization than for the inverted organization, and that the query costs for conjunctive

Table 5.1

Timing Parameters

Symbol	Definition
L	Average list length
N_T	Average number of terms in a single query product
N_P	Average number of nonnegated terms in a single query product
T_N	Time to decode a key value in an n-level index
L_S	Shortest list length in a query (average)
ρ	Ratio of the number of records that satisfy a query to L_S (average)
N_A	Number of data record addresses per physical record
T_A	Average time to access a record and move it to internal memory

queries with long lists are less for the inverted organization than for the multilist organization. Now that query processing for the inverted organization has been discussed, it seems appropriate to derive, in a somewhat formal manner, the relationship between query costs for the two file organizations. The query costs are measured in terms of the retrieval times. The logical processing of inverted lists is not included in the cost for the inverted organization since this cost is negligible when compared to the cost of accessing records from external memory.

Expressions for the retrieval times for the two organizations are given in Table 5.2, and the symbols used in the expressions are given in Table 5.1. The formulations are based on a single query product. If a query is a sum of products, then the times for the products must be summed. Since the time to access a record depends on the particular storage device on which the record is stored, access time is simply indicated by the symbol T_A. For a disk device, T_A includes the seek time, latency time, and data transfer time.

For the multilist organization, the query cost, with the directory decoding cost ignored, is

$$Q_{CM} = L_S T_A \tag{5.8}$$

For the inverted organization $[L/N_A]$ physical records must be accessed for each of the N_T key values in the product. Thus, the time to retrieve the N_T inverted lists involved in the list intersection is $[L/N_A]N_T T_A$. For the multilist organization, every record in the shortest list, that is, the list of length L_S, must be accessed, but for the inverted organization only those ρL_S records that satisfy the key value logic must be accessed. Therefore, the query cost for the inverted organization, with the directory decoding cost ignored, is

$$Q_{CI} = (\rho L_S + [\frac{L}{N_A}] N_T) T_A \tag{5.9}$$

Substituting (5.8) into (5.9) produces the following relationship between the query costs for the multilist and inverted organizations

$$Q_{CI} = (\frac{N_T}{L_S} [\frac{L}{N_A}] + \rho) Q_{CM} \tag{5.10}$$

When

$$\rho < (1 - \frac{N_T}{L_S} [\frac{L}{N_A}]) \tag{5.11}$$

then $Q_{CI} < Q_{CM}$, and when

$$\rho > (1 - \frac{N_T}{L_S} [\frac{L}{N_A}]) \tag{5.12}$$

then $Q_{CI} > Q_{CM}$. Analyzing (5.10), (5.11), and (5.12) shows that the larger the number of physical records per inverted list, $[L/N_A]$, the larger the amount of time to access the inverted lists. In addition, the smaller the length of the

Table 5.2

Retrieval Times for the Multilist and Inverted Organizations

Action	Multilist	Inverted
Directory decoding	$N_P T_N$	$N_T T_N$
List intersection (retrieval of lists only)	–	$[\frac{L}{N_A}] N_T T_A$
Record transfer	$L_S T_A$	$\rho L_S T_A$

shortest list L_S, the more likely Q_{CM} will be less than Q_{CI}. This result supports the informal argument presented in Section 5.6.1.3.

5.7.3   Updating Inverted Files

Updating inverted files is more difficult than updating multilist files because the variable length inverted lists must be maintained in sorted order to facilitate list intersection and list union. The maintenance of variable length lists and the requirement that they be ordered contribute to certain programming complexities that are absent from the multilist organization.

When a new address is added to an inverted list, some of the addresses in the list may have to be moved to make room for the new address. Since the variable length records representing the inverted lists may increase in length during an update, extra space should be provided in each list at file load time. The extra space is important if real-time updating is to be allowed.

5.7.3.1   *Whole Record Addition*

An algorithm for whole record addition with n key values $KV_1, KV_2, \ldots, KV_n$ is given below. The record to be inserted has been assigned address x in external memory, and the record addresses in the inverted list corresponding to KV_i are designated as $y_{i_1}, y_{i_2}, \ldots, y_{i_m}$.

Algorithm ADD_IRECORD

1. [Initialize] $i \leftarrow 1$.
2. [Decode KV_i in the proper index] $a_i \leftarrow DS(Key, KV_i)$. If a_i is a valid pointer (possibly null), then go to Step 3; otherwise, allocate space for an inverted list for KV_i (at a_i) and $DS(Key, KV_i) \leftarrow a_i$.
3. [Insert address x in the inverted list pointed to by a_i] $FS(Key, KV_i, y_{i_j}) \leftarrow x$, $y_{i_j} < x < y_{i_{j+1}}$.
4. [Update the list length, if any] $length(KV_i) \leftarrow length(KV_i) + 1$.
5. [Test] $i \leftarrow i+1$, if $i \leqslant n$, then go to Step 2; otherwise Exit.

Step 2 in Algorithm ADD_IRECORD is essentially the same as it is for Algorithm ADD_MRECORD in Section 5.6.2.1. In Step 3 address x is added to the inverted list stored at address a_i. The addition of x to this inverted list requires that addresses $y_{i_{j+1}}, y_{i_{j+2}}, \ldots, y_{i_m}$ be moved forward to make room for x. Then, the updated inverted list is rewritten to external memory.

5.7.3.2 Key Value Addition

A key value can be added to an existing record by using Steps 2, 3, and 4 in Algorithm ADD_IRECORD. The key value is assumed to have already been added to the record and rewritten to external storage at address x. If more than one key value is added to an existing record, then Steps 2, 3, and 4 in Algorithm ADD_IRECORD are repeated for each distinct key value.

5.7.3.3 Key Value and Whole Record Deletion

The deletion of a whole record with address x requires that x be removed from all inverted lists of which it is an element. Record deletion for the inverted organization can be time-consuming since all appropriate inverted lists must be updated. If record x has n key values, $KV_1, KV_2, \ldots, KV_n$, then whole record deletion is performed in the following manner.

Algorithm DELETE_IRECORD

1. [Initialize] $i \leftarrow 1$.
2. [Decode KV_i in the proper index] $a_i \leftarrow$ DS(Key, KV_i).
3. ' [Remove x from the inverted list pointed to by a_i]
    FS(Key, KV_i, y_{i_j}) = $y_{i_{j+1}}$, $y_{i_j} < x < y_{i_{j+1}}$
4. [Update the list length, if any] length(KV_i) $\leftarrow$ length(KV_i)-1.
5. [Test] $i \leftarrow i+1$, if $i \leq n$, then go to Step 2.
6. [Delete record x] Delete record x from the file.

The function FS in Step 3 of Algorithm DELETE_IRECORD is used to remove address x from the inverted list pointed to by a_i. This use of FS does not cause the record with address y_{i_j} to be retrieved. The deletion of one or more key values from an existing record at address x is done by repeating Steps 2, 3, and 4 of Algorithm DELETE_IRECORD for each key value to be deleted. One additional step that may be performed is to delete key values from a record, if key values are kept in records. This last step is not necessary unless a programmer desires a file to reflect its true content when it is printed.

The cost of an update for the inverted organization depends on which update is being performed. The cost may include

1. The cost to decode and/or modify one or more directory entries.
2. The cost to modify one or more inverted lists.
3. The cost to update the affected data records.

5.8   THE CELLULAR MULTILIST FILE ORGANIZATION

The performance of multilist files, with respect to query processing, suffers when the lists are lengthy. The cellular multilist organization is derived from the multilist organization, and it is an attempt to arrange the records for more optimal retrieval. The length of each list in a cellular multilist file is restricted so that records in the list do not extend beyond certain hardware boundaries or cells. A cell can be a track, cylinder, volume, or any other zone delimited by a natural hardware boundary such that the time required to access data increases by a step function when data extend beyond cell boundaries. When data can be read simultaneously from more than one cell at a time, the cells are referred to as parallel cells. When the data records in a list are restricted to a single cell, the lengthy seeks incurred when traversing lists that span more than one cell are avoided and fast responses result.

Each index entry for a cellular multilist file consists of one or more "list head pointer/list length pairs"; one such pair exists for each cell containing records indexed by a key value. A directory for a cellular multilist file is larger than the directory for the corresponding multilist file, but the data record area for the two files requires the same amount of space. Figure 5.11 illustrates the DEPARTMENT index, organized for a cellular multilist file, for the data records in Figure 5.5. The index entry for key value 'AUTO' has three list head pointer/list length pairs, each one corresponding to a list in a single cell. That is, the 'AUTO' list in Figure 5.5 is subdivided into three shorter lists: one of length two in cell 1 with the head at address 1.5, one of length three in cell 2 with the head at address 2.2, and one of length one in cell 3 with the head at address 3.7.

Updating cellular multilist files is essentially the same as updating multilist files; therefore, the reader is referred to Section 5.6.2.

5.8.1   Answering Queries

Even if the cells in a cellular multilist file are not parallel cells, the cell concept can be used to provide good response times. As an example, suppose that the query

$$\text{DEPARTMENT} = \text{'AUTO'} \wedge \text{DEPARTMENT} = \text{'HDWE'} \quad \text{(Q5.7)}$$

is initiated by a programmer. Records having key value 'AUTO' reside in cells 1, 2, and 3, and records having key value 'HDWE' can be found in cells 0, 1, and 2. The only records that can be common to both lists are located in cells 1 and 2. The length of the list in cell 1 is two for 'AUTO' and it is three for 'HDWE'. The 'AUTO' list for cell 1 is traversed, since it is shorter, and each record is examined for the existence of the key value 'HDWE'. Record 1.5 belongs to both lists. In cell 2, the 'HDWE' list is the shortest so each record in it is accessed and examined for the occurrence of 'AUTO'. There are no

DEPARTMENT INDEX

AUTO	FURN	HDWE	SHOE
	0.9/1	0.3/2	0.6/3
1.5/2	1.4/2	1.4/3	1.2/2
2.2/3	2.1/1	2.0/1	2.3/1
3.7/1	3.8/2		3.5/1

Figure 5.11.   Cellular multilist file index corresponding to the multilist file in Figure 5.5.

records in cell 2 common to both lists. Thus, only record 1.5 satisfies query Q5.7.

The important thing to note in the above example is that only three data records are accessed during the processing of query Q5.7. On the other hand, if the file had been organized as a multilist file, then six data records would have been accessed and examined. The cellular multilist can lead to lower response times at the expense of more space for a larger directory. If the cells are parallel cells, then the response time for Q5.7 can be reduced even further because the records in the 'AUTO' list in cell 1 can be accessed in parallel with the records in the 'HDWE' list in cell 2. An operating system is usually responsible for scheduling access requests to external storage devices, and it determines to some extent how much parallelism can be effected.

The cellular multilist organization offers no particular advantages over the multilist organization for disjunctive queries unless the cells are parallel.

5.9 HYBRID LIST FILE ORGANIZATIONS

Since the number of records in a file is usually large and each query typically retrieves only a small portion of the records, the file should be organized in such a way as to minimize the system search effort in answering a query. The analysis of query costs (Sections 5.6.1.3 and 5.7.2.1) for both inverted and multilist organizations suggests that a file organization that would process a query according to the procedure used in the inverted organization when length (L_{ij}) $(L_{ij}$ is defined in Section 5.2) is large, while using an organization similar to a multilist organization when length(L_{ij}) is small, would out-perform both pure inverted and pure multilist organizations. A class of list-structured file organizations called hybrid list organizations, that includes the inverted and multilist organizations as special cases (degenerate cases) in the class have been developed.

The class of hybrid list organizations is defined in the following manner. A hybrid list organization of parameter L_{th} is a list structure that stores a set of pointers to records containing the key value in term T_{ij} as a separate inverted list if length(L_{ij}) $> L_{th}$; otherwise, the set of pointers is embedded in the data records as a multilist organization. In the special case in which $L_{th} = 0$, all lists are implemented as inverted lists and the hybrid organization degenerates to a pure inverted organization. At the other extreme, $L_{th} = \infty$ (infinity), a pure multilist organization is produced. As L_{th} increases from 0 to ∞, more and more lists are stored as multilists. Figure 5.12 illustrates a hybrid organization.

The cost of updating for the class of hybrid files lies somewhere between that for the two pure (degenerate) organizations since it is easier to update a multilist file than an inverted file. The more lists that are stored as multilists, the easier it is to perform updates. The cost of updating a hybrid list file oscillates between the cost of updating a corresponding inverted file and a corresponding multilist file.

A simplified simulation model of the hybrid file organizations has been used to determine the L_{th} values that produce hybrid organizations that are simultaneously better than pure inverted and pure multilist organizations with respect to both query costs and update costs combined. The list lengths were simulated by beta and exponential distributions. The result of simulating 400 queries with a mean list length of 20 using the exponential distribution

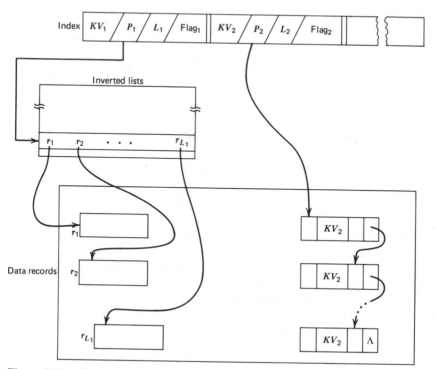

Figure 5.12.   Structure of a hybrid list organization with parameter L_{th} and $L_1 > L_{th}$ and $L_2 \leq L_{th}$.

demonstrated that as L_{th} moves from zero to infinity, the percentage improvement in query cost over both the inverted and multilist organizations climbed to positive peaks. In fact, the improvement was 27.5 percent over inverted and 12.3 percent over multilist when $L_{th} = 8$. Similar results were observed for the beta distribution. Other simulation results showed that hybrid list organizations may out-perform both pure organizations when both query and update costs are considered. The amounts of improvement of a nondegenerate organization over the pure ones are dependent on the particular environment in which the files are used.

5.9.1 Answering Queries

When all the lists corresponding to the key values in a query in a hybrid list file are stored as inverted lists or when they are all stored as multilists, retrieval is done in straight inverted or multilist fashion. Each index entry for a key value, however, must have a flag indicating how the corresponding list is organized: inverted list or multilist. Comparing the list length stored in an index entry against L_{th} is not sufficient for determining how a list is organized. The flag is necessary because of the way updating is done; updating will be discussed in the next section.

When one or more of the lists are inverted and one or more of the lists are multilist, as is the case for KV_1 and KV_2 in Figure 5.12, query processing is performed in the manner adopted for the multilist organization in Section 5.6.1. That is, for a conjunctive query, the shortest list is traversed and the records examined for the occurrence of the other key value(s), and for a disjunctive query redundant record accessing is avoided.

5.9.2 Updating Hybrid List Files

When a hybrid list file is updated, the list associated with a key value does not have its organization changed because of updating. If the list is an inverted list (or if it is a multilist) before an update, then it remains so after the update is performed. After several updates, a hybrid organization of parameter L_{th} may possess some multilists that are longer than L_{th}, and some inverted lists that are shorter than L_{th}. For this reason, each index entry should contain the flag mentioned earlier indicating how the list is organized so that updating can be done properly, using either the inverted organization update procedures or the multilist organization update procedures.

Even though some multilists are longer than L_{th} and some inverted lists are shorter than L_{th}, system performance is usually not seriously degraded. Simulation results show that a reasonably large range of L_{th} values whose corresponding hybrid organizations all have near optimal performances exist. The lists in a hybrid list file are restructured, if necessary, at file reorganization time.

5.10 EVALUATING SECONDARY KEY RETRIEVAL FILE ORGANIZATIONS

The kind of file organization used has a very important effect on the performance and associated costs of retrieval systems. These costs usually include total storage costs, query costs, and update costs. Also of concern is whether real-time or batched systems are involved.

The multilist file organization is satisfactory for systems that respond to simple and range queries and do not require extremely fast response times. The simplicity of programming a system using multilist structures is an added benefit. For most large retrieval systems, especially on-line real-time systems, the inverted organization is the best organization to use. Table 5.3 lists some advantages and disadvantages of the two organizations.

The most important factor affecting the overall performance of secondary key retrieval file organizations is the manner in which the indexes and associated lists are actually organized and managed in storage. In large files, highly inverted to increase accessing speed, the index itself becomes another file problem, possibly of the same magnitude as the file of data records. Many designers have stored an index as a sequentially organized file, which can be searched using a binary search algorithm. However, this is not an appropriate way to organize indexes for highly inverted files with several keys and many

Table 5.3

Comparison of Multilist and Inverted File Organizations

Organization	Advantages	Disadvantages
Multilist	Easily programmed. Conjunction queries are efficiently handled for short lists. Easily updated since complete reorganization of lists is avoided. Good for simple and range queries.	Conjunctive queries are inefficiently handled for long lists. The number of records that satisfy a query bears no relation to the number of records accessed.
Inverted	Low response time for conjunctive queries. Efficient use of storage space if key values are removed from data records. Satisfactory for real-time retrieval.	Updating is complex since the inverted lists are variable in length and must be ordered. Work space in internal memory is required to perform the logical processing of inverted lists.

different key values that are subjected to realistic multikey queries. Large directories should be organized as multilevel structures like the one illustrated in Figure 5.1, and they should reside in fast access external memory.

Another important decision, especially for inverted files, is whether or not to remove the key values from the data records. This storage saving possibility may not be followed for the following reasons:

1. The entire contents of the file are printed frequently.
2. The programming problems associated with compacting records, that is, removing key values as the records are written to external storage.
3. The query response time degradation that can result if data records have to be reconstructed to answer a query, that is, if a programmer wants the value of a data item that is a key and its value has been removed from the data record.

Another question of interest involves the selection of secondary keys on which to index. Some systems have been implemented in which every data item is treated as a key and every key value is indexed. Other systems have been implemented in which a programmer can specify which data items are keys and indexing is done on the key values of these keys. A basic premise is that secondary indexes should exist only for those keys that are frequently referenced and that require minimum search times. Even if a key meets these criteria, it does not always pay to index its values.

The major purpose of any secondary key index is to reduce the number of records that must be examined during access requests. The efficiency of a search is measured by its selection ratio, that is, the ratio of the number of hits (good records) to the number of records examined. The larger the selection ratio by sequential scan, the smaller the payoff in having a secondary key index. In general, the decision to create an index for a secondary key should also take into account the ratio of the number of distinct values of a key to the number of records in a file. For a large set of personnel records, it would probably not pay to index on the data item SEX. The reason for this is that the selection ratio would be relatively high, possibly 0.5 or higher for a query like SEX = 'MALE'; hence, it would be best to scan the file sequentially.

The multilist organization provides a seemingly satisfactory solution for simple and range queries, but when Boolean queries are involved, the search time may bear no relation to the number of records satisfying the query. For instance, the query

$$K1 = X \land K2 = Y \tag{Q5.8}$$

may lead to a list of length m for key value X and a list of length n for key value Y. Then $\min(m,n)$ data records will be retrieved and tested against the query. It is possible that none or only a very small number of these records satisfy Q5.8. This problem can be remedied somewhat by combined attribute indexes.

As an example, consider queries using keys K_1, K_2, and K_3. In some specific cases access speed may be faster by indexing on all three keys combined. In a combined index on the keys K_1, K_2, and K_3, each index entry contains a pointer to a list of data records in which each data record has a key value for each of the three keys. In other cases, access speed may be faster by indexing on each of the three keys individually. Matters become complex for combined indexes when maintenance aspects are considered. Combined indexing has not seen much actual practice. The reason for this lack of use is that time performance is very sensitive to changes in the contents of a file and to the type and logical complexity of queries issued against the file.

Since the costs of programming are very high, it is important to have some knowledge about which file organizations may be appropriate for a given application. For on-line retrieval systems, considerable care should be taken in selecting a file organization. General guidelines for file organization selection are difficult to establish and more often each situation has to be examined individually.

The problem of selecting an appropriate file organization can be approached by modelling file organizations and then simulating their performance under various conditions. Three very important quantifiable performance measures for selecting a file organization are:

1.   Total storage costs.
2.   The average time to answer a typical query.
3.   The average time to perform an update.

The best or most appropriate file organization for on-line secondary key retrieval depends on the particular users and their environment.

A basic methodology for comparing and selecting file organizations appropriate for secondary key retrieval is:

1.   Obtain measures of the relevant characteristics of the actual file or of a representative sample of it and of the requirements of the programmers.
2.   Take into account storage device related performance specifications supplied by a manufacturer.
3.   Estimate, by simulation, the minimum storage requirements and the minimum average access time to answer an average query for various alternative file organizations.
4.   Estimate the frequency and cost of file update operations.

On this basis, an appropriate file organization can be selected using the cost function given below.

The specific file statistics considered most pertinent to be measured are:

1.   Number of records.

2. Minimum record length.
3. Maximum record length.
4. Average record length.
5. Average key value length.
6. Minimum key value length for each key.
7. Maximum key value length for each key.
8. Average key value length for each key.
9. Number of unique key values for each key.

The relevant user requirements provided by a user are:

1. Frequencies of queries.
2. Frequency of update.
3. Mode of retrieval, mode of update—real-time or batched.
4. Type of update—insert, delete, modify.
5. Average number of records retrieved for a typical query—an estimate.
6. Key values of records to be printed—yes or no.
7. File organization desired, if any.
8. The number and names of keys used to access records.

The relevant device specifications taken into account are:

1. Block (or sector) length.
2. Average time to access a track.
3. Average time to compare a key value.
4. Average time to retrieve consecutive blocks.
5. Cost per track per unit period.
6. Machine cost per second.

When the measurements (or statistics) listed above have been collected, the best file organization may be one that minimizes the cost function (this cost function assumes the use of a disk)

cost/unit period = [(cost per track/unit period) × (total storage in tracks)]
+ [(cost/second) × (access time in seconds per typical query)
× (number of queries/unit period)] + [an update cost function]
+ [other highly unquantifiable cost functions]

The unit period may be a day, week, etc. The unquantifiable costs include the costs of programming, software maintenance, documentation, etc.

In summary, two final comments are worthy of mention. First, file organizations that have the best access time performance generally have higher storage and update costs, that is, as access times decrease, storage and update costs go up. In a fully inverted file, the access time to answer any query is minimal, but storage and update costs tend to be maximal compared to other organizations. Second, two important questions that should be considered are: (1) how much degradation in average access time and storage cost should be tolerated before reorganizing a file?, and (2) how sensitive is performance to the three sets of measurements, that is, relevant user requirements, etc., listed above.

EXERCISES

1. Describe several applications that require secondary key retrieval.
2. Use the file organizations supported by the computer system on which you normally work to implement an inverted file organization.
3. Examine some application systems that use large files and determine the type of file organizations used and how they are implemented.
4. It was suggested in Section 5.2 that the record address list in Figure 5.1 be a list of record addresses.

    (a) Should these record addresses be absolute or symbolic addresses?
    (b) If a file is reorganized, what happens to the record address list?
    (c) If the record addresses are symbolic, what would they be?

5. Read Hsiao and Harary's paper given in the references and compare it with the discussion in Section 5.3.
6. Examine a large file application system to determine the mode in which updating is done and determine how and when space is reclaimed as a result of updating.
7. Explain why the ring structure in Figure 5.4 is not a hierarchical ring structure. Start by defining a hierarchical structure.
8. In Section 5.6, it was suggested that a multilist system that stores only key values and not key/key value pairs will operate less efficiently since some longer list searches may result when queries are answered. Why?
9. Give an informal argument similar to that given for formula 5.6 in Section 5.6.1.3.1 to justify formula 5.7.
10. Draw the multiring structure indexed on the SALARY and DEPART-MENT keys for the following data records:

SALARY	DEPARTMENT	NAME
$10,000	SHOE	JONES
10,000	HDWE	SMITH
15,000	SHOE	BLACK
20,000	HDWE	WHITE
20,000	SHOE	JAMES
15,000	SHOE	BROWN

11. Describe a situation in which a multilist file is preferable to an ISAM file. The situation that you describe should be clearly related to the fundamental differences between these two file organizations.

12. You have been hired as a highly paid consultant for a merchandising firm to design a file structure that contains data records describing the products that they sell. Each data record contains the following information:

   (a) A product number (unique integer).
   (b) A list of suppliers who supply this product to the firm (for example, Goodyear, Acme Tool, etc.).
   (c) A list of customers who purchase this product from the firm (for example, Boeing, Ford, etc.).
   (d) The cost of the product.
   (e) The number of units of this product in stock.

   The file structure must permit rapid processing of the following types of queries:

   (a) Find all the products supplied by a given supplier.
   (b) Find all the products purchased by a given customer.
   (c) Output the recorded information about a given product, having been provided with its product number.

   Also, once a day you must output, in product number order, a list of all of the parts whose number of units in stock is less than a specified value.

   Describe the file structure that you would recommend and how it meets the above requirements.

13. Several commercial database management systems use the file organizations described in this chapter. For the ring, multilist, and inverted organizations select a database management system (see the references at the end of Chapter 9) and write an overview of the system describing the query language used and the techniques employed in implementing the file organizations.

REFERENCES

5.1   Cardenas, A.F. "Analysis and Performance of Inverted Database Structures," *Commun. ACM,* Vol. 18, No. 5, May 1975, pp. 253–263.

   A model for the inverted file organization is presented and analyzed to obtain estimates of the average access time and total storage requirements.

5.2   Bachman, C.W. and Williams, S.B. "A General Purpose Programming System for Random Access Memories," *Proceedings of 1964 FJCC,* Vol. 26, pp. 411–422.

This paper describes a system called IDS (Integrated Data Store) that uses rings to organize data. IDS is a set of procedures for processing rings. Some of the concepts in IDS later had a large influence on the CODASYL network database data model.

5.3   Dodd, G.D. "Elements of Data Management Systems," *ACM Computing Surveys,* June 1969, pp. 117–133.

A tutorial survey of several file organizations is presented. This early paper is recommended reading for Chapter 5.

5.4   Shneiderman, B. "Reduced Combined Indexes for Efficient Multiple Attribute Retrieval," *Information Systems,* Vol. 2, No. 4, 1977, pp. 149–154.

This paper discusses an alternative to combined indexes that can significantly reduce the size of combined indexes. This improvement leads to shorter response times for conjunctive queries but it does not improve the update problem that arises with combined attribute indexes.

5.5   Hsiao, D.K. and Harary, F.D. "A Formal System for Information Retrieval from Files," *Commun. ACM,* Vol. 13, No. 2, February 1970, pp. 67–73.

This paper describes a generalized model for file organizations and presents a general algorithm for tracing both sorted and unsorted multilists.

5.6   Lefkovitz, D. *File Structures for On-Line Systems,* Spartan Books, New York, 1969.

This book discusses in detail the multilist, inverted, and cellular multilist file organizations.

5.7   Claybrook, B.G. and Yang, C-S. "Efficient Algorithms for Answering Queries with Unsorted Multilists," *Information Systems,* Vol. 3, No. 2, 1978, pp. 93–97.

Three algorithms for the parallel traversal of unsorted multilists are given and analyzed.

5.8   Yang, C-S. "A Class of Hybrid List File Organizations," *Information Systems,* Vol. 3, No. 1, 1978, pp. 49–58.

Presents a new class of list-structured file organizations, which includes the inverted list and multilist organizations as special cases in the class. The query cost for organizations in the class is analyzed.

5.9   Cardenas, A.F. *Data Base Management Systems*, Allyn and Bacon, Boston, 1979.

A brief introduction to multilist and inverted list file organizations is given.

6
File Systems

6.1 INTRODUCTION

An important task of an operating system is the maintenance of files. Certain facilities are provided by an operating system for creating, destroying, organizing, reading, writing, modifying, moving, copying, and controlling access to files. The component of an operating system that provides these facilities is usually referred to as a file system. In this chapter, the basic functions performed by a typical file system are discussed. No attempt, however, is made to describe any particular file system.

A file system is usually the largest component of an operating system. It performs two important functions:

1. It gives the programmer the ability to create name spaces.
2. It is responsible for accessing, storing, and managing data stored in external memory.

Several features and mechanisms are usually incorporated into a file system; it provides:

1. A mechanism for mapping logical files into physical locations.
2. The ability to share common files.
3. The ability to allocate, deallocate, and administer external storage effectively.
4. Flexibility and versatility for accessing files.
5. Machine and device independence to as large a degree as possible.
6. Security and integrity mechanisms.

A question appropriate to ask at this time is: Where is a file system with respect to an operating system, user programs, and data files? One role that a file system plays is an interface between a program and the files that the program expects to access. Another role of a file system is a supervisor that monitors data management. These two roles are illustrated in Figures 6.1 and 6.2, respectively.

6.2 ACCESS METHODS

A programmer communicates indirectly with a file system via an operating system through a set of predefined commands commonly called a *job command language,* assembly language programs, or programs written in a high-level programming language. A job command language permits a programmer to identify: (1) the file on which operations are to be performed, (2) the device on which a file is located, (3) the manipulations to be performed on a file, and (4) the attributes of a file. An assembly language program can invoke macros that permit communication with the file system. A high-level language program indirectly invokes an access method (or routine) via a GET, PUT, READ, or WRITE statement. The execution of these statements causes an access method routine to be invoked that performs the requested I/O operation on the indicated file.

Access method routines are file system procedures that interpret and satisfy user requests for storage or retrieval of data. As indicated in Figure 6.2, access method routines are the "go-between" for a user program and a file. Figure 6.3 illustrates some of the characteristics of access methods.

Access methods handle buffering, blocking, and deblocking and serve as interfaces with devices. Access methods presume a particular file organization. For example, an access method for a sequential file is different than an access method for an indexed sequential file. However, some distinct access methods can share common code. A primary objective of the access method concept is to provide a degree of independence between a program that accesses a file and the device on which the file is stored.

Application programs and access method routines execute in the problem state (versus the supervisor state). However, I/O operations must be initiated in the supervisor state so that I/O processing can be managed on a system-wide

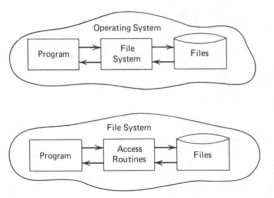

Figure 6.1. The file system as an interface.

Figure 6.2. The file system as a supervisor.

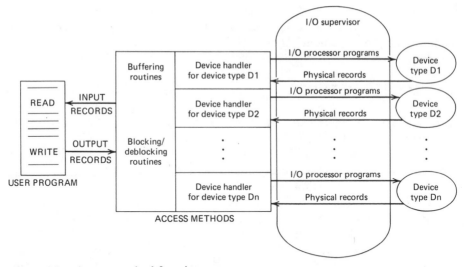

Figure 6.3.   Access method functions.

basis. The overall I/O system on most modern computing systems is organized as follows:

1. An operating system includes an I/O supervisor that issues all privileged I/O instructions. The I/O supervisor executes in the supervisor state.
2. When an access method needs the services of the I/O supervisor, it initiates a supervisor call interruption that changes the state of the processing unit from the problem state to the supervisor state and transfers program control to the I/O supervisor, which initiates the I/O operation.
3. Program control is returned to the access method and it continues processing, waits, or returns control to the application program.
4. When an I/O operation is complete, an interrupt is generated by the hardware I/O system. The interruption is processed by the I/O supervisor and the operation is marked as being complete.
5. Program control is given to the access method to complete the original I/O operation requested by a user program.

The above description of the overall I/O process is illustrated pictorially in Figure 6.4. The FCT (file control table) shown in Figure 6.4 is discussed later in Section 6.6. The FCT holds the address(es) of I/O buffer(s) and the address of the access method associated with the file being processed.

6.3   THE OPEN AND CLOSE FUNCTIONS

The major contemporary file systems require a user program to notify the I/O system of its intent to process a particular file. This intent is realized in a user

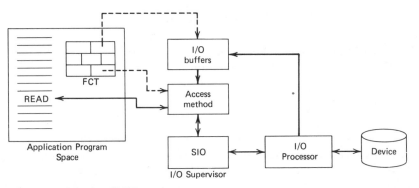

Figure 6.4.   The overall I/O process.

program via a system call named OPEN. In a high-level language, the OPEN call is an OPEN statement that includes the name of the file being OPENed. In assembly language, the OPEN call is realized in the form of an OPEN macro with a set of parameters that includes the file name. CLOSE is the related partner of OPEN and performs postprocessing tasks on the specified file.

Not all high-level programming languages have explicit OPEN and CLOSE statements. For example, FORTRAN has neither. With FORTRAN programs, a compiler automatically generates an OPEN for each file to be processed and the REWIND statement performs some of the functions performed by an explicit CLOSE. COBOL and PL/I have OPEN and CLOSE statements.

6.3.1   The OPEN Function

The major responsibilities of the OPEN function are to ready a file for processing, initialize system tables as required, and generally check on several details to ensure that record and block processing can be performed correctly and efficiently. The activities that can result from issuing an OPEN statement include:

1.   Mounting the medium on which a file is stored.
2.   Positioning the storage medium for file access.
3.   File label verification.
4.   Initializing internal memory tables (this includes initializing the address(es) of buffer(s) and the address of the access routine).
5.   Initially filling buffers if anticipatory reading is appropriate.

6.3.2   The CLOSE Function

The CLOSE function is less complex than the OPEN. It performs the following functions:

1.   Empties all buffers for output files.
2.   Repositions files, usually back to the first record in a file, if the file is a sequential file.

3. Modifies file descriptors (see Section 6.5).
4. Resets flags in file tables (see Section 6.6).
5. Releases access method routines that were loaded to process the file.
6. Releases main storage space required for file tables.

6.4 DIRECTORIES

A *directory* performs an important function within a file system called *name mapping*. This particular phenomenon permits a user to create name spaces and to store (retrieve) data in (from) them. Name mapping converts a symbolic file name into a physical file address that identifies where the file is stored.

Each user may have a directory of his own files and may create subdirectories to contain groups of files conveniently treated together. A directory normally behaves like an ordinary file. A file system controls access to the contents of directories; however, anyone with the appropriate authorization can access a directory just like any other file.

In designing a system of file directories, it is natural to think in terms of a hierarchy with the entries in the higher levels of a directory being other directories. The entries in the lower levels are a mixture of files and directories. The directory entries in a hierarchically structured directory can contain either system directories or user directories. Data files are at the lowest level.

The most important system directory is the master directory (or root directory). Files created by users are usually located by tracing a path through a chain of directories, starting with the master directory, until the desired file is found. Figures 6.5 and 6.6 illustrate typical directory organizations. The directory structure in Figure 6.5 is a typical UNIX* user directory and the directory structure in Figure 6.6 is a general directory organization that illustrates file naming and file sharing across users.

An interactive user or a program running on behalf of a user references a specific file via a symbolic file name. A symbolic file name is usually in the form of a path name that is a sequence of names separated by some specially designated character such as a period ('.') or slash ('/'). For example, in Figure 6.5, file 14 has the symbolic name mail/inbox/msgl. In Figure 6.6, data file 13 has name R.R1.R5, directory file 10 has the name R.R1.R2, and data file 3 has two names P.P2 and R.R1.R2.R8. In the simplest case there is a one-to-one correspondence between symbolic file names and files. However, in more advanced file systems the same file may appear in several directories under possibly different names; that is, a single file may be shared by two or more user groups, with each group having a different path through the directories to the file itself.

The directory structures in Figures 6.5 and 6.6 imply that the output of a directory search for a file is the file itself. This is slightly misleading, because the terminal nodes of the hierarchical structure, rather than containing the file,

*UNIX is a trademark of Bell Laboratories.

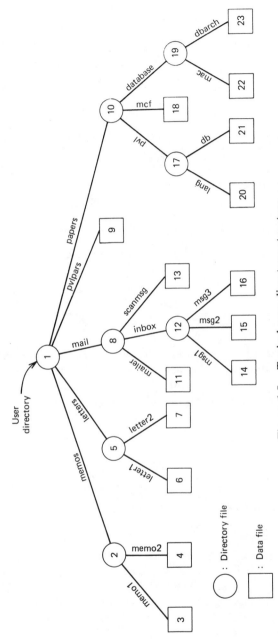

Figure 6.5. Typical user directory structure.

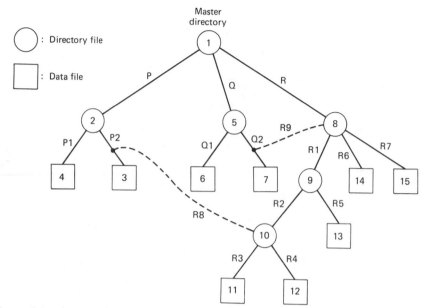

Figure 6.6.   A general directory structure.

normally contain an object commonly referred to as a file descriptor or a pointer to a file descriptor. A file descriptor contains information concerning the physical location of the file and the physical characteristics of the file. File descriptors are discussed in detail in the next section.

6.5   FILE DESCRIPTORS

A *file descriptor* permits the final mapping step from a symbolic file name to a file to be completed. A file descriptor is established when a file is first created and it is updated by a file system when the file is moved, compacted, expanded, or accesssed. In simple file systems in which there is a one-to-one correspondence between file names and files, a file descriptor is usually kept in a directory. If, however, a file system permits more than one symbolic name to map to a single file, a file descriptor should be stored in a single place on the device where the file resides. In this case, a directory entry usually holds a file identifier that is treated as an index into a system-maintained table of contents on the device on which the file resides. All directory entries corresponding to the same file contain the same file identifier.

Several pieces of important information are stored in a file descriptor. Among these are:

1. The physical address of the file—that is, the location and length of the file (for files that are not stored in contiguous blocks, the address of

each physical record (or block) must be specified, either by a pointer to the first record of a linked list of records or by the use of an index or file map).

2. The access control information—authorization information, specifying who can access the file and how they can access it.
3. The date of the file's creation.
4. The date of the last change.
5. The frequency of access.
6. The disposition, permanent or temporary.
7. The file organization (sequential, indexed sequential, etc.).
8. The record format (fixed or variable length records).
9. The file's owner.
10. The number of links to the file (or the number of paths to the file).
11. A bit indicating whether the file is a directory or a data file.

6.6 FILE TABLES

A program is connected to the file(s) that it uses via a set of system-generated tables. These tables act as an interface (or communications) mechanism between a program and its files. The tables contain information needed by a user's program and by the access routines for retrieving data. The first of these tables is the file control table (FCT) located in a user's program area. It serves as a communications area for a user program and the access method routines of the file system.

When a high-level language program is compiled, a FCT is generated for it. There is one entry in a FCT for each file declared or used by a program. Languages such as COBOL and PL/I have explicit file declaration statements, whereas other languages such as FORTRAN do not. In either case, a compiler adds an entry to the FCT for each file used in a program and program code generated by the compiler references a file via its entry number in the FCT.

The information contained in a FCT entry comes from as many as three sources: (1) the file descriptor, (2) job command language statements, and (3) the user program. This information is augmented with other information such as buffer size, buffer location(s), the address of an access method routine, etc. A typical FCT entry is illustrated in Figure 6.7.

Most of the information about a file is placed in its FCT entry when the file becomes active, that is, OPENed. FCT entries are interrogated and updated by the file system during file processing activities. When a file becomes inactive, that is, CLOSEed, changes in pertinent file descriptor information stored in the FCT entry are used to update the file descriptor itself.

Another table, the active file table (AFT), is used by a file system to keep track of all active files in a computer system. An AFT resides in supervisor memory where it is protected from user programs. For each active program in the system, an entry is made in the AFT for each file OPENed. An entry is

Symbolic file name			
Number of buffers		Size of buffers	
Pointer to buffer			
Pointer to buffer			
.			
.			
.			
Pointer to buffer			
Status: Open/Closed		Device type	Device number
Physical address		Address of access routine	
Access control information			
Creation date		Date of last change	Frequency of access
Disposition: Perm/Temp	File org	Record format	Number of links to file
Owner		Directory file or Data file	
Size of block or physical records		Address of current record	
Number of records per block		Address of AFT entry	

Figure 6.7. A typical FCT entry.

removed when a file is CLOSEed. An AFT entry is illustrated in Figure 6.8.

Another function of a file system is to relate each user file to the I/O device on which it resides. The file system uses the device unit table (DUT) that resides in the supervisor area of internal memory to complete this function. The DUT identifies all I/O devices available in a computer system. Each entry in the DUT for an I/O device gives a unit address, device type, device status

Name of file	File type
Name of program to which file is assigned	
Address of the FCT	
Address of DUT	
Address of file	Current file position
File protection information	Processing priority
Address of access routines	

Figure 6.8. An AFT entry.

(busy/not busy), device number, current device identifier (for example, volume number), etc.

Figure 6.9 illustrates the use of a FCT, an AFT, and a DUT in connecting a user's program to a file. Link 1 is established by the language processor that processes a user's program. Links 2 and 3 are established by OPENing the file and link 4 is established at system generation time.

6.7   STORAGE MANAGEMENT IN EXTERNAL MEMORY

Another important function that a file system performs is storage management. This includes allocating, deallocating, and maintaining external storage. The techniques for managing external memory are similar to those used in managing internal memory; however, for external memory, it is important to minimize the number of accesses to external memory that are necessary to perform the storage management.

6.7.1   Allocation of File Space

A file system may allow a user to participate in the allocation of space for files. For example, a file system may allow, or actually require, a user to estimate the storage space required for a file. This estimate is normally made via job command statements, and space can be requested in cylinders, tracks, sectors, blocks, records, or even bytes in some cases. Cylinders, tracks, and sectors are natural subdivisions of space for disks, but for some storage devices such as

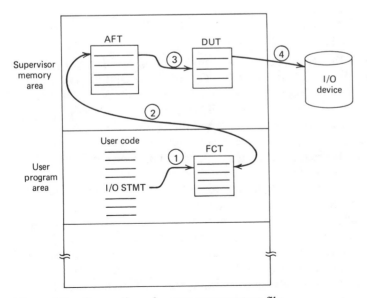

Figure 6.9.   Connection of a user program to a file.

charge-coupled devices and magnetic bubble memories, these subdivisions may not be meaningful. The specification of storage space in terms of blocks, records, or bytes is not affected by the choice of a storage device.

In some cases a file system will take complete responsibility for allocating space. In other cases, a user may have to specify a primary quantity, which is allocated initially, and a secondary quantity, which is assigned repeatedly (to some limit) whenever the space already assigned is exhausted.

Storage space may be assigned contiguously or noncontiguously. This decision is usually left to the file system; however, some systems allow a programmer to specify that space be allocated contiguously. For efficiency of access, it is generally best to contiguously allocate storage; on the other hand, it is usually easier to deallocate and maintain storage if the contiguous requirement is removed. A basic strategy associated with allocating storage is to do it in a manner such that subsequent access requests can be made efficiently. With respect to disks, this means minimizing rotational delay time and seek time. Since file size is often not known in advance, a static allocation policy must frequently rely on upperbound size estimates. Unless much wasted space can be tolerated, a dynamic storage allocation method seems necessary for some files; for example, for spooled input and output files.

Noncontiguous file space can be implemented by chaining physical records (or blocks) together or by using file maps. A file map maps each logical record address to its physical record address. File maps can be implemented as indexed tables and they may, depending on file size, be stored entirely within a file's file descriptor. When a file is opened, all or part of its file map is copied into memory possibly as part of the AFT information.

6.7.1.1 File Maps

Sometimes, the file mapping technique employed depends on the type of accesses made on a file. Sequential files can be realized on secondary storage by either contiguous or linked methods. The most straightforward method maps logically contiguous records into physically contiguous ones. The records of a linked organization are not, in general, stored with identical logical and physical orders. Instead, they may be scattered throughout a secondary storage media. Each record is linked to the next one by a forward pointer. If backspacing is also desired, a backward pointer can also be employed.

If we assume that records $R_0, R_1, \ldots, R_m$ of a file are ordered and it is required to directly access an arbitrary record R_i, then a linked allocation scheme is not as practical as other techniques.

If a file is logically organized, as in Figure 6.10a, then the direct address of record R_i can be computed by $B + i \times n$ where i is the record number, B is the location of R_0 in external memory (this calculation assumes that logical and physical records are the same size), and n is the record length. If, however, the records in a file are of variable length, as illustrated in Figure 6.10b, then the address of the ith record cannot be directly computed. A sequential search

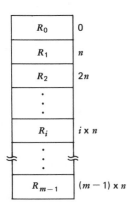

(a)

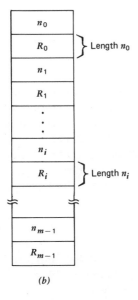

(b)

Figure 6.10. Fixed and variable length record files. (a) Fixed-length records. (b) Variable length records.

through the file could be made until the desired record is reached, but in general, this, like linked allocation, is too inefficient for direct accessing.

To handle direct addressing in a suitable manner for variable length records stored contiguously or noncontiguously, an index table with entries of the form

ith entry:

Length of block i	Address of block i

can be employed. Figure 6.11 illustrates this approach.

When the index table technique is used for file mapping, a logical record number acts as an index into an index table (see Figure 6.11) to retrieve a

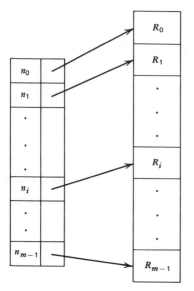

Figure 6.11.   The use of an index table for file mapping.

pointer to the corresponding physical record. The index table technique works well when records are not stored contiguously and when secondary storage is dynamically allocated and deallocated. The index table technique also allows an efficient implementation of partially filled files. In this case, each index table entry has a tag bit indicating whether or not the corresponding record has been allocated and is being used. Files that are sequential in nature can also be accessed with the index table method; one just moves sequentially through the table.

6.7.1.2   *The Hasp II System*

One of the most widely used systems for I/O spooling on the IBM 360s and 370s is the Hasp II system. This system is briefly described below to illustrate a simple scheme for allocating and freeing external storage space.

The Hasp II system allocates disk space on a cylinder basis for a file, but on a track basis for a request. When a request for disk space is issued, the allocator will supply the next track from the cylinder. When a cylinder has no more free tracks (or the request is the first request), a new cylinder is allocated to the job making the request, and the first track is allocated. Hasp II attempts to allocate cylinders in a contiguous manner.

Available space on devices (disk and drum) is maintained by using a Master Cylinder Map (MCM). A MCM contains a bit map for each device. A bit value of "1" in a bit map for a device means that the corresponding cylinder is free and a bit value of "0" means that the cylinder has already been allocated. The bit map is kept in internal memory.

Associated with each job is a Job Cylinder Map (JCM). There is one bit map per file associated with a job. A bit value of "1" in a file bit map means that a cylinder on the device on which the file resides is allocated to the file; whereas a bit value of "0" means that the corresponding cylinder is not allocated to the file. The JCM is stored on disk until the associated file becomes active. The space for a file can be released by "ORing" the bit map for the file with the bit map for the device on which the file resides.

6.7.2 Keeping Track of Space

There are two problems involved in keeping track of space: (1) maintaining a record of the available space on a device, and (2) maintaining a record of the space allocated to each file on the device. A file system uses a table sometimes referred to as the *device block space table* (DBST) to keep track of blocks that are available for use, that is, free blocks. There is one DBST for each device, and, while the device is being used, the DBST is kept in supervisor memory. At other times it is stored on the storage device itself.

Figure 6.12(*a*) illustrates a DBST for fixed-size blocks. The first entry in word one gives the total number of file blocks available on the device and the second entry gives the number of file blocks available at any given time. The remainder of the table is a bit map that indicates which blocks are available for allocation and which are unavailable. For each block, there is a bit in the map. If a bit is 0, then the block is available, and if it is 1, it is unavailable.

The above scheme is appropriate only for keeping track of fixed-size blocks. If the blocks can be variable in size, then an index table similar to the one in

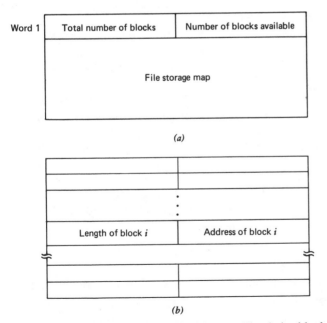

Figure 6.12. Device block space tables. (*a*) Fixed-size blocks. (*b*) Variable size blocks.

Figure 6.11 is used to keep track of available blocks (see Figure 6.12b). An alternative to using an index table is to link all available blocks together forming a list of available blocks. If blocks are fixed in size, then allocating a block means taking the first one on the list, and deallocating a block means positioning the block at the head of the list. However, if the blocks are of variable size, then a dynamic storage allocation algorithm may be necessary to avoid the inefficient use of space, and the deallocation process may involve the consolidation of adjacent blocks.

While a DBST maintains a record of the available space on a particular storage device, a file block table (FBT) keeps track of the blocks assigned to a particular file. The length of a FBT depends on the number of blocks allocated to a file. The list of blocks allocated to a file can be recorded using a bit map if the blocks are fixed in size. If the blocks are variable in length, then an index table with entries like those in Figure 6.12b can be used.

EXERCISES

1. Describe the functionality of the file system of your computer system. Trace the steps from the time that a high-level program output statement, for example, a WRITE statement, is executed to the time that data are written on an external storage device.
2. What access methods does your operating system support? Describe the functions that the access methods perform.
3. Describe the actions that occur when OPEN and CLOSE macros are executed in an assembly language that you know.
4. Describe the directory organization on two computer systems with which you are familiar or for which you have documentation. Can user files be readily shared via the directories? Describe the naming conventions for giving symbolic names to files.
5. How are the names of files used in programs written in high-level languages such as PL/I and Pascal mapped to the symbolic names of files that are stored on external storage devices on your computer system?
6. Where are the equivalent of file descriptors stored in your computer's file system?
7. Describe in detail the location and content of file tables in your computer system. When are they created and what piece of software creates them?
8. How is external memory allocated and maintained in your file system?

REFERENCES

6.1 Madnick, S.E. and Donovan, J.J. *Operating Systems,* McGraw-Hill, New York, 1974, 640 pages.

Chapter 6 of this book describes a general model of a file system.

6.2 Feieritag, R. J. and Organick, E. I. "The Multics Input/Output System," Third ACM Symposium on Operating System Principles, Stanford University, October 1971, pp. 17–23.

This paper describes a device interface module for MULTICS.

6.3 Shaw, A.C. *The Logical Design of Operating Systems,* Prentice-Hall, Englewood Cliffs, New Jersey, 1974, 306 pages.

Chapter 9 of this book covers most of the topics covered in this chapter.

6.4 Freeman, D.E. and Perry, O.R. *I/O Design: Data Management in Operating Systems,* Hayden, Rochelle Park, New Jersey, 1977, 374 pages.

This book is recommended reading for this chapter. It presents detailed discussions on input/output systems, channel programming, device allocation, opening and closing files, and the I/O supervisor.

6.5 Simpson, T. H., et al. Houston Automatic Spooling Priority System-II (Version 2), IBM Type III Program No. 360D-05.1.014, IBM Corporation, Program Information Department, Hawthorne, New York.

This paper, as the title suggests, describes features of the Hasp II spooling system.

6.6 Ritchie, D.M. and Thompson, K. "The UNIX Time-Sharing System," *Commun. ACM,* Vol. 17, No. 7, July 1974, pp. 365–375.

This paper discusses the implementation of the UNIX file system and the user language interface.

7

Sorting

7.1 INTRODUCTION

Sorting is the process of arranging (ordering) records in a table or file into ascending or descending sequence. The sorting problem can be stated precisely as follows: given n records $R_1, R_2, \ldots, R_n$, with key values $KV_1, KV_2, \ldots, KV_n$, respectively, order the records on the KV_i.

Sorting is an important topic in computer science because about twenty-five percent of all computer time is spent sorting. Programs developed for some application areas, such as business data processing, may spend the majority of their computation time in sorting and/or searching activities to produce reports, formatted tables, etc.

Sorting is of primary interest in file processing because, in general, a sorted file is easier to search than an unsorted file. Almost all operations, for example, insert, delete, etc., on a file involve searching and they are made simpler if the file is sorted.

There are several factors that influence the effectiveness of a sorting algorithm; thus, in general, there is no single sorting algorithm that is best for every situation. Some of these factors are:

1. The number of records to be sorted.
2. Whether or not all records will fit into the available internal memory.
3. The degree to which the records are already sorted.
4. The type of storage media on which the records are stored.
5. The complexity and storage requirements of the sorting algorithm.
6. Whether or not records are likely to be periodically deleted or added.

Some of the internal sorting algorithms discussed below can be improved by the proper selection of data structures. In particular, the efficiency of algorithms that involve the movement of records from one place to another in a table can be substantially improved by arranging the table as a simple linked list. Additional memory is required for a pointer field but this becomes less significant as the record length increases.

Sorting algorithms are generally classified as *internal sorting* algorithms, in which the list of records can be kept entirely in internal memory during the sort, or as *external sorting* algorithms in which there are more records to be sorted than can be kept in internal memory at any given time. The records to be sorted by an internal sorting algorithm are contained in a table in internal memory, and, for external sorting, the records are kept in a file in external memory. Internal sorting algorithms are presented in this chapter because the initial phase of external sorting algorithms usually requires an internal sort to create a set of runs. A run is a sorted sequence of records.

No attempt is made to provide a comprehensive survey of sorting algorithms; instead, only those algorithms that are practical for external sorting and a few internal sorting algorithms are presented. Each algorithm is accompanied by an example and its space and time complexities are given.

7.2   INTERNAL SORTING ALGORITHMS

The algorithms described below can be classified as exchange sorting, insertion sorting, partition exchange sorting, binary tree sorting, and merge sorting algorithms. As is characteristic of most algorithms in computer science, the sorting algorithms that are the least complex and require minimal storage are the most inefficient, and the complex algorithms with higher storage requirements are the most efficient. The internal sorting algorithms discussed below are the bubble sort, insertion sort, quicksort, binary tree sort, and merge sort.

7.2.1   Exchange Sorting

Exchange sorting is a phrase used to describe a collection of minimal-storage sorts that interchange records in a list when an earlier key value is found to be larger than a later key value. The bubble sort and the quicksort are examples of exchange sorting, and both methods are discussed below.

7.2.1.1   *Bubble Sort*

For the bubble sort, a list of records can be examined first to last or last to first. The bubble sort algorithm given below begins at the end (bottom) of the list and "bubbles" the record with the smallest key value to the top and then begins at the bottom again and bubbles the next smallest to the second position in the list, etc.

Essentially, a bubble sort tries to place one record of a list in its final sorted position during each pass over the list. The first pass places the record with the smallest key value in the first position in the list. The method may be reversed so that the first pass places the record with the highest key value in the last position; the algorithm described below follows the first alternative. On the first pass, the last member of the list is compared with its immediate predecessor, and if the predecessor is larger, the two are exchanged. The smaller key value, now in position $n-1$, is compared with the element in position $n-2$. An exchange is made, if necessary, to place the smaller of these in position $n-2$, etc. When position 2 is compared with 1, the pass ends.

Bubble Sort Algorithm The following bubble sort algorithm sorts a list containing N records. The FLAG variable is used to indicate whether or not any exchanges have taken place in a pass. If not, the sort is over.

Algorithm BUBBLE_SORT

1. Repeat Steps 2 and 3 for $i = 1, 2, \ldots, N-1$.
2. [Initialize FLAG] FLAG $\leftarrow$ 0.
3. Repeat for $j = N-1, N-2, \ldots, i$
   If $K_{j+1} < K_j$, then FLAG $\leftarrow$ 1, $R_{j+1} \leftrightarrow R_j$.
   If FLAG = 0, then exit.
4. [Sort completed] Exit.

Example

Initial List	Pass 1	Pass 2	Pass 3	Pass 4	Pass 5	Pass 6	Pass 7	Pass 8
19	1	1	1	1	1	1	1	1
13	19	2	2	2	2	2	2	2
5	13	19	5	5	5	5	5	5
27	5	13	19	9	9	9	9	9
1	27	5	13	19	11	11	11	11
26	2	27	9	13	19	13	13	13
31	26	9	27	11	13	19	16	16
16	31	26	11	27	16	16	19	19
2	16	31	26	16	27	21	21	21
9	9	16	31	26	21	27	26	26
11	11	11	16	31	26	26	27	27
21	21	21	21	21	31	31	31	31

Eight passes are required to sort the above list of numbers. No exchanges are made on pass eight and the algorithm terminates.

Number of Comparisons The number of comparisons for a bubble sort depends on the number of passes required to order the data. For each subsequent pass, there will be one less comparison than the preceding pass. The total number of comparisons is given by

$$(N-1) + (N-2) + (N-3) + \dots$$

and the number of terms represents the number of passes. There is a minimum of one pass and in this case the number of comparisons is $(N-1)$. In the worst case, there will be $N-1$ passes; so the maximum number of comparisons is $N(N-1)/2$ or the maximum number of comparisons is $O(N^2)$. An approximation of the expected number of comparisons is $N^2/2 - 3N/4$.

Number of Exchanges The number of exchanges varies with the degree to which a list is already ordered. There are no exchanges for an ordered list. The maximum number of exchanges occurs when a list is in reverse order; this produces an exchange for every comparison or $N(N-1)/2$ exchanges. The expected number of exchanges is half this, or $N(N-1)/4$.

Space Required This minimal-storage sorting algorithm requires storage space equal to the size of the list to be sorted.

7.2.1.2 *Quicksort*

The quicksort is a partition exchange sort and is one of the most efficient sorting algorithms in existence. The quicksort algorithm is inherently recursive.

The quicksort algorithm works as follows. A record in the list to be sorted is selected as the "pivot." After the sort's first phase, the pivot record occupies the position that it will occupy when the list is completely sorted. The records with key values smaller than the pivot record's key value precede it in the list and those records with key values greater than the pivot record's key value follow it in the list. Each record is compared against the pivot record and their positions are exchanged if the record's key value is larger and the record precedes the pivot record, or if the record's key value is less and the record follows the pivot record. This constitutes one phase of the quicksort.

The position of a pivot record at the end of a phase partitions a list into two sublists, each of which in turn must be sorted. If the pivot record's key value is a good approximation of the median of the list, then the two partitions will be about equal in size. If the pivot record's key value is the worst possible approximation of the median, then the partitions at the end of the first phase will be of lengths 1 and $N-1$.

These are several variations to the quicksort and they usually involve different methods for selecting the pivot record for each phase. Pivot selection determines the size of the partitions generated by a phase, and the method is optimum when each phase's pivot is the median of the partition to be sorted.

Quicksort Algorithm In Algorithm QUICKSORT given below, the pivot record is selected as the first record in a partition, and the smaller of the two partitions is processed in the next phase. The larger partition is stacked and sorted later. A partition is specified by the indexes (l and r) indicating its beginning and end. Processing the smaller of two partitions ensures that there will be no more than $\log_2 N$ partitions on the stack. Another sort algorithm for example, the bubble sort, may be combined with quicksort to sort partitions of length $\leq M$ (where M is some relatively small number). The bubble sort is a minimal-storage algorithm, and it is efficient for small sets of records, especially when they are partially ordered.

Algorithm QUICKSORT

1. [Initialize] $l \leftarrow 1, r \leftarrow N$.
2. [Sort partition $R_l \ldots R_r$] If $r < l + 1$, then go to Step 8; otherwise, $i \leftarrow l, j \leftarrow r, K \leftarrow K_l, R \leftarrow R_l$.
3. [Compare $K : K_j$] If $K < K_j$, then $j \leftarrow j - 1$ and repeat this step.
4. If $j \leq i$, then $R_i \leftarrow R$ and go to Step 7; otherwise, $R_i \leftarrow R_j$ and $i \leftarrow i + 1$.
5. [Compare $K_i : K$] If $K_i < K$, then $i \leftarrow i + 1$ and repeat this step.
6. If $j \leq i$, then $R_j \leftarrow R$ and $i \leftarrow j$; otherwise, $R_j \leftarrow R_i$, $j \leftarrow j - 1$ and go to Step 3.
7. [Push partition indicies on stack] If $r - i \geq i - l$, then push $(i + 1, r)$ on stack and $r \leftarrow i - 1$; otherwise, push $(l, i - 1)$ on the stack and $l \leftarrow i + 1$.
    Go to Step 2.
8. [Pop stack] If the stack is empty then exit; otherwise, remove the top entry $(l', r'), l \leftarrow l', r \leftarrow r'$ and go to Step 2.

Example

```
[19   13    5    27    1    26    31    16    2    9    11    21]
 i = 1                                            j=11 j=12
```

1st exchange

```
 11    13    5    27    1    26    31    16    2    9    19    21
      i=2  i=3  i=4                               j=11

 11    13    5    19    1    26    31    16    2    9    27    21
            i=4                           j=10
```

2nd exchange

```
 11    13    5    9    1    26    31    16    2    19    27    21
            i=5  i=6                      j=10
```

3rd exchange

```
 11    13    5    9    1    19    31    16    2    26    27    21
                 i=6                 j=9

 11    13    5    9    1    2    31    16    19    26    27    21
                          i=7          j=9
```

4th exchange

   11   13   5   9   1   2   19   16   31   26   27   21

                                     $i=7$ $j=8$

5th exchange

   [11   13   5   9   1   2   16]   19   [31   26   27   21]

                                       $j=8$

                                     $i=8$

Number of Comparisons   The expected number of comparisons ranges from $1.1N\lceil\log_2 N\rceil$ to $1.4N\lceil\log_2 N\rceil$, depending on pivit selection. The minimum number of comparisons occurs when the pivot selected is a perfect median every time; in this case, the number of comparisons is less then $N\lceil\log_2 N\rceil$. The maximum number of comparisons occurs when the pivot is the worst choice in each phase. When this occurs, only one valid partition is produced per phase and it is only one record smaller than the partition being sorted. An example of the worst case occurs when the records are already sorted and the pivot is selected as the first record in each partition. The number of comparisons in the worst case is $N(N-1)/2$. In order to protect against the worst case, a list of records may be randomly ordered prior to sorting.

Number of Exchanges   The number of exchanges is difficult to compute. There cannot be more exchanges than comparisons. An estimate of half the number of comparisons may be a reasonable guide.

Space Required   Algorithm QUICKSORT requires space for N records and a stack of size no greater than $\log_2 N$. Note that in the worst case, no stack is required.

7.2.2 Insertion Sorting

An insertion sorting algorithm places a new record into an already ordered list by traversing the list starting at the head until the proper position for the new record is found. The simplest insertion sort is linear insertion and it is the kind of sort used to insert cards into a bridge hand. The binary tree sort, described in Section 7.2.4 is usually referred to as a tree insertion sort and is a generalization of list insertion.

    Insertion sorting works as follows. The first record is placed in the first position in a list. The key value of the next record to be placed in the already ordered list is compared with the key value of the first record. If the key value of the new record is greater, it is positioned after the first record. Otherwise, the first record is moved to position 2 in the list and the new record is placed in position 1. All succeeding new records are compared to each record of the list in order from the first position until a higher key value is found. That higher record and all records of the list that follow it are then moved one position to the right. This operation makes available the position into which the new record is inserted.

Insertion Sort Algorithm   The value n is the number of records R_i that have already been sorted at any given time, and N is the number of records R'_j that are to be sorted.

Algorithm INSERTION_SORT

1. [Initialize] $R_1 \leftarrow R'_1, n \leftarrow 1$.
2. Repeat Steps 3, 4, and 5 for $i = 2, 3, \ldots, N$ and then exit.
3. $j \leftarrow 1$.
4. If $K'_i < K_j$, then for $l = n + 1, n, \ldots, j + 1$ do $R_l \leftarrow R_{l-1}$; otherwise, $j \leftarrow j + 1$ and if $j \leqslant n$, repeat Step 4.
5. $R_j \leftarrow R'_i, n \leftarrow n + 1$.

Example

The key values of the records to be sorted arrive in the order 19, 13, 5, 27, 1, 26, 31, 16, 2, 9, 11, 21.

Initial list:	19											
Add 13:	13	19										
Add 5:	5	13	19									
Add 27:	5	13	19	27								
Add 1:	1	5	13	19	27							
Add 26:	1	5	13	19	26	27						
Add 31:	1	5	13	19	26	27	31					
Add 16:	1	5	13	16	19	26	27	31				
Add 2:	1	2	5	13	16	19	26	27	31			
Add 9:	1	2	5	9	13	16	19	26	27	31		
Add 11:	1	2	5	9	11	13	16	19	26	27	31	
Add 21:	1	2	5	9	11	13	16	19	21	26	27	31

Number of Comparisons   The number of comparisons on any pass of an insertion sort is a function of the number of records in the sorted list. If the number of records to be placed in the list is N, then, in general, the expected number of records on the list at any given time is $N/2$. In the worst case, each new record will be placed at the end of the list and the expected number of comparisons in each pass is $N/2$. The worst case (for comparisons) occurs when the records arrive in sorted order. There are $N(N-1)/2$ comparisons in the worst case.

If records arrive in reverse order, only $N-1$ comparisons are required. If records arrive in random order, then one-half of the list will be searched before a higher key value is found. The expected number of comparisons in this case is $N(N-1)/4$ or $O(N^2)$.

Number of Data Movements   The minimum number of record movements, zero, occurs when records arrive in sorted order, and the maximum number of record movements occurs when records arrive in reverse order. In this latter case, the first record is moved $(N-1)$ times; the second record is moved $(N-2)$ times, etc. Thus, for $(N-1)$ records (the last record is not moved), there will be $N(N-1)/2$ record moves. When records arrive in random order, the expected number of moves is $N(N-1)/4$.

Space Required   The space required is equal to the number of records to be sorted.

7.2.3   Merge Sorting

In general, merging means combining two or more ordered lists (runs) into a single ordered list. The straight two-way merge sort algorithm is discussed in this section; it is typical of merge sort algorithms. The merge sort merges longer and longer runs until everything is merged into one list. Initially, all runs are of length one, and the first pass merges these N runs to form $\lceil N/2 \rceil$ runs of length two (if N is odd, the last run has only one record.) For simplicity, we assume that N is a power of 2. The first pass merges N runs of length one to form $N/2$ runs of length two. The second pass merges $N/2$ runs of length two to form $N/4$ runs of length 4. The number of runs and the size of runs after pass i are $N/2^i$ and 2^i, respectively.

   Another way to describe the merge sort is to picture it as a binary tree (see Figure 7.1) with runs of length one at the terminal nodes and the root as the final sorted list. The internal nodes are intermediate sorted runs.

Merge Sort Algorithm   As stated above, a merge sort algorithm merges longer and longer runs until everything is merged into one list. Algorithm MERGE_ LISTS given below merges two ordered lists $x_1 \le x_2 \le \ldots \le x_n$ and $y_1 \le y_2 \le \ldots \le y_n$ to produce the ordered list $z_1 \le z_2 \le \ldots \le z_{n+m}$. The remainder of the merge sort algorithm is left as an exercise to the reader.

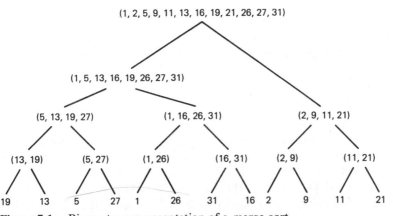

Figure 7.1.   Binary tree representation of a merge sort.

Algorithm MERGE_ LISTS

1. [Initialize] $i \leftarrow 1, j \leftarrow 1, k \leftarrow 1$.
2. [Find smallest element and output to z list]
   While ($i \leq n$ and $j \leq m$) do
      if $x_i \leq y_j$, then $z_k \leftarrow x_i$, $i \leftarrow i+1$, $k \leftarrow k+1$;
         otherwise, $z_k \leftarrow y_j$, $j \leftarrow j+1$, $k \leftarrow k+1$.
3. [Copy either the remainder of the x list or y list to the z list]
   If $i > n$ then $(z_k, \ldots, z_{n+m}) \leftarrow (y_j, \ldots, y_m)$;
      otherwise $(z_k, \ldots, z_{n+m}) \leftarrow (x_i, \ldots, x_n)$.
4. [Exit the algorithm] Exit.

Example

19	13	5	27	1	26	31	16	2	9	11	21

Pass 1 13 19 | 5 27 | 1   26 | 16   31 | 2   9 | 11   21

Pass 2 5 13 19 27 | 1   16   26   31 | 2   9   11   21

Pass 3 1   5   13   16   19   26   27   31 | 2   9   11   21

Pass 4 1   2   5   9   11   13   16   19   21   26   27   31

Number of Comparisons   The number of comparisons for a straight two-way merge is $O(N\log_2 N)$. This expression is derived from the fact that there are $\log_2 N$ passes (see the binary tree representation of the sort in Figure 7.1), and during every pass, each of the N records is involved in a comparison. There are N movements in each pass, but there are not always N comparisons because if one of two runs is completely moved, then the remainder of the other run is simply moved to the merge run with no comparisons involved. The expression $N\log_2 N$ therefore represents an upper bound for the number of comparisons.

The efficiency of the merge sort can be improved somewhat by using a linked list to represent each run. Merging is then performed by modifying links rather than moving records.

Space Required   The 2-way merge sort algorithm requires space for $2N$ records with only half of this space being used at any given time.

7.2.4   Binary Tree Sorting

The binary tree sort consists of two phases: a construction phase and a traversal phase. The construction phase consists of successively inserting new records into a binary tree according to the following rule. For each node X in a sorted tree, all key values in the left subtree of node X are less than the key value of node X and all key values in the nodes in the right subtree of node X are greater than or equal to the key value in node X. The tree is then traversed in postorder to produce a linear ordered list. The binary tree sort is particularly appealing because records can be added to a tree dynamically and one does not have to know, a priori, the number of records to be sorted.

Example   The key values of the records to be sorted are assumed to arrive in the order 19, 13, 5, 27, 1, 26, 31, 16, 2, 9, 11, 12.

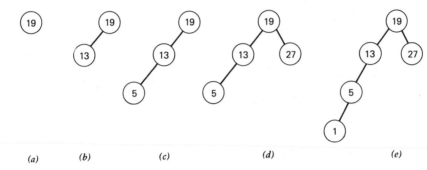

(a)   (b)   (c)   (d)   (e)

Finally,

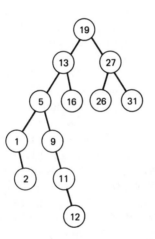

Binary Tree Sort Algorithm   An algorithm for creating a sort tree is essentially the same as Algorithm TREE_INSERT given in Section 4.3.1 for creating binary search trees. However, a sort tree can have records with identical key values. A complete binary tree sort algorithm includes a tree insertion algorithm and a tree linearizing algorithm.

Number of Comparisons   The closer a binary tree, created using algorithm TREE_INSERT, is to being a balanced tree, the less is its height and the fewer the number of comparisons required to insert a new record into the tree. The worst case occurs when the resulting tree is a degenerate tree. This occurs when the records to be sorted arrive either in ascending or descending order. The number of comparisons in the degenerate case is $N(N-1)/2$. The average number of comparisons along a degenerate path is $N/2$ and this occurs $(N-1)$ times. The best case occurs when a tree is balanced and the number of levels is $\log_2 N$. The number of comparisons in this case is $N\log_2 N - N$. The expected number of comparisons for a tree whose records arrive in random order is between $N(\log_2 N - 1)$ and $N(N-1)/2$.

Space Required   the space required by a binary tree sort algorithm is equal to the space required for the N records and the $2N$ pointers used to construct the tree.

7.2.5   A Comparison of the Internal Sorting Algorithms

The time and space complexities of the five internal sorting algorithms described earlier are given below in Table 7.1.

7.3   EXTERNAL SORTING

External sorting methods are applicable to files of data that are too large to wholly fit into internal memory during the sorting process. The internal sorting algorithms discussed earlier are impractical for external sorting. With external sorting, care must be taken to minimize the amount of time spent accessing external memory. The sorting problem changes from writing a very efficient sort procedure (for example, for internal sorting) to determining the proper balance between I/O and CPU utilization and blocking and buffering techniques.

The efficiency of an external sort is measured in terms of the total amount of time required to read, sort, and write all data records. The most common form of external sorting is the sort/merge. It consists of two separate phases: a sort phase and a merge phase. A sort phase distributes runs of records over two or more files that later provide input to the merge phase. The sort phase reads as much data as can be held in internal memory in a sort area and, using an internal sort routine, develops runs. The runs are then written onto two or more files stored in external memory. All data records in the input file are processed

Table 7.1

Time and Space Complexities of the Internal Sorting Algorithms

Method	Time (average)	Space
Bubble sort	$O(N^2)$	N
Linear insertion sort	$O(N^2)$	N
Quicksort	$O(N\log_2 N)$	$N + \log_2 N$
Binary tree sort	$O(N\log_2 N)$	$N(1 + 2p)$ (p is pointer space)
Straight 2-way merge sort	$O(N\log_2 N)$	$2N$

by the sort phase before the merge phase is undertaken. The primary purpose of a sort phase is to reduce the number of merge passes.

The merge phase is executed similarly to the merging of runs in the straight two-way internal merge sort. The efficiency of the merge phase is affected by the following sort phase-related items:

1. The number of runs produced by the sort phase.
2. The size of the runs and whether all runs are of the same size.
3. The blocking and buffering characteristics used during the sort phase.
4. The distribution of runs to files.

7.3.1 Sort Phase Considerations

The available storage for performing the sort phase must be split among:

1. An internal sort procedure.
2. A sort area.
3. The I/O procedures.
4. The I/O buffers.

The critical factors in determining the size of a sort area are the record size and the effect that run size has on the merge phase. In order to determine the impact of run length on the efficiency of the merge phase, it is important to know the number of records in a file because this can be used to determine how long runs should be to attain various merge phase efficiency levels. An initial run size, which is more or less controlled by the size of the sort area, is important because it determines the number of passes during the merge phase. The exact number of records to be sorted is often unknown and the number of initial runs must often be estimated.

The amount of memory required to support I/O activities, for example, I/O procedures and I/O buffers, is determined at the same time as an internal sort algorithm is selected and the size of the sort area is estimated. The blocking factor at both input and output and the degree of CPU-I/O overlap attainable with various buffer sizes and buffer techniques are important considerations in determining the memory area size to support I/O activities.

The output block length is determined by considerations in the design of the merge phase. The block length most efficient for the merge phase is the one that provides for the best balance of CPU-I/O overlap during the merge within the constraints of I/O device performance. If there are no overlap possibilities on the computer system for the sort phase, then all space can be assigned to the sort procedure and its sort area. In this case, the pattern of the sort procedure is to fill memory with input records, sort them, and then write the complete run using a block size appropriate for the merge phase.

Another important determination that must be made by the sort phase designer is the pattern in which runs will be distributed across files, that is, input files for the merge phase. There are two basic types of algorithms for distributing runs: balanced and unbalanced. A balanced distribution places an equal number of initial runs on each file. An unbalanced distribution places runs on files to achieve an ideal merge level (or as high a degree of efficiency as possible given the initial run length.)

7.3.2   The Balanced Two-Way Merge Sort

The balanced 2-way merge sort is described using a simple example. This example should clarify some of the comments made in Section 7.3.1 concerning sort area size and block size.

In this example the input file contains 7000 records $R_1, R_2, \ldots, R_{7000}$ and each record is 160 characters in length. The amount of memory available for the sort area limits the number of records that can be in internal memory at any given time to 1000. The sort phase creates initial runs of length 1000 and places them alternately on tapes 1 and 2 until the input is exhausted (see Figure 7.2). Then, tapes 1 and 2 are rewound and the runs merged from these two tapes, producing runs that are twice as long as the initial runs. The new runs produced are written alternately on tapes 3 and 4. Then all tapes are rewound and the contents of tapes 3 and 4 used to produce runs for tapes 1 and 2. This process continues until only one run is left (the entire sorted file). Each pass in the merge phase is illustrated in Figure 7.2.

It is probably apparent to the reader that the merge phase illustrated in Figure 7.2 is not the best way to handle sorting the 7000 records. The total number of records read and written (counting the creation of the initial distribution of runs) is 28,000 reads and 28,000 writes. Instead of going from pass 1 to pass 2 and rewinding all tapes, the first merging pass could have stopped after tapes 1, 3, and 4 contained:

Tape 1 $R_{6001-7000}$
Tape 3 $R_{1-2000}, R_{4001-6000}$
Tape 4 $R_{2001-4000}$

with tape 1 ready to read $R_{6001-7000}$. Then tapes 2, 3, and 4 could be rewound and a 3-way merge performed using the first run of tapes 1, 3, and 4. These runs would be merged onto tape 2. Then tape 2 could be rewound and merged with the final run on tape 3 to produce the final sorted tape, tape 1. The total number each of read and writes is 7000 + 6000 + 5000 + 5000 + 2000, or 25,000 reads and 25,000 writes.

Balanced merging can be generalized to T tapes, where $T \geq 3$. The number of tapes onto which the initial runs are distributed is P where $1 \leq P < T$. The runs are distributed as evenly as possible onto the P tapes and then a P-way merge is done. The choice of P usually turns out to be $\lceil T/2 \rceil$.

The 7000 records can be sorted using 5 tapes (that is, $T = 5$). The above merge sort can now be done more efficiently by distributing the runs as follows and performing a 4-way merge onto tape 5.

Sorting pass	Tape 1	$R_{1\text{-}1000}$, $R_{2001\text{-}3000}$, $R_{4001\text{-}5000}$, $R_{6001\text{-}7000}$
	Tape 2	$R_{1001\text{-}2000}$, $R_{3001\text{-}4000}$, $R_{5001\text{-}6000}$
	Tape 3	empty
	Tape 4	empty
Merge pass 1	Tape 1	empty
	Tape 2	empty
	Tape 3	$R_{1\text{-}2000}$, $R_{4001\text{-}6000}$
	Tape 4	$R_{2001\text{-}4000}$, $R_{6001\text{-}7000}$
Merge pass 2	Tape 1	$R_{1\text{-}4000}$
	Tape 2	$R_{4001\text{-}7000}$
	Tape 3	empty
	Tape 4	empty
Merge pass 3	Tape 1	empty
	Tape 2	empty
	Tape 3	$R_{1\text{-}7000}$
	Tape 4	empty

Figure 7.2. Merge phase of a balanced 2-way merge sort.

Tape 1 R_{1-1000}, $R_{4001-5000}$
Tape 2 $R_{1001-2000}$, $R_{5001-6000}$
Tape 3 $R_{2001-3000}$, $R_{6001-7000}$
Tape 4 $R_{3001-4000}$
Tape 5 empty

After the first runs on tapes 1, 2, 3, and 4 are merged onto tape 5 using a 4-way merge, the following tape configuration exists:

Tape 1 $R_{4001-5000}$
Tape 2 $R_{5001-6000}$
Tape 3 $R_{6001-7000}$
Tape 4 empty
Tape 5 R_{1-4000}

Next, rewind tapes 4 and 5 and perform a 4-way merge onto tape 4. The total number each of reads and writes is 7000 + 4000 + 7000 or 18,000 reads and 18,000 writes.

It should be clear from the two examples of merging given earlier that for tapes it is important to try to keep the number of reads and the amount of rewinding to a minimum. Reading tape backwards in some merges can avoid excessive rewinding; however, the merge sort algorithm must be capable of dealing with runs sorted in both ascending and descending orders.

The higher the order of merging, that is, the larger the value of P, the more computer processing time used, but this time is usually negligible compared to the time required to read, write, and rewind tapes.

The balanced 2-way merge sort does not try to optimize the distribution of initial runs to reduce the number of passes over the records; however, the polyphase merge sort, described in the next section, does distribute initial runs, in an unbalanced fashion, so that fewer passes over the data are required.

7.3.2.1 Analysis of Balanced Merge Sort

If s initial runs are produced during the internal sorting phase and if $2^{k-1} < s \le 2^k$ the balanced 2-way merge sort makes $k = \lceil \log_2 s \rceil$ merging passes over all the data. Notice that k is the same as the number of levels in a balanced binary tree with s nodes. One pass includes both reading and writing.

The first merge in a balanced 2-way merge produces $\lceil s/2 \rceil$ runs and the second merge produces $\lceil s/4 \rceil$ runs. Thus, if s is in the range $17 \le s \le 32$, there will be one distribution pass and five merge passes. If $s > 1$, then the total number of passes over all the data is $\lceil \log_2 s \rceil + 1$. In general, a balanced m-way merge using 2m tapes makes $\log_m s + 1$ passes over all the data. On the other hand, an m-way merge using $m+1$ tapes requires $\log_m s$ merge passes and $\log_m s - 1$ redistribution passes. So the total number of passes over the data, counting the initial distribution pass, is $2\log_m s$.

7.3.3 Polyphase Merge Sort

To make the polyphase merge sort work, a "perfect" Fibonacci distribution of runs must be on the tapes after each phase. For example, when the number of tapes T is 5, the following distributions of runs are generated (this table is called the distribution table).

Level	T1	T2	T3	T4	Total	Final output will be on:
0	1	0	0	0	1	T1
1	1	1	1	1	4	T5
2	2	2	2	1	7	T4
3	4	4	3	2	13	T3
4	8	7	6	4	25	T2
5	15	14	12	8	49	T1
6	29	27	23	15	94	T5

n	a_n	b_n	c_n	d_n	t_n	
$n+1$	$a_n + b_n$	$a_n + c_n$	$a_n + d_n$	a_n	$t_n + 3a_n$	

Before describing how these distributions are determined, we interpret how they are employed using the distribution table. If the total number of runs is 94 as given in the above table, then 29 runs are placed on T1, 27 on T2, 23 on T3, and 15 on T4. A 4-way merge is performed that requires six merge phases after the initial distribution. The maximum level number in the distribution table gives the number of merge phases to complete a sort; the final output tape is

Table 7.2

Polyphase Merge with 13 Runs

Phase	T1	T2	T3	T4	T5
1	1,1,1,1	1,1,1,1	1,1,1	1,1	
2	1,1	1,1	1		4,4
3	1	1		7	4
4			13		

determined by moving backward cyclically from tape 1. Each merge phase does not make a pass over all records; thus, a phase and pass are not the same thing. The fact that each phase does not pass over all data is the reason for the polyphase merge sort's improved performance over a balanced m-way merge, even when unnecessary copying is avoided in the m-way merge sort.

Two examples are given in merge Tables 7.2 and 7.3 to illustrate how a polyphase merge proceeds after the initial runs have been distributed. In Table 7.2, there are 13 initial runs of length one (indicated by a 1 in Phase 1 of the table). The distribution of runs is 4, 4, 3, 2 on tapes T1, T2, T3, and T4, respectively. In Table 7.3 there are 25 initial runs of length one.

At the end of phase 2 in Table 7.2, there are two runs of length one on tapes T1 and T2, one run of length one on T3, T4 is empty, and T5 contains two runs of length four. The number of merge phases in Table 7.2 is three (phase one is the initial distribution) and the sorted list of records is on tape T3. If the reader computes the initial distributions for the case of 13 runs, the maximum level number in the distribution table is three and the final output tape is tape T3.

In the polyphase merge illustrated in Table 7.2 not all of the records are processed in each merge phase. For example, in phase 1, 13/13 of the records are read; in phase 2 only 8/13 of the records are read; 7/13 in phase 3 and 13/13 in phase 4. This amounts to 3 2/13 passes or slightly over three complete passes over all records. A balanced 2-way merge using four tapes would make five passes over the records (including the distribution pass).

Table 7.3

Polyphase Merge with 25 Runs

Phase	T1	T2	T3	T4	T5
1	1,1,1,1,1,1,1,1	1,1,1,1,1,1,1	1,1,1,1,1,1	1,1,1,1	
2	1,1,1	1,1,1	1,1		4,4,4,4
3	1,1	1		7,7	4,4
4	1		13	7	4
5		25			

If $P = T-1$, that is, a P-way merge with T tapes, the polyphase merge distributions for T tapes correspond to p^{th} order Fibonacci numbers (the value of p is P). The pth order Fibonacci numbers $F_n^{(p)}$ are defined by the rules:

$$F_n^{(p)} = F_{n-1}^{(p)} + F_{n-2}^{(p)} + \ldots + F_{n-p}^{(p)} \text{ for } n \geq p$$

$$F_n^{(p)} = 0 \text{ for } 0 \leq n \leq p - 2; \quad F_{p-1}^{(p)} = 1$$

When $p = 2$, this is the usual Fibonacci sequence defined by $F_{n+1} = F_n + F_{n-1}$ where $F_0 = 0$ and $F_1 = 1$. In the nth level distribution, the kth tape, for $1 \leq k \leq P$, gets

$$F_{n+p-2}^{(p)} + F_{n+p-3}^{(p)} + \ldots + F_{n+k-2}^{(p)}$$

initial runs. For example, when $T = 5$ and $P = 4$, tape 3 on level 3 gets three runs. The number of runs on each tape at level n and the total number of runs can be computed by the expressions for a_n, b_n, c_n, d_n, and t_n given in the last line of the above distribution table. A general expression for the total number of initial runs on all tapes is

$$T_n = pF_{n+p-2}^{(p)} + (p-1) F_{n+p-3}^{(p)} + \ldots + F_{n-1}^{(p)}$$

When the number of runs, s, is not exactly equal to one of the T_n then $T_n - s$ artificial dummy runs are added, and s is assumed to be perfect.

An analysis of the polyphase merge sort is more complex than for the balanced m-way merge sort. A detailed analysis can be found in Knuth (see the reference list at the end of this chapter).

EXERCISES

1. Suppose you are doing an insertion sort on a sequential file that initially has 100 records. You are going to insert 100 new records during the sort. What is the expected number of records that must be passed over in the sequential file in finding the proper location for each insertion? (Do not worry about how the data are moved over to accommodate each insertion.) Compute your answer as an expected value averaged over all the insertions.

2. Consider doing an insertion sort on a hypothetical device (using a hypothetical file structure) with the following characteristic: the cost (in terms of performance as measured by the number of basic operations such as addition) to insert an item into a list is $2k+3$, where k is the number of items already in the list. Derive an expression for the cost (in similar operations) for an insertion sort of n items. To get started, use n as the cost to look at every item in the unsorted list. Use a linear search of the k items already sorted, to find where to insert each new item.

3. Sort the following list of key values using the bubble sort:

   83 64 72 86 14 28 37 94 108 33 17 24 14

   Choose a data structure to represent the set of key values that will make the bubble sort as efficient as possible. The expected number of exchanges for the bubble sort is $N(N-1)/4$. Does your choice of data structure reduce the number of exchanges? If so, does it increase the storage requirements?

4. Sort the list of key values in Exercise 3 using the Quicksort algorithm twice. First, use the first key value in a partition as the pivot and second, use the median of the partition as the pivot. Which pivot selection produced the most efficient sort? Explain your answer.

5. The expected number of moves in an insertion sort is $N(N-1)/4$ when key values arrive in random order. Describe a data structure for representing lists of key values to be sorted by an insertion sort that can decrease the number of moves.

6. Complete the remainder of the merge sort algorithm using the MERGE_ LISTS algorithm (see Section 7.2.3).

7. Rewrite Algorithm TREE_INSERT in Section 4.3.1 so that it can be used in a binary tree sort algorithm. Develop a tree linearizing algorithm that can be used as the second part of the binary tree sort algorithm.

8. Develop a balanced 2-way merge sort algorithm that takes advantage of reading a tape backwards.

9. Determine the distribution table corresponding to Table 7.3, that is, develop the distribution table for a 4-way polyphase merge on 5 tapes with 25 runs.

10. Obtain the distribution table for a 2-way polyphase merge on 3 tapes assuming 987 runs. Show the polyphase merge for this merge sort.

11. Develop algorithms and programs for performing a balanced 2-way merge sort and use it to merge two sorted input files.

REFERENCES

7.1 Lorin, H. *Sorting and Sort Systems,* Addison-Wesley, Reading, Massachusetts, 1975, 373 pages.

7.2 Knuth, D.E. *Sorting and Searching,* Vol. III, Addison-Wesley, Reading, Massachusetts, 1973, 723 pages.

These two books provide more than adequate coverage of file sorting algorithms.

7.3 Martin, W.A. "Sorting," *ACM Computing Surveys,* Vol. 3, December 1971, pp. 147–174.

A comprehensive survey of sorting algorithms is given.

Protection

8.1 INTRODUCTION

One of the functions of an operating system is to protect a computer system's resources from unauthorized users and uses. This function is usually fulfilled by two protection mechanisms: an identification/authentication mechanism and an access control mechanism. An identification/authentication mechanism verifies a user's claimed identity, and it is designed to prevent unauthorized users from gaining access to a computer system. This mechanism can be considered a "front end" protection mechanism. An access control mechanism is normally located in the file system component of an operating system. When an authenticated user attempts to access a file, the request is mediated by the access control mechanism. The access control mechanism determines whether the user is authorized to access the file in the way that he requests. An access control mechanism can be considered a "back end" protection mechanism.

The term *protection* refers to all mechanisms in an operating system that control the access of users and programs executing on the behalf of users to stored information. On the other hand, *security* is a general concept that deals with preventing users from accessing and modifying data in unauthorized ways by utilizing protection mechanisms internal to a system and physical security measures such as locking doors to rooms filled with computer terminals, etc.

In discussing protection, it is convenient to think of a system as having subjects (for example, users and processes) that require access to objects. In general, an object can be any resouce within a computer system. In this chapter, however, the subjects of interest are users, and the objects of interest are files. A more general discussion of protection and security is outside the scope of this chapter.

An important topic that arises when protection and security in computer systems are discussed is the relationship between mechanism and policy. *Security policy* is defined as a statement of the rules that describe how the security requirements of a community of users can be fulfilled. The relationship between mechanism and policy is: a protection mechanism enforces a security policy. After various types of identification/authentication and access control mechanisms are discussed, two types of security policies, discretionary and nondiscretionary (or mandatory), are discussed.

8.2 IDENTIFICATION/AUTHENTICATION MECHANISMS

As stated earlier, an identification/authentication mechanism verifies a user's claimed identity. The mechanisms discussed below are satisfactory for use in situations in which a user is trying to gain access to a computer system from a computer terminal. Authentication mechanisms, however, can be used in other environments. For example, fingerprint matching and voice control are useful as security measures to control access to restricted buildings or restricted areas of buildings.

8.2.1 Passwords

One of the most common identification/authentication techniques involves using passwords. With this technique, a user specifies his user identification (or the user identification of the user that he claims to be) to the system. The computer system requests that the user input a password to prove that he is the user that he says he is. To implement a password authentication scheme, the system maintains a list of user identifier-password pairs. The user must supply the password corresponding to the user identifier that he used during log in, or he is denied further access to the system and its resources.

The list of passwords is a resource of the system that must be protected. If an intruder gains access to the password list, then he has easy access to information stored in the computer system. In some systems, passwords are transformed using a transformation, which is hard to duplicate, before being stored. When a user provides his password, the system transforms it and compares this transformed password with the stored transformed version. The transformation technique reduces the chances that someone who gains access to the password list can use it to access another user's data.

Passwords have some serious defects. The most common defect involves the process of choosing passwords. If a user chooses his own password, he usually chooses something easy to remember, for example, he derives a password from his name. For this reason, some systems have programs that generate, in a random manner, passwords. These passwords are then assigned to users. In some situations, all passwords are frequently changed. But frequently changed passwords involving random sequences of letters are difficult to remember; thus, users tend to make written copies of their passwords. This exposure of a password invites compromise.

Another basic defect of passwords is that a password may be seen by others when it is used. This has lead to situtions where a password is valid for only one use. In this case, a user has a list of passwords and he crosses each one off the list as it is used. Other attempts to limit the period of usefulness of a compromised password have lead to attaching an expiration date or usage count to passwords. Passwords may also be exposed in a more subtle way than via typing at a terminal. A password is sent through a communication system and a wiretapper may be able to intercept it during this passage.

Another problem with passwords is that their use is based on secrecy. An alternative approach to secrecy that has been successfully used for interactive users is unforgeability. A user is given a difficult-to-fabricate plastic card that is coded with his password. The terminal has a code transmitter device that reads the code and forwards the code to the computer system. The code is treated as the user's password. Anyone who gains access to the plastic coded card may, however, compromise the system. Other techniques that have been used and are more difficult to forge than coded cards are fingerprint readers and signature readers.

A problem common to both the password and unforgeable object approaches is that authentication is only one-way. They do not authenticate the computer system to the user. A computer can be programmed to "act like" the computer system that a user has intended to use. To do this, an intruder intercepts all communications to and from the user's terminal and directs them to a computer program under his control. The intruder's program asks the user to input his password. Once the intruder has the password, he terminates communication with the user's terminal by issuing a common error message. The user never suspects that his password has been stolen.

8.2.2   Encryption

Another authentication technique that has received some use is encryption. An encryption device scrambles input signals from a terminal and this encrypted information is communicated to the computer system. The exact encrypted signals are determined by the value of a transformation key. Different keys produce different encrypted signals. In order for the computer system receiving the encrypted signals to decipher (understand) them, it must have a deciphering device that uses the same key as the encrypting device.

Encryption is normally used in unprotected communications systems to provide a degree of security. However, encryption can be used for authentication in the following manner. The user bypasses the enciphering device on his terminal by sending his identifier unencrypted to the computer system. The system uses the identifier to determine a secret transformation key. The computer system loads this key into its enciphering device and attempts to communicate with the user. At the same time, the user loads his copy of the transformation key into his terminal's enciphering device. If the user's key and the computer system's key are identical, the user can communicate intelligibly with the system. If the user and the computer system can communicate intelligibly, then the system is certain of the identity of the user and the user is certain of the identity of the computer.

8.3 A PROTECTION MODEL

In this section a simple model is briefly described in which access control mechanisms are viewed. The assumption here is that data of interest to users are stored in mutually exclusive files. Conceptually, then, it is necessary to: (1) build an impenetrable wall around each distinct file that warrants separate protection; (2) construct a door in the wall through which access can be obtained; and (3) post a guard at the door to control its use.

The guard must have some way of knowing which users are authorized to have access and each user must have some reliable way of identifying himself to the guard. This authority check is usually implemented by requiring that the guard demand a match between something he knows and something the prospective user possesses. Figure 8.1 illustrates two possible approaches. In the first protection mechanism (Figure 8.1a), the user presents his unique USERID to the guard along with his request. The guard examines the list to determine if the USERID is included in the list. If not, the request is disallowed. If the USERID appears on the list, the guard then determines if the

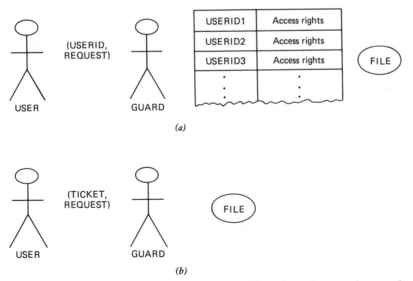

Figure 8.1. Two models of protection. (a) List-oriented protection mechanism. (b) Ticket- (or capability-) oriented protection mechanism.

user has the right to perform the requested operation on the object being guarded. If so, the user's request is allowed; otherwise, the request is denied.

In the ticket- (or capability-) oriented protection mechanism illustrated in Figure 8.1b, a user presents a capability along with an operation request to the guard. A capability is assumed to contain a set of access rights to a file and a reference to the file. The possession of a capability to the file is evidence that the user has access to the file; however, the guard must determine if the requested operation is in the rights list of the user's capability.

8.4 ACCESS CONTROL MECHANISMS

Once a user gains access to a system (that is, he is authenticated), he normally tries to use the resources of the system to do work. One of the important resources of the system is data stored in files on external storage devices. Access requests to data can occur via application programs executing in internal memory or via users working at a terminal and submitting requests using an interactive command (or query) language. An access control mechanism functions in essentially the same manner regardless of how an access request originates. Figure 8.2 illustrates the potential sources of access requests.

Each request for data, regardless of how the request originates, has a unique user id (USERID) associated with it. An interactive user supplies his USERID when he logs onto the system and an application program has the USERID of the user on whose behalf the program is executing. When requests for data, either to retrieve it or to update it, are made, a USERID is assumed to be attached to the request.

The access control mechanisms discussed in this section are designed to protect the data in files from unauthorized users. The protection models

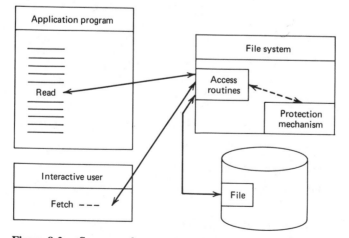

Figure 8.2. Sources of access requests.

illustrated in Figure 8.1 are typical of the mechanisms used by file systems to control access to stored data. The control mechanism at the gate, referred to as a guard in Figure 8.1, must allow only authorized users to access the file he is guarding. Sometimes the control mechanism is also referred to as a *protection monitor*. In addition to checking the identity of the user or program that is attempting an access, the protection monitor can also examine data in cases where access control is data-dependent.

To control access attempts, a protection monitor is logically located in the path between a user and a file. The monitor can be local to a file; that is, each file has its own protection monitor. Normally, it is inefficient for each file to have its own monitor to enforce protection. An alternative approach (and the normal approach) uses a central protection monitor in the file system that mediates all access attempts to files in the file system. However, since each access is mediated by a single protection monitor, this approach may generate a bottleneck in the system.

8.4.1 Protection Status Model

The protection status of a system can be abstractly described by using a simple matrix model. At any given time there is a set of users (U), each with a unique USERID, and a set of files (F). The protection status is described by the mapping

$$M: U \times F \rightarrow A$$

where A is a set of access rights.* The protection status is dynamic. Users and files are continually created, deleted, and changed. If the mapping M depends only on the identity of U and F, then the protection status can be described as an *access control matrix* with rows associated with users and columns associated with files. If $u \in U$ and $f \in F$, then rights(u, f) is an element in the matrix. In this chapter this set of rights is referred to as

rights(USERID, FILE)

where USERID is the unique identifier of a user $u \in U$ and FILE is the symbolic file name of a file $f \in F$.

An access control matrix is illustrated in Figure 8.3. The rows are associated with user identifiers and the columns are associated with symbolic file names. For example, rights(USERID2, D) = {copy, delete}. An access control matrix gives the access specifications of users to files, and it is used by the file system to enforce access controls in sharing schemes.

A file system normally does not keep a copy of the access control matrix because the matrix is usually sparse and the storage of a sparse matrix in the

---

*A right is represented by the name of the operation that it allows to be performed on the object. Typical operations that can be exercised on files are read, write, modify, delete, and copy.

File Name / Userids	A	B	C	D	...
USERID1	read, write		copy, read		...
USERID2	write, delete			copy, delete	...
USERID3			delete, write		...
. . .					

Figure 8.3. An access control matrix.

form suggested by Figure 8.3 would waste storage space. The matrix could be stored as 3-field entries in a table. The fields are

(user identifier, filename, access rights)

For example, the portion of the access control matrix illustrated in Figure 8.3 could be stored as illustrated in Figure 8.4. This representation of the matrix also wastes space because only a small percentage of the entries in the table are

User Identifier	File Name	Access Rights
USERID1	A	read, write
USERID1	B	
USERID1	C	copy, read
USERID1	D	
USERID2	A	delete, write
USERID2	B	
USERID2	C	
USERID2	D	copy, delete
USERID3	A	
USERID3	B	
USERID3	C	delete, write
USERID3	D	

Figure 8.4. Table representation of the access control matrix in Figure 8.3.

being used at any given time. While each user may potentially have access to every file under the control of a file system, in practice this is unrealistic. Thus, alternatives for representing the access control matrix are sought.

Two alternatives are:

1. Store the access rights with a file, that is, store the access control matrix, column by column, in access control lists; the entries in an access control list are of the form $(u, M(u, f))$.

2. Store the access rights with the user, that is, store the matrix row by row, with each element in a row stored in a simple data structure called a capability.

To place these two implementations of an access control matrix in the proper perspective, alternative one is often referred to as a *list-oriented* (or access control list) implementation, and it corresponds to the protection model in Figure 8.1*a*. The second alternative is referred to as a *capability-oriented* implementation, and it corresponds to the protection model in Figure 8.1*b*. A capability contains a set of access rights to a file and a reference to the file (the reference is indicated by the symbolic file name). The structure of a capability is illustrated in Figure 8.5.

With respect to the access control matrix in Figure 8.3, the access control list stored with file A would contain the two entries

USERID1, {read, write}

USERID2, {delete, write}

For the second alternative suggested above, the user with user identifier USERID2 owns the two capabilities

delete, write	A

copy, delete	D

8.4.2 List-Oriented Implementation

As was stated earlier, with a list-oriented implementation of an access control matrix, the protection information is stored with the file itself. The access control list for the file contains a list of identifiers of authorized users and the access rights for each authorized user. When an access request to a file is made, the list is checked by the protection monitor to determine if the USERID attached to the request is on the list. If the USERID is on the list, then the protection monitor checks to determine if the user possesses the right

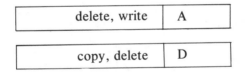

access rights	reference to file

Figure 8.5. Capability structure.

necessary to perform the requested operation. In a controlled sharing environment, the access control list for a shared file must contain the USERIDs of all users who have access to the file.

An example of how access control lists are employed is given below. Suppose user $U1$ is executing procedure A and procedure A is attempting to read file F. The entry for file F in $U1$'s directory contains a pointer to the access control list for file F. The file system uses the pointer to locate the access control list, and the protection monitor determines that the read right is contained in rights($U1$, F). Associated with file F's access control list is a pointer to the physical location of F. The access control list for F and the pointer giving the location of F are normally part of the data stored in a file descriptor (see Chapter 6).

8.4.3 Capability-Oriented Implementation

A capability contains a set of access rights to a file and a reference to the file (see Figure 8.5). In a capability-oriented system, a user is authorized to access a file if he holds a capability to the file. A capability references a file by its symbolic name and the file system maps the file name via a directory to its physical address.

When a user desires access to a file, a capability is presented, on behalf of the user, to the protection monitor via the file system along with the operation to be performed on the file. The protection monitor compares the operation request with the access rights in the capability to ensure that the user has been authorized use of the operator. If access is allowed, then the file name in the capability is used to obtain the physical address of the file and the access request is realized.

The primary differences between capabilities and access control lists can be described as follows:

1. Employing capabilities is analogous to passing out keys for a door and everyone with the correct key may enter.
2. Using access control lists is analogous to having a guard stand at the door with a list of all he will allow to pass through the door.

8.4.4 Modifying Access Specifications

An access control matrix, regardless of how it is actually implemented, is usually dynamic in a file system with files being added, modified, and deleted. This means that access control lists and capabilities must be modifiable. While capabilities are more efficient to use during retrieval requests, access control lists are easier to modify when the authorization specifications must be altered.

Access specification modification is discussed below with respect to:

1. Granting access rights.
2. Revoking access rights.

8.4.4.1   *Granting Access Rights*

The granting of access rights occurs when a programmer such as programmer *A* wishes to allow programmer *B* to access a file *F* owned by *A*. Some security policies do not allow a user to grant more rights than he holds and the grantor must have the USERID of the grantee. When access control lists are used to implement protection, *A* tells the file system protection monitor to add *B* to the list for *F* and give *B* certain access rights such as read, copy, etc. Programmer *A* must obtain programmer *B*'s USERID and *B* must obtain the name of the file, namely *F*.

The problem of granting access is more complex in a capability-based system. If programmer *A* can cause a capability to be written into programmer *B*'s directory, then obviously *A* has the power to overwrite any capability in *B*'s directory. On the other hand, if *B* can read a capability directly from *A*'s directory, then *B* can probably read *A*'s remaining capabilities. A mailbox type operation can be used to protect both programmers involved in the granting of access.

The mailbox scheme consists of three steps:

1. *A* and *B* exchange identifiers by some path that is outside the protection monitor.
2. *A* gives *B*'s identifier to a job running with *A*'s identifier and has the job transmit the capability to *B* by placing it in the mailbox that is designated for *B*.
3. *B* gives *A*'s identifier to a job that looks in the mailbox to find a capability labeled as coming from *A*.

Anyone who has a capability for a file can give the capability to another programmer.

8.4.4.2   *Revoking Access Rights*

The dynamic modification of access specifications also includes the ability to revoke access to a file. With an access control list, anyone who can modify the list can remove the identification of a user from the list, blocking further access. Revoking access in a capability system is much trickier. A user does not have access to a capability given away and may not even know how many copies of the capability have been made. Thus, in general, capability-based systems do not aid in the revocation of access.

Revocation of access in a capability-based system can be performed if indirect capabilities are used. In this case, a user does not give a copy of a capability to a file to other users; instead, a capability to the capability for the file is given. Now, the original owner of the capability retains control over the only capability to the file and can revoke all access to the file by destroying his capability.

8.4.5   Access Control Mechanism Implementation Issues

Several important differences exist between the access control list and capability-oriented implementations of access control matrices. The list-oriented protection mechanism requires that the protection monitor examine an access control list at the time access is requested. This implies that some kind of associative search must accompany each access to a file. Because associative matching is slow unless associative memory is used to hold access control lists (this possibility is not always practical because of the relatively high cost of associative memory), various methods have been suggested to reduce the overhead incurred by the protection monitor while checking an access control list. One way is to check the list only on the first access to a file. If access is permitted, some form of a temporary pointer is given to the program accessing the file. This temporary pointer directly accesses the file without the protection monitor checking the access control list, but the program is not allowed to keep the pointer between invocations. The result of utilizing the temporary pointer is a hybrid system with the power of access control lists and the speed of capabilities. The temporary pointer scheme is practical only in situations where a user's rights to a particular file are not altered during the execution lifetime of the program making the request.

As another expansion to access control list systems, it is helpful to place a number of users into a group and provide equal access to each member of the group. In this case, a university professor may want to allow all students in his class to use a single data file. The professor does not want to place the entire class in the access control list only to have to change the list for the next quarter. Users can be grouped by adding one or more identifiers onto the user identifier field, both in the access control list and the USERID that is associated with each process. When checking the access control list, the protection monitor looks for either a USERID match or a GROUPID match.

Since checking access control lists may be slow and a bottleneck, list-oriented implementations are not often used in situations where the number of access requests is high. On the other hand, capability-oriented mechanisms typically require considerable technology to control the forgery of capabilities and to control passing capabilities around from one user to another.

As a rule, most real systems contain both kinds of sharing implementations: a list-oriented system at the human interface and a capability-oriented system in the underlying implementation. This kind of arrangement is accomplished by providing at the higher level a list-oriented protection monitor whose only purpose is to assign temporary capabilities that the lower level (capability-oriented) protection monitors will honor.

The degenerate cases of list- and capability-oriented systems are as follows. In a list-oriented system, if each protection monitor's list of authorized users can contain only one entry, then a complete isolation kind of protection system exists in which no sharing of information among users can take place. Similarly, in a capability-oriented system, if there can be only one capability for each file in the system, a complete isolation kind of protection system exists.

8.5 DISCRETIONARY AND NONDISCRETIONARY SECURITY POLICIES

As stated earlier, two types of security policies may be enforced by the protection mechanisms in an operating system: discretionary and nondiscretionary (or mandatory). Almost all operating systems enforce some type of discretionary security policy. Only recently, however, have manufacturers at the urging of the Department of Defense begun to consider the problem of enforcing mandatory security policy in commercial operating systems. The access control mechanisms described in Section 8.4 are suitable for enforcing discretionary security policies; however, they must be augmented to handle mandatory security policies.

8.5.1 Discretionary Security Policy

In most discretionary security policies, the owner or creator of a file determines who should be granted access to a file and the access rights that the grantees should have. That is, the process of granting access to a file remains at the discretion of the owner of the file. In some policies, the owner can grant owner status to another user, thus allowing the new owner to grant access to the file at his discretion. In this type of policy, the owner of a file also has the right to revoke the access rights previously granted to any other user. Typical discretionary access rights that can be granted by the owner of a file include: read, write, copy, delete, etc.

Another common discretionary security policy utilizes two privileges referred to as grant and revoke. The creator of a file automatically receives the two privileges. The policy prohibits a user from granting access rights unless he holds the grant privilege himself; in addition, the policy may prohibit him from granting more rights than he holds. A user who has the grant privilege can give this privilege to another user. The holder of the revoke privilege can revoke access rights; however, the security policy may allow the revoker to revoke only those access rights that he has granted.

The implementation of a mechanism suitable for enforcing the first discretionary security policy discussed above can be relatively simple. The second security policy involving the grant and revoke privileges will require a more complex mechanism. One of the references (Griffiths and Wade) at the end of this chapter describes the implementation of mechanisms suitable for enforcing this type of discretionary security policy.

8.5.2 Nondiscretionary Security Policy

The best known nondiscretionary security policy is the Department of Defense (DoD) security policy. With a nondiscretionary security policy, access to a file is not left to the discretion of the creator of the file. The owner of a file cannot arbitrarily grant access to anyone that he desires; instead, a user gains access to a file based on a predetermined system-wide, mandatory policy.

Each file in a computer system (that enforces a mandatory security policy) has a security tag associated with it. The security tag contains the classification of the file determined by a security officer according to the sensitivity of the data in the file. In the military classification system, classification is defined as the pair

$$(security\ level,\ category)$$

The security levels are taken from the list TOP SECRET, SECRET, CONFIDENTIAL, and UNCLASSIFIED and they are ordered as follows:

$$TOP\ SECRET > SECRET > CONFIDENTIAL > UNCLASSIFIED$$

Category is defined as a set (possibly empty) of compartments. Compartments have no ordering but subsets of compartments are ordered by set inclusion. Tagging a file with a set of one or more compartments indicates that the file contains data that should be visible to only a subset of those users cleared to the security level of the data. Compartmentalization is a form of need-to-know.

Each user has a clearance that is also defined as the pair

$$(security\ level,\ category)$$

Users have clearances and files have classifications. Security classes comprised of security levels and categories form a lattice with the partial ordering relation "$\geq$". For clearances $X = (SL1, C1)$ and $Y = (SL2, C2)$, $X \geq Y$ if and only if $SL1 \geq SL2$ and set $C1$ contains set $C2$. A user with clearance W is allowed to access a file with classification Z if and only if $W \geq Z$.

The DoD security policy contains two rules: the simple security rule and the *-property (pronounced star property). The simple security rule prohibits a user from "reading up"; that is, it prohibits a user from reading a file that has a classification higher than the user's clearance. The *-property prevents a user from "writing down." This means that if a user is logged onto the system with clearance X, then he cannot write data into a file with classification W when $W < X$. The intent of the *-property is to prevent the disclosure of information to those who are not cleared to access it. If the *-property is not enforced, then a user with security level SECRET could copy a file with SECRET classification to a file with CONFIDENTIAL classification. Thus, users with a CONFIDENTIAL clearance could effectively gain access to SECRET information.

The DoD lattice model can be adapted to many commercial security requirements. The category can be used to compartmentalize information within a company. Compartments for accounting, shipping, personnel, research, manufacturing, etc., are possible. Security levels are also useful in commercial applications. Proprietary (or classified) documents are frequently generated in business activities.

8.6 SUMMARY

Regardless of the type of computer system, the usefulness of a set of protection mechanisms depends upon the ability of a system to prevent security violations. Security violations are usually placed into three categories:

1. *Unauthorized release of information*—An authorized user is able to read and take advantage of information stored in the computer by releasing it to unauthorized people.
2. *Unauthorized information modification*—An unauthorized person is able to make changes in stored information by bypassing the protection mechanisms.
3. *Unauthorized denial of use*—An intruder can prevent an authorized user from using or modifying information even though the intruder may not be able to access or modify the information.

In the third category, an intruder may tie up system resources, cause a system crash, or disrupt service in other ways.

In practice, producing a system at any level of functionality that actually does prevent all security violations is extremely difficult, if not impossible. Design and implementation flaws often provide paths that permit access controls to be circumvented. These flaws are usually in the form of operating system code segments that are incorrect. Experience has provided some useful principles that can guide the design and contribute to an implementation without security flaws. Below are seven design principles that apply to protection mechanisms:

1. Economy of mechanism—Keep the design as simple and small as possible; otherwise, unwanted access paths may develop because of large amounts of code.
2. Base access decisions on permission rather than exclusion—The protection scheme identifies conditions under which access is permitted.
3. Every access to every object must be authorized.
4. Open design—The design should not be secret; the protection mechanisms should not depend on the ignorance of potential attackers.
5. Separation of privilege—When feasible, a protection mechanism that requires two keys is more flexible than one that allows access to the presenter of only a single key.

6. Least privilege—Every program and every user of the system should operate using the least set of privileges necessary to complete the job; primarily, this principle limits the damage that can result from an accident or error.
7. Psychological acceptability—The human interface must be designed for ease of use, so that users routinely and automatically apply the protection mechanisms correctly.

Another design principle that applies to computer systems involves something referred to as the "work factor." The work factor involves comparing the cost of circumventing a mechanism with the resources of a potential intruder. For example, the number of experiments needed to try all possible 5-letter alphabetic passwords is $26^5 = 11,881,376$. If a potential intruder tries to enter each possible password at a terminal, one might consider a 5-letter password adequate. On the other hand, if the intruder could use a computer capable of generating and trying millions of passwords per second, a 5-letter password would be a minor barrier.

EXERCISES

1. What protection is afforded on the computer system that you use for controlling access to system resources such as files?
2. For the computer system in Exercise 1, where is the protection enforcing mechanism that mediates accesses to files located?
3. Write a report describing the authorization and protection mechanisms available in the System R database management system.
4. Using your computer system, determine three possible ways that you can violate the security of the system, that is, gain access to resources for which you have not been authorized access. This type of study is referred to as a "penetration study."
5. This chapter briefly addresses the topic of Department of Defense (DoD) security policy. Write a short paper describing DoD security policy.
6. What is a security kernel?
7. Security and integrity are two concepts that are closely related. Discuss the relationship between them.
8. List some hardware architectural features that appear to be important for implementing an operating system with a relatively high degree of security.
9. Describe how a capability-based system such as CAP or SWARD enforces security.

REFERENCES

8.1   Hoffman, L.J. "Computers and Privacy: A Survey," *ACM Computing Surveys,* Vol. 1, June 1969, pp. 85–103.

This tutorial-level paper surveys the problem of access control and privacy in computer systems. Some suggested legal and administrative safeguards are given.

8.2 Lampson, B.W. "Protection," *Operating Systems Review,* Vol. 8, January 1974, pp. 18–24.

Presents some abstract models for protection systems.

8.3 Saltzer, J.H., and Schroeder, M.D. "The Protection of Information in Computer Systems," *Proceedings of the IEEE,* Vol. 63, September 1975, pp. 1278–1308.

Excellent review of protection mechanisms in computer systems. Much of the material in this chapter is based on this paper.

8.4 Denning, D.E. and Denning, P.J. "Data Security," *ACM Computing Surveys,* Vol. 11, September 1979, pp. 227–249.

Internal security mechanisms, how they work, and their inherent limitations are discussed. This is a good, easy-to-read introduction to protection and security concepts.

8.5 Needhan, R.M. and Walker, R.D.H. "The Cambridge CAP Computer and Its Protection System," *Proceedings of 6th Symposium on Operating Systems Principles,* in *Operating Systems Review,* Vol. 11, November 1977, pp. 1–10.

8.6 Wulf, W.A., et al. "HYDRA: the Kernel of a Multiprocessor Operating System," *Commun. ACM,* Vol. 17, No. 6, June 1974, pp. 337–345.

8.7 Feiertag, R.J. and Neumann, P.G. "The Foundations of a Provably Secure Operating System (PSOS)," *Proceedings of 1979 NCC,* Vol. 48, pp. 329–334.

These three papers describe attempts to develop operating systems potentially capable of providing a high degree of security.

8.8 Neumann, P.G. "Computer System Security Evaluation," *Proceedings of 1978 NCC,* Vol. 47, pp. 1087–1095.

8.9 Lipner, S.B. "A Panel Session—Security Kernels," *Proceedings of 1974 NCC,* Vol. 43, pp. 973–980.

8.10 Linden, T.A. "Operating System Structures to Support Security and Reliable Software," *ACM Computing Surveys,* Vol. 8, December 1976, pp. 409–455.

These three papers focus on system structuring concepts that support security. In addition, they collectively refer to many other security-related papers.

8.11 Lempel, A. "Cryptology in Transition," *ACM Computing Surveys,* Vol. 11, December 1979, pp. 285–303.

This paper presents a survey of the evolving state of the art of cryptology.

8.12 Astrahan, M.M., et al. "System R: Relational Approach to Database Management,"*ACM Transactions on Database Systems,* Vol. 1, June 1976, pp. 97–137.

8.13 Griffiths, P.P. and Wade, B.W. "An Authorization Mechanism for a Relational Database System," *ACM Transactions on Database Systems,* Vol. 1, September 1976, pp. 242–255.

The first paper on System R contains a description of the architecture and design of the system. The second paper describes protection and security mechanisms and the granting and revocation of authorization within the context of System R.

8.14 Lipner, S.B. "Non-discretionary Controls for Commercial Applications," *Proceedings of the 1982 Symposium on Security and Privacy,* April 1982, pp. 2–10.

This paper describes the notion of the lattice model developed from the Department of Defense's security policies and examines commercial requirements for information security and derives an application of the lattice model suitable for these requirements.

Introduction to Database Management Systems

9.1 INTRODUCTION

In the past several years database management systems (DBMSs) have received much attention as a means for storing and accessing large volumes of data. A DBMS can be defined as a large piece of software running on top of an operating system that accesses a database. A functional definition of a DBMS is the following. A DBMS is software that facilitates the use and control of large information files normally maintained on external storage devices, includes the availability of a data description language (DDL) and a data manipulation language (DML) that permits the insertion, deletion, and modification of data, provides for data and system integrity, and allows security control and data administration. A database itself should be distinguished from a DBMS. A database is usually defined as a collection of files.

A database system has the following properties that distinguish it from a file processing system:

1. It is integrated, with different applications using the same database.
2. It eliminates or reduces data duplication.
3. It enhances data independence by permitting application programs to be insensitive to changes in the database.
4. It permits concurrent (shared) usage.
5. It permits finer granularity.
6. It provides for the centralized control of accessing and security control functions.

Logical data independence is the ability to insulate application programs from changes in the logical organization of the database used. A DBMS that provides data independence ensures that application programs can continue to run, perhaps at reduced performance, if the stored data are reorganized to accord other applications higher performance. Granularity refers to the unit of manipulatable data that can be locked during accessing and updating operations.

The primary purposes of this chapter are to discuss some of the similarities, differences, and relationships between DBMSs and file management systems (FMSs), introduce database architectures, and show how the file organizations discussed in previous chapters of this book are used in physical database design. No attempt is made in this chapter to discuss in detail the three major data models: the hierarchical, network, and relational models. Only the relational model is presented, with a minimum of detail, in order to discuss the relationships between the different views of data represented in a database architecture (see Figure 9.2) and to discuss physical database design.

One important thing to remember when reading this chapter is that the major role of a DBMS is to allow the user to deal with an abstraction of the data stored in a database rather than the computer-stored data itself.

9.2 COMPARISON OF DBMSs AND FMSs

In today's computer systems, users access data through either a FMS or a DBMS. In both cases, the user focuses on the logical structure of the data and not on the physical aspects. Both FMSs and DBMSs utilize access methods to handle the details of physical access to/from storage devices. An access method is a layer of software whose function is to conceal all device-dependent details from the FMS and DBMS. Since DBMSs are normally built on top of an operating system, they may use the same access methods as the operating system's FMS (see Figure 9.1).

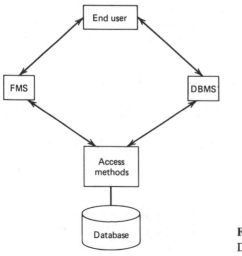

Figure 9.1. Relationship of FMSs and DBMSs.

In conventional FMSs, the logical aspects of data and some physical characteristics (hopefully none) are specified within an application program. There may be a close coupling of the logical and physical aspects of data; this tends to expose more of the access method to the application program. Other application programs requiring access to the same data must do one of the following:

1. Adopt the same view by adhering to the same logical aspects of the originating application.
2. Duplicate the data into other file(s) in which the organization is more suitable.

In some cases, unfortunate side effects can result from sharing data across applications:

1. Applications become unnecessarily complex because of involvement in the physical aspects of stored data.
2. Duplicating data may lead to data inconsistency problems.

Data inconsistency problems result when data are duplicated and an update might fail to modify all instances of the duplicated data. FMSs provide a flexible mechanism for describing the requirements of a particular application; however, when a requirement to share data across applications, exists, problems can result.

One of the main problems with the file management facilities available in conventional operating systems, for example, the sequential, indexed sequential, and random file organizations, is that they suffer from the inability to provide data independence. For example, a change in the logical record description of a file involves reloading the whole file and modifying and recompiling every program using that file. Changing various physical structure aspects of a file may cause similar problems; for instance, changing to a new storage device or changing from fixed-length physical records to variable length records may make alterations to a program necessary.

The DBMS approach affords a solution to the problems of data independence and the sharing of data across application programs that are encountered with FMSs. It provides a centralized mechanism for control of all data in the database (not just for a single application) and makes provisions for different application views of the data. Problems of data redundancy and thus data inconsistency are greatly reduced. Standards can be enforced across applications, security restrictions can be uniformly applied, and conflicting application requirements can be balanced through an integrated approach.

The description of data, its logical relationships and physical attributes, is separated from an application program via a DBMS. There may be a considerable difference between the perceived view of data as it relates to an application program and what is actually represented to the database system. Because of the separation of data definition from an application program, programs may change or data requirements grow without necessarily affecting the other.

9.3   DATABASE ARCHITECTURE

In DBMSs, the separation of data requirements and application specifications is accomplished through two or three levels of data definitions and mappings. When a database architecture consists of three levels (views) of data, the views are usually referred to as the external, conceptual, and internal views. Figure 9.2 illustrates the relationship of the three views of data via the ANSI/SPARC three-level database architecture.

9.3.1   Views in a Database Architecture

Each view in a database architecture represents a level of abstraction. The *internal view* is not at the level of bits stored on an external storage device, but it may be considered to be a collection of files. The *conceptual view* is an abstraction of the internal view, and the internal view can be considered an implementation of the conceptual view. Likewise, *external views* are abstractions of the conceptual view with each implemented in terms of the conceptual view.

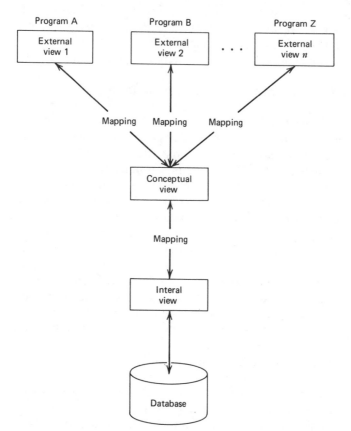

Figure 9.2.   ANSI/SPARC three-level database architecture.

An internal view record and a stored record are the same, but the internal view is still at least one level of abstraction above the physical database since it does not deal in terms of physical records or blocks. An internal view specifies what indexes exist, how stored items are represented, the physical sequence of stored records, etc. The internal view is implemented on physical storage devices.

A conceptual view is a collection of objects representing all the entities, properties, and relationships of interest in a database. A conceptual view record is not necessarily the same as either an external view record or a stored record.

An external view is a collection of objects representing the entities, properties, and relationships of interest to a specific application. The object that models an entity may, for example, be a logical record in COBOL or a tuple in a relation. An external view is a user view and represents an application program's database.

The correspondence between the objects in one view and the objects in another view are established through mappings as illustrated in Figure 9.2. Each mapping represents an implementation of one view in terms of another. If data independence is an attribute of the database architecture, then a change to a view, say to the internal view, should result only in changes to the conceptual/internal mapping, thus leaving the conceptual view unchanged.

It should be pointed out that most commercial DBMSs combine conceptual and internal views and hardly provide any external views. Thus, they achieve only a limited degree of data independence.

9.3.2 Data Description Languages

Each view in Figure 9.2 is specified via a language called the data description language (DDL) that is provided as part of a DBMS. The DDL is used to describe entity types and relationships among entities in terms of a particular data model, for example, the relational data model. In general, the DDL and data model may vary for each level of abstraction. In fact, there could be several DDLs, each using a different data model just for specifying external views. In practice, however, the two views of most importance to a user, the conceptual view and an external view, are based on the same data model and use similar DDLs. The reason for the use of a single data model at these two levels of abstraction is that the more similar the conceptual view and an external view, the easier it is to define a mapping between the two views; in addition, using the same data model usually ensures that this will happen.

A description of a view is called a *schema*. A schema consists of the definition of all entity types, the relationships among the entity types, and the mappings between the abstract objects at one level and the more concrete objects at the next lower level. The DDL used to specify a conceptual schema is sometimes referred to as the schema DDL. An external view is defined via a *subschema* and the DDL at this level is referred to as the subschema DDL. In this book, the various levels of abstraction are referred to as views and the terms schema and subschema are used only in certain contexts where they are appropriate.

9.3.3 Data Manipulation Languages

A data manipulation language (DML) is a language used to retrieve data from a database and to update a database. A DDL and a DML, when considered together, are often referred to as a *data sublanguage* (DSL). A DSL can be embedded in a host programming language such as COBOL or PL/I, or in other cases, the functions of a DSL may be embodied in an interactive query language. A DML is closely aligned with the data model used to define views of data. For example, if the data model is a graph model, then the DML is designed to manipulate graphs.

A DML may be *procedural* or *nonprocedural*. To manipulate a database using a procedural DML, a user has to specify what is wanted plus how to obtain it. With a procedural DML, a user writes segments (usually short) of code that traverse database structures in order to locate the record(s) to be retrieved or updated. A procedure to traverse a database to locate a record can be likened to a procedure to search a linked list for an element with a particular value.

The network and hierarchical data models usually support procedural DMLs because, in general, it is too inefficient to perform database accesses in a strictly nonprocedural manner with these two data models. Such procedural DMLs require that the user know the details of the underlying database structures in order to search the database. Requiring this knowledge, to some extent, nullifies the advantages that can be gained via abstraction to remove details of no interest to the user.

Nonprocedural DMLs are easier for a user to use in manipulating a database. With a nonprocedural DML, the user does not have to traverse a database; instead, he specifies only what is wanted and allows the system to decide how to obtain it.

The relational data model usually supports nonprocedural DMLs because table searching is naturally associative and this is easily expressed in a nonprocedural manner. Indexes are used to speed up table searching but the user is not aware of this.

The more procedural a DML, the simpler it is to implement since the user directs the DBMS, step by step, on how to obtain data. A nonprocedural DML is more complicated to implement since it places the responsibility of determining how to obtain the data, and therefore how to optimize the search, on the DBMS.

9.3.4 A Close Look at Database Architecture

Figure 9.3 presents a more detailed view of a database architecture than Figure 9.2. A user can interface with a database either via an application program as

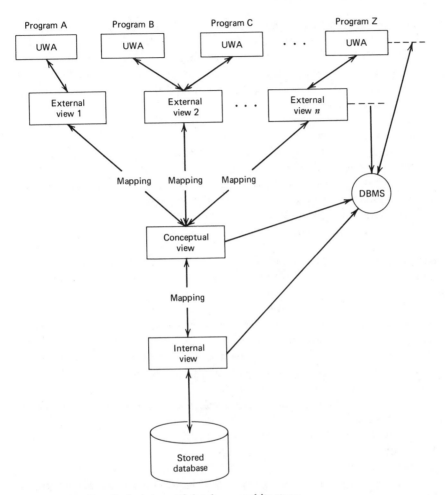

Figure 9.3. Detailed picture of database architecture.

depicted in Figure 9.3 or via an interactive query language (not depicted). Each application program has its own external view; several programs, however, can use the same external view. Each application program has its own user work area (UWA) in which data associated with retrieval and update requests against the database are stored. In Figure 9.3, each external view is specified using a DDL and each application program uses a DML to access the database.

All of the retrieval and update actions expressed via a DML are executed under the control of the DBMS. To obtain a better understanding of the sequence of actions that can take place in a DBMS, a retrieval request is traced.

1. An application program issues a retrieval request to the DBMS indicating the data to be accessed.
2. The request is validated against the proper external view to ensure that the application program has access to the data requested.

3. The DBMS may check its buffers to determine if the request can be satisfied with currently available data. If so, Step 8 is executed next.
4. The DBMS requests that the operating system perform a transfer between the external storage device containing the requested data and the system buffers. This request is handled by the access routines of the operating system.
5. The operating system initiates the transfer between external memory and internal memory.
6. The data are placed in the system buffers in internal memory.
7. The operating system notifies the DBMS that the transfer is complete.
8. The DBMS places the data and some status information in the UWA of the application program that issued the request.
9. The application program may access the data and status information in the UWA in the course of its execution.

Status information reveals whether or not an access request was successful. As illustrated in Figure 9.3, the DBMS monitors each step in an access against the stored database.

In addition to the above steps that are performed in a retrieval request, mappings between views also enter into any request made against a database. The mappings are important because there is no data directly associated with any of the views; that is, views are not materialized. Data exist only in the stored database. A mapping takes one or more object(s) at one level of abstraction and transforms them into one or more object(s) at the next higher level of abstraction. Thus, data requested against an external view via an application program are materialized for the requester through a series of mappings between each level of abstraction. The mappings, in effect, transform stored data into data as the user sees it in his application program. A mapping specification may involve type conversions, the merging of two or more records at one level to form a record at the next higher level, and the subsetting of records at one level to form a record at the next higher level.

If the conceptual view is a tree-structured collection of records (of some type) called TREE and an external view is an ordered list of records (of the same or different type as in TREE) called LIST, then the conceptual/external mapping in this case would transform a tree into an ordered list. A mapping is a function and if the mapping in this case is called TREEMAP, then it can be expressed in functional form as

$$\text{TREEMAP: TREE} \rightarrow \text{LIST}$$

External view definitions (or subschemas) are typically stored in files and are not physically part of an application program. Each external view has a name and it is linked to an application program via its name. Storage space must be allocated in an application program to contain external view objects (this may be the UWA alluded to above).

9.4 WHAT DOES A DBMS KNOW ABOUT ITS DATA?

If a DBMS is defined as a collection of files, then the DBMS knows:

1. What stored files exist.
2. The structure of stored records.
3. The stored field(s) on which a file is sequenced.
4. The stored fields that can be used as search arguments for direct access.

The above four items are usually specified as part of the internal view definition.

A DBMS does not know:

1. Anything about physical records or blocks.
2. How stored fields are associated to form stored records (fields in a record are normally adjacent but they could be linked).
3. How sequencing is performed (for example, by means of physical contiguity, an index, a pointer chain, or maps).
4. How direct access is performed, for example, via an index, sequential scan, hash addressing, etc.

These last four items are also part of the internal view but they are used by access methods and not by the DBMS.

9.5 A LOOK AT DATABASE ARCHITECTURE VIA THE RELATIONAL MODEL

To illustrate some of the important aspects of database architecture, the relational data model is used. The relational model was selected because it is the simplest to describe and to understand. With the relational model, a view of data is a set of relations (tables) containing tuples (rows) that correspond to records of a flat file. A flat file contains no repeating groups, that is, each value at every row and column position is exactly one value and never a set of values. A table represents one entity type and each row represents a particular entity of that type. Columns are attributes, with all values in a column having the same domain.

9.5.1 A Mathematical Description of the Relational Model

Given sets $D_1, D_2, \ldots, D_n$ (not necessarily distinct), a relation R is a set of n-tuples each of which has its first element from D_1, second element from D_2, etc. The sets D_i are called domains. The number n is called the degree of R and the number of tuples in R is the cardinality of R.

The properties of a relation (derived from the mathematical definition of a relation), if we assume a table representation, are:

1. No two rows are identical.
2. The ordering of rows is not significant.
3. The ordering of columns is significant (however, this is a matter of debate since columns are usually referenced by name in access requests).

9.5.2 A Relational Example

With the hierarchical and network data models, relationships among entity types are represented by hierarchical structures and by database sets, respectively. However, with the relational data model, relationships are represented via data values. To illustrate this feature of the relational model and to illustrate some of the concepts discussed in Section 9.3, consider the following simple example.

The conceptual view of a database consists of two relations EMPLOYEE and DEPARTMENT with the following attributes

EMPLOYEE(EMPNO, NAME, DNO, JOB, SAL, COMM)

DEPARTMENT(DNO, DNAME, LOC)

EMPNO and DNO are the primary keys (underscored) for relations EMPLOYEE and DEPARTMENT, respectively. DNO in relation EMPLOYEE is referred to as a *foreign key* in EMPLOYEE since DNO is the primary key in another relation, DEPARTMENT. The two entity types in the conceptual view are employees and departments. The relationship between these two entity types is defined via the DNO attribute. The relationship is a one to many relationship since each department may have 0,1, or more employees.

9.5.2.1 A Relational DDL

The following **define** construct defines the DEPARTMENT relation.

```
define DEPARTMENT as
    row  DNO:        character(3),
         DNAME:      character(12),
         LOC:        character(20)
    key  DNO
    nulls LOC
end DEPARTMENT;
```

The EMPLOYEE relation can be defined similarly as
```
define EMPLOYEE as
    row  EMPNO:      character(5),
         NAME:       character(30),
```

```
          DNO:        character(3),
          JOB:        character(10),
          SAL:        real,
          COMM:       real
     key  EMPNO
     nulls JOB, SAL, COMM
end EMPLOYEE;
```

The **nulls** attribute defines which column elements can have null values.

Various external views can be derived from the simple conceptual view defined above. For simplicity purposes, each of the three external views specified below are assumed to consist of a single relation; however, this need not be the case. In general, an external view may consist of several relations; the syntax of the **define** construct used above would have to be altered slightly, however, to accommodate this. Three possible external views, VIEWA, VIEWB, and VIEWC, are defined as follows:

```
define VIEWA as
     row        EMPNO:      integer,
                EMPNAME:    character(30),
                DNO:        character(3),
                DNAME:      character(12),
                EMPJOB:     character(10),
                EMPLOC:     character(20)
     key        EMPNO
     derivation <EMPNO, NAME, DNO, DNAME, JOB, LOC>:
                EMPLOYEE, DEPARTMENT where
                EMPLOYEE.DNO = DEPARTMENT.DNO
end VIEWA;


define VIEWB as
     row        EMPNO:      character(5),
                NAME:       character(30),
                SALARY:     real
     key        EMPNO
     derivation <EMPNO, NAME, SAL>: EMPLOYEE
end VIEWB;


define VIEWC as
     row        EMPNO:      character(5),
                NAME:       character(30),
                DNO:        character(3),
                DNAME:      character(12),
                LOC:        character(20)
     key        EMPNO
```

derivation   <EMPNO, NAME, DNO, DNAME, LOC>:
                EMPLOYEE, DEPARTMENT **where** JOB =
                'SALESMAN' **and** EMPLOYEE.DNO =
                DEPARTMENT.DNO
end VIEWC;

The qualification of attributes is used when necessary to distinguish between attributes with identical names in different relations. Brackets ('<', '>') are used to indicate the derived tuple in each external view. The tuple element names in an external view **row** do not have to agree with the corresponding names in the underlying conceptual (or source) relations nor do they have to agree in type. Notice that EMPNO is of type **character**(5) in EMPLOYEE and of type **integer** in VIEWA. The tuple element names in the **derivation** of an external view are, however, the source relation tuple element names. The names of the source relation(s), for example, EMPLOYEE and/or DEPARTMENT, are defined in a derivation following the colon ("":"") and preceding the **where** clause, if any. A **where** clause, if one exists in a **derivation**, defines which tuples from the source relation(s) are used to derive tuples in an external view relation.

The mapping from the source relations, EMPLOYEE and DEPART-MENT, to the abstract relation VIEWA, is relatively simple. It involves the derivation of tuples for relation VIEWA, the mapping of names, for example, EMPNO to EMPNO, NAME to EMPNAME, etc., and converting EMPNO of type **character**(5) to type **integer.**

9.5.2.2 A Relational DML

In this section a simple DML developed for embedding in host languages is used to illustrate how relations can be accessed and updated. With this DML, there are essentially two ways to access relations defined in external views. The first way is to use the **open** and **fetch** statements. To use the **fetch** statement to retrieve rows from a table, a tuple variable, for example, x, must be opened on the table using an **open** statement* as in

open x **on** VIEWA

In host languages such as COBOL and PL/I, a tuple variable can be represented by a record variable or a structure name, respectively. A variable can be opened on only one relation at a time.

An **open** statement establishes currency for a tuple variable on a relation. The current tuple is the last one fetched. Currency can be implemented by a cursor that moves from row to row in a table. The **fetch** statement

fetch x

---

*The **open** and **close** statements discussed in this chapter should not be confused with the OPEN and CLOSE statements discussed in Chapters 1 and 6 although the functions that they perform are somewhat similar.

fetches the next tuple from VIEWA, binds it to x, and updates the currency associated with x. Variable x serves a dual role here; it acts as a copy for the current tuple and also as the address of the current tuple. The role that x plays depends on the context in which it is used. It never plays both roles simultaneously. A **close** statement permits the currency for a variable to be reset as in

close x

An external view definition establishes a set of tuples that are of interest to a user. The **fetch** statement is merely used to sequence through them one at a time.

Since relations cannot be sorted, as this would violate the definition of relation in the relational model, a **sort** attribute can be attached to an **open** statement as in

open x **on** VIEWA **sort**(EMPNO)

Tuples fetched from VIEWA are bound to x in sorted order, sorted on EMPNO.

A second way to retrieve tuples from a relation is via an iteration statement in the host language such as a **for** statement. For example,

for y **in** VIEWA **where** EMPNO = 10637 **do**
put list (y .EMPNAME, y .EMPJOB)

for z **in** VIEWA **where** EMPLOC = 'BOSTON' **do put list**(z)

The first **for** statement outputs the EMPNAME and EMPJOB for the employee with EMPNO equal to 10637. The second **for** statement streams tuples from VIEWA, one at a time, and binds them to z for all tuples in VIEWA with EMPLOC equal to 'BOSTON' and then outputs them. The scope of variables y and z is limited to the **for** statement and they are implicitly declared to be of the type necessary to hold VIEWA's tuples.

Relations can be updated via an **update** statement. Operations APPEND, DELETE, and REPLACE are available for updating relations. If only the current tuple in a relation is to be updated, then the following **update** statement is written

```
update x
  do
    x.DNAME = 'SHOE';
    REPLACE x
  end;
```

Only the DNAME tuple element in current tuple x is updated. In the statement

x .DNAME = 'SHOE'

tuple variable x acts like a copy of the current tuple, whereas in the above REPLACE statement, x acts like the address of the current tuple. In the above

update statement it is assumed that x has been opened on VIEWA and at least one **fetch** statement involving x has been executed prior to the update statement's execution.

An **update** statement can also be a loop as in the following statement:

update y **in** VIEWA **where** DNO = 'A16' **do** DELETE y **end**

In this **update** statement, all tuples in VIEWA with DNO equal to 'A16' are deleted.

The REPLACE and DELETE operations must be used within the context of an **update** statement, whereas the APPEND operation does not. The APPEND operation permits tuples to be added to a relation. For example, if y is a tuple variable, then the following sequence of statements adds a new tuple to VIEWA:

y.EMPNO = 13021;
y.EMPNAME = 'JONES C.';
y.DNO = 'A17';
y.DNAME = 'SALES';
y.EMPJOB = 'SALESMAN';
y.EMPLOC = 'DALLAS';
APPEND y **to** VIEWA;

9.6 PHYSICAL DATABASE DESIGN

The objectives in this section are: (1) to discuss some of the elements included in an internal schema, and (2) to discuss how file organizations are utilized in database design. The access paths to records, the files stored in a database, the stored record definitions, the fields on which stored records are sequenced, etc., are part of an internal schema definition. Most of the material presented in this section comes from a paper describing the implementation of the INGRES relational DBMS (see the reference list).

The file selection problem that occurs in the design of an integrated database is far more complex than in file systems. In file systems, file selection is analyzed in the context of choosing one main access path to a collection of one or more records; the correlation between records in two or more files is done externally in an application program. In an integrated database, several access paths to a given set of records may be desirable to efficiently satisfy the various types of requests that may be made against a database. Selecting the appropriate access path involves access path optimization. The main problem involving access path optimization is to select the access path(s) to desired data that result in minimal search time.

The primary data access facilities provided by DBMSs are retrieval, insertion, modify, and deletion. Inherent in all of these operations is search. Searching is obviously required for retrieval, but it is also important for other

DBMS operations. In some cases, when inserting data, it is necessary to locate the correct place to perform the insertion. Modify and deletion operations must also locate the data that is to be modified or deleted. Thus, many implementation considerations for a DBMS are reduced to developing good search mechanisms. Most of the file organizations used in the implementation of DBMSs are special cases of search mechanisms. For instance, an index is a search mechanism that is usually implemented as a B-tree.

The remainder of the comments in this section are directed at the design of access paths in relational systems. There are two types of access paths: *content addressibility access paths* used to select sets of tuples based on their contents, and *data relatability access paths* used to relate tuples of one relation to tuples of another relation.

Content addressibility (or associative) access paths can be implemented using indexes that act as associative access aids. A relation may be indexed on any or all domains (or columns). Indexes can be used to scan a table in order by the indexed values or to directly access the rows that match a particular value or range of values. Data relatability access paths are usually implemented using "links" that are pointers stored with a tuple that connects it to related tuples in the same table or different tables.

Pointers are represented by tuple identifiers (TIDs). TIDs are not visible to users. They are customarily implemented as a concatenation of a page number and a line number (or byte offset from the bottom of a page) within a page. In this implementation, a tuple must fit entirely on a single page. The line number is an index into a line table whose entries contain pointers to tuples in the page. By using indirection, the physical arrangement of tuples in a page can be reorganized without affecting the TIDs. This technique allows the efficient utilization of space within data pages, since space can be compacted and tuples moved with only local changes to the pointers in the slots of a line table. A TID can also be considered the byte offset of a tuple in a file. This scheme is used primarily for small or temporary relations.

An access path giving value ordering and associative access on one or more attributes to a relation is conveniently implemented and maintained through the use of a multipage index structure that contains pointers to the tuples themselves. The pages of a given index can be organized into a B-tree. For nonleaf nodes, an entry consists of a (key value, pointer) pair. For leaf nodes, an entry is a combination of a key value and a variable length ascending list of TIDs for tuples having the key value. One or more such entries exist in each leaf page. In addition, the leaf pages may be chained in a doubly linked list, so that sequential access can be supported from leaf to leaf.

As stated previously, relationships between tuples in the same relation or different relations are represented using links (or binary links) implemented as TIDs. For example, links may be maintained by storing the TIDs of the NEXT, PREVIOUS, and OWNER tuples in the prefix of the member (or child) tuples and by storing at least the TID of the first child tuple in the parent tuple. The prefix may contain other information such as the number of stored data fields and the number of pointer (TID) fields.

As an example of the use of links to relate tuples, consider the DEPART-MENT and EMPLOYEE relations that compose the conceptual view defined above. A tuple from DEPARTMENT can be considered the owner of 0 or more EMPLOYEE tuples. This is natural since a department contains employees. Suppose the DEPARTMENT and EMPLOYEE relations have data as illustrated in Figure 9.4 with the TIDs for tuples written to the left of each row of each relation. The DEPARTMENT tuple with TID DTID2 is related to all employees having a DNO equal to 108. The link structure illustrating this relationship is given in Figure 9.5. If a tuple is a member of more than one chain, then multiple sets of NEXT, PREVIOUS, and OWNER fields will appear in the prefix of the stored tuple. This linked structure is similar to the multilist organization discussed in Chapter 5. These chains are used primarily for navigational access.

There are two important things to note in the examples of Figures 9.4 and 9.5:

1. The relationships depicted by links in Figure 9.5 are expressed explicitly by attribute values in the relational model.
2. Some of the implementation details such as the B-tree indexes and the links concept are part of an internal schema definition; however, this information is used by access routines and not by the DBMS.

DEPARTMENT	DNO	DNAME	LOC
DTID1	116	SALES	BOSTON
DTID2	108	PURCHASING	BOSTON
DTID3	102	REPAIR	DALLAS
DTID4	124	ADVERTISING	NEW YORK

EMPLOYEE	EMPNO	NAME	DNO	JOB	SAL	COMM
ETID1	12846	SMITH, L.	108	PURCH	20000	0
ETID2	10021	JONES, C.	116	SALESMAN	35000	.06
ETID3	10011	WILLS, D.	116	SALESMAN	40000	.07
ETID4	16248	JACKSON, M.	108	PURCH	22000	0
ETID5	37260	MILLER, W.	124	ADVERT	50000	.10
ETID6	41000	JOHNSON, D.	108	PURCH	20000	0
ETID7	76378	GAREAU, W.	102	MECHANIC	14000	0
ETID8	01002	HARRIS, E.	108	PURCH	25000	0

Figure 9.4. DEPARTMENT and EMPLOYEE relations.

	NEXT	PREVIOUS	OWNER						
DTID2	ETID1	—	—	108	PURCHASING	BOSTON			
ETID1	ETID4	DTID2	DTID2	12846	SMITH, L.	108	PURCH	20000	0
ETID4	ETID6	ETID1	DTID2	16248	JACKSON, M.	108	PURCH	22000	0
ETID6	ETID8	ETID4	DTID2	41000	JOHNSON, D.	108	PURCH	20000	0
ETID8	—	ETID6	DTID2	01002	HARRIS, E.	108	PURCH	25000	0

Prefix

Figure 9.5. Binary link representation.

In some implementations of relations, all data are stored in segments that are used to control physical clustering. The internal schema defines this clustering and if clustering is used, then all tuples of any relation must reside within a single segment. A single segment, however, may contain several relations. Each segment consists of a sequence of equal sized pages.

In INGRES, initially a file contains a number of primary pages holding all previously loaded tuples. A tuple must fit within a single page. If the relation grows and these pages are filled, then overflow pages are allocated and chained by pointers to the primary pages with which they are associated. The location of a tuple in the file is a function of the value of the tuple's key value. The key value determines the page of the file on which the tuple will be placed.

There are two possible modes of key-to-address transformation used in INGRES: hashing and order preserving. Hashing needs no explanation but the order preserving mode does. The order preserving scheme is similar to IBM's ISAM file organization. A relation is sorted to produce an ordering on a particular key. A multilevel directory, which is static, is created that records the high key value on each primary page. The directory resides on several pages following the primary pages within the file itself. A primary page and its overflow pages are not maintained in sort order (the reason for this decision involves locking). The ISAM implementation is useful for queries in which the key value is specified as falling within a range of values.

If a relational DBMS provides at least the two types of access paths described above, then an optimizer can, for a given request, try to determine which of the access paths should be used.

9.7 SUMMARY

The purpose of this chapter has not been to provide an in-depth look at the relational data model; however, some important features of the relational model were reviewed. The relational model was used to discuss database architecture and to show the importance of studying file organizations since they are an important part of physical database design and implementation.

EXERCISES

1. Sketch the database architecture of a DBMS that is available for your use and compare it with Figures 9.2 and 9.3. Does it permit external views to be defined via its DML?
2. Using an available DBMS, perform some retrievals and updates against a database supplied by your instructor.
3. Read the articles in the special issue of *Computing Surveys* given in the reference list at the end of this chapter. Represent the DEPARTMENT and EMPLOYEE relations given in Figure 9.4 using CODASYL networks and hierarchical structures.
4. Describe how external user views protect a database.
5. Using the view definitions VIEWA, VIEWB, and VIEWC in Section 9.5 and the source relations in Figure 9.4, materialize the relation (defined by each view) that represents the data visible via the view.

REFERENCES

9.1 Codd, E. F. "A Relational Model of Data for Large Shared Data Banks," *Commun. ACM,* Vol. 13, No. 6, June 1970, pp. 377–387.

Paper introduces the relational model of data.

9.2 Cardenas, A. F. *Data Base Management Systems,* Allyn and Bacon, Boston, 1979, 519 pages.

9.3 Date, C. J. *An Introduction to Database Systems,* 3rd Edition, Addison-Wesley, Reading, Massachusetts, 1981.

9.4 Tsichritzis, D. C. and Lochovsky, F. H. *Data Base Management Systems,* Academic Press, New York, 1977, 388 pages.

These three books provide in-depth discussions of database data models and descriptions of several database management systems such as IMS, IDMS, TOTAL, ADABAS, and System 2000.

9.5 Sibley, E. H. "The Development of Database Technology," *ACM Computing Surveys,* Vol. 8, March 1976, pp. 1–5.

The issue of *Computing Surveys* containing this article is a special issue on database management systems. It includes other tutorial articles on the relational, hierarchical, and network data models. It is recommended reading for this chapter.

9.6 Stonebraker, M., et al. "The Design and Implementation of INGRES," *Transactions on Database Systems,* Vol. 1, September 1976, pp. 189–222.

This paper presents a good description of some of the design and implementation strategies of INGRES. INGRES was one of the first implementations of the relational model. This paper is recommended reading. Most of the material in Section 9.6 was taken from this paper.

Index